✳

THE NEW BUDDHISM

⚜

THE NEW BUDDHISM
The Western Transformation of an Ancient Tradition

James William Coleman

OXFORD
UNIVERSITY PRESS

2001

OXFORD
UNIVERSITY PRESS

Oxford New York
Athens Auckland Bangkok Bogotá Buenos Aires Calcutta
Cape Town Chennai Dar es Salaam Delhi Florence Hong Kong Istanbul
Karachi Kuala Lumpur Madrid Melbourne Mexico City Mumbai
Nairobi Paris São Paulo Shanghai Singapore Taipei Tokyo Toronto Warsaw

and associated companies in
Berlin Ibadan

Copyright © 2001 by James William Coleman

Published by Oxford University Press, Inc.
198 Madison Avenue, New York, New York, 10016

Oxford is a registered trademark of Oxford University Press

All rights reserved. No part of this publication
may be reproduced, stored in a retrieval system, or transmitted,
in any form or by any means, electronic, mechanical,
photocopying, recording, or otherwise, without the prior
permission of Oxford University Press.

Library of Congress Cataloging-in-Publication Data
Coleman, James William 1947–
The new Buddhism : the western transformation of an ancient tradition / James William Coleman.
p. cm.
Includes index.
ISBN 0-19-513162-2
1. Buddhism—United States—History—20th century. 2. Religious life—Buddhism. 3.
Monastic and religious life (Buddhism)—United States. I. Title.

BQ734.C65 2000
294.3'0973—dc21
00-024981

2 4 6 8 9 7 5 3 1

Printed in the United States of America
on acid-free paper

Contents

�֍

THE NEW BUDDHISM

One
❋

WHAT IS THIS?

Everything changes. This fundamental fact lies at the marrow of Buddhist realization, and throughout its 2,500-year history Buddhism itself has certainly lived up to this dictum. First in India and then throughout the Asian world, Buddhism has continually adapted to the changing circumstances of time and place. Yet against the panoramic diversity of the Buddhist tradition, what may be the most sweeping change in its long history is passing unnoticed by most of the world. After fading out in the land of its birth centuries ago and teetering on the edge of twentieth-century extinction in Tibet and China, a new Buddhism is now emerging in the industrialized nations of the West. This Buddhism is fundamentally different from anything that has gone before, yet, in the best tradition of Buddhist logic, it remains at its core completely unchanged from the moment of Siddhartha Gautama's great realization under the bodhi tree.

A slim, thirtyish woman comes home from work to her New Jersey apartment. After a suitable greeting for the cat and a quick shower, she changes into some loose-fitting clothes and goes barefoot into her extra bedroom. The room is bare of furniture except for a multishelved altar against the far wall that holds a bewildering assortment of statues, icons, religious objects, and photographs. She lights a long stick of incense and plants it in an intricately carved pot full of fine white sand. In the center of the altar is a photograph of her guru—a Tibetan man with a brilliant smile who looks to be in his middle sixties and is wearing brightly colored monastic robes. She bows and moves back a few feet. Placing a thick pad on the floor in front of her, she puts her hands together with palms and fingertips touching and brings them over her head. She quickly drops to the floor, her knees landing on the pad and her hands sliding until her body lies flat—arms outstretched, head, chest, and hips touching the ground. After she lurches back up to the standing position, she repeats the whole thing over again, quietly reciting a prayer with each prostration. After about ten minutes she is glistening with a thin film of sweat, but she continues until the incense has burned out and she has repeated this ritual more than two hundred times. When she is done, she records the total in a book she keeps in the corner and goes to the kitchen for a cold drink.

The Buddhist Tradition

Before we can understand the new face Buddhism is assuming in the West, we must look at the old. For most Westerners a mention of Buddhism is likely to bring to mind head-shaven monks in exotic robes, a kung fu master dispensing wise sayings after vanquishing evildoers in a cloud of kicks and punches, or some other image of the mysterious and foreign. Some Western scholars have even questioned whether or not Buddhism is really a religion, since it doesn't give the kind of attention to God (or gods) that many assume to be the sine qua non of all religious life.

Buddhism is certainly *not* a Western religion, but only the most ethnocentric observer could attend a Buddhist service, with its robed priests, its rituals, and its devoted followers, and fail to see the similarities with Western practice. From its very beginning the central goal of Buddhism was, nonetheless, radically different from that of the Western faiths. Instead of glorifying or praising a deity or seeking to live in accord with the divine will, the goal of Buddhism is personal awakening: even the gods bow to the truly enlightened one. Many Western mystics have trodden a path familiar to the Buddhist seekers. But mystics have always remained on the margins of the Western religious establishment; in Buddhism they are its core. The Buddha made no claim to be any kind of deity or to have some special message from God. He said he was simply someone who woke up and saw things as they are. His goal was not to teach a new creed or new way of life but to help those who gathered around him to see the truth for themselves.

The Buddha was, in other words, not a Buddhist. It was the institutional structures and traditions that grew up around Siddartha Gautama's teachings that made Buddhism into what we traditionally call a religion. As the great German sociologist Max Weber pointed out, once any charismatic religious teacher dies, the message must be "routinized" if it is to continue. The inevitable result is a more formalized doctrine and some sort of established institutional structure. The paradox, often evident in Asian Buddhism, is that those same structures too easily become an end in themselves, preserving the letter but not the spirit of the founder's teachings.

What was the Buddha's message? Spiritual seekers, scholars, and intellectuals have struggled over that question for centuries. Although it is relatively easy to describe what Siddhartha Gautama (the Buddha) said or at least what the surviving texts claim he said, the point was not to learn a set of doctrines but to experience the reality that underlies them. When they become an end in themselves, the fine words and the intellectual knowledge can actually become a barrier to true understanding.

The marrow of Buddhism is the actual experience of the awakened state, but the words that describe it can at least give us some clues if we don't confuse the description of the food for the actual meal. Looking through awakened eyes, everything is a vast interdependent stream of changing phenomena. Things arise from an infinite chain of past causes and produce effects that have endless consequences. Everything is related to and dependent upon everything else. Nothing, including ourselves, has any independent being or unchanging essence. We are simply an ever changing stream of experience. In realizing this great truth, Siddhartha also saw the origins of human suffering in our deepest desires and attachments. We cling to one passing phenomenon after another and struggle endlessly to hold back the inevitable tides of change. We vainly strive to colonize our experience: to create an artificial world of safety and pleasure and to exclude the inevitable human experiences of pain and uncertainty. The Buddha was not, however, the life-denying pessimist that he is sometimes pictured to be, for he also saw the end of suffering through the cultivation of ethical behavior, meditation, and transcendent wisdom.

As Buddhism developed into an institutionalized religion, the struggle to wake up to those great truths fell primarily to the monks who gave up their everyday lives and dedicated themselves to the pursuit of enlightenment. But of course everyone can't be a monk, and it was left to lay Buddhists to lead ethical lives and provide the material support the monastics needed, so that in some future time (perhaps in a future life) they might have their own opportunity to realize enlightenment. Thus Buddhism came to be split into two institutional realms. The monastic elite continued on Gautama's quest for enlightenment, while new forms of mass Buddhism sprang up that were more concerned with earning an auspicious rebirth—usually by accumulating merit through good works, by faith, or by chanting some magic formula. Although the Buddha never laid claim to any kind of divinity, the stories of his incredible abilities and accomplishment grew over the years, and he became an object of popular worship in many forms of Buddhism. In the Mahayana tradition, which became dominant in northern Asia, a retinue of godlike bodhisattvas (powerful beings who dedicated themselves to help others on the road to enlightenment) joined the Buddha in the popular pantheon. In exchange for their material support, the priests and monks came to fulfill the same kind of functions for lay Buddhists that priests in other religions did. They officiated at ceremonies, gave advice, and performed rituals.

Of course, the lay/monastic distinction was not quite as clear-cut as I have made it seem. Many lay Buddhists certainly attained deep realization, while many monks and priests, particularly during the periodic eras of institutional decline, showed little interest in following the arduous path to enlightenment that the Buddha laid out. But this division between the masses of laypeople and the monks and priests who at least in theory are following the path to enlightenment remains central to the Asian Buddhist tradition. Over the years, this elite group of men (and a few women) came to be vested with great prestige that set them off from their lay followers and made them the object of tremendous respect and authority.

Buddhism in the West

Just a century and a half ago, Buddhism was virtually unknown in the West except to a few travelers and intellectuals. As Thomas Tweed has shown in his excellent study of the early American encounters with Buddhism, many of the American Christians who first heard about Buddhism were puzzled by how a religion with no God and no immortal soul attracted so many of the world's people. But as time went by, Buddhism gained a following among a small group of intellectuals who saw it as a more tolerant, more rational alternative to Christianity and among some of the growing numbers of people interested in spiritualism and the supernatural. Much of this early interest was, however, stimulated by books and stories about Buddhism that were often of questionable accuracy.

The World Congress of Religion, held in Chicago in 1893, is often credited with the introduction of the first traditional Buddhist denominations to North America. In actual fact, however, there were already a substantial number of Asian immigrants in North America who had brought various versions of popular Buddhism with them—even if they were too far removed from the cultural elites who attended such meetings to be given much attention. To this day, the most obvious division in Western Buddhism is between the "ethnic Buddhism" of Asian immigrants and the "new Buddhism" pursued by Western converts who, interestingly enough, are often the same kind of people as those who attended the World Congress of Religion back in 1893.

Faster and easier travel, virtually instant communication, and a growing tide of migration brought the East and the West inextricably closer together than ever before. As ethnic Buddhism became more common in the West, it made numerous adaptations to its new environment, but it nonetheless maintained its Asian traditions and its Asian outlook. Unlike the new Buddhism that has such a strong appeal to the sophisticated and the highly educated, the other stream of Western Buddhism seeks to serve the needs of average people. Monks are few and far between, and rituals and ceremonies abound. Its followers are found mostly in the ethnic enclaves of the big cities, and among some of the more suburbanized descendants of earlier Asian immigrants. Ethnic Buddhism's primary role is to minister to the social and spiritual needs of the Asian communities of the West, much as the Christian churches and Jewish synagogues serve their communities, often providing a taste of the comfort and security of home in the process.

The first Buddhist tradition to make the leap to a Western audience was Japanese Zen. A Japanese Rinzai master, Soyen Shaku, spoke at the World Congress of Religion, and the writings of his student D.T. Suzuki introduced paradoxical Zen thought to many fascinated Western intellectuals. By the 1950s, most educated Westerners had at least heard of Zen Buddhism, even though it continued to be seen as something hopelessly strange and exotic. During that era, the young Bohemians of the "beat generation" took up Zen as a kind of intellectual talisman and challenge to the existing view of things. The next two decades saw something of a "Zen boom" when, for the first time, significant numbers of Westerners began actual Buddhist practice. By the time this first wave of enthusiasm had died down, residential Zen centers had sprung up in most of the major urban areas of North America, and Zen had firmly established itself as a religious presence in the West.

The headwaters of the second stream of the new Buddhism are in the remote Himalayan mountains of Tibet. For centuries, Tibet was one of the most isolated countries on Earth. But the Chinese conquest of the 1950s and the brutal repression that followed sparked a Tibetan diaspora that brought their culture and especially their religion onto the world stage. The first Tibetan teachers reached the West during the 1960s, but they didn't build much of an institutional presence for another decade. Fueled by a seemingly inexhaustible supply of charismatic Tibetans, symbolized by the Dalai Lama with his combination of compassionate presence and political importance, Tibetan Vajrayana has exploded on the Western Buddhism scene in the last two decades. Culturally, the extroverted Tibetans could hardly have been more different from the proper Japanese. Zen monks wear robes of black and brown, decorate their temples with elegant simplicity, and tend to display a measured emotional mien. Tibetan temples, on the other hand, are a riot of bright colors and exotic images. They commonly include paintings and sculptures depicting multiarmed gods engaging in fiery sexual intercourse, and unlike the Japanese, the Tibetans do not hesitate to display passionate emotion.

The newest stream of Western Buddhism actually has the most ancient roots. Known in the West as Vipassana, this style of practice derives from the Theravadan tradition predominant in the southern parts of Asia, and most scholars would agree that it adheres more strictly to the Buddha's original teachings than any of the world's other Buddhist sects. One of the most important differences between Vipassana and the other traditions of the new Buddhism is as much as anything a matter of historical accident. The Zen and Tibetan traditions were carried to the West by Asian teachers, but Vipassana teachings were brought back by Westerners who went to Thailand or Burma to seek them out. As a result, the Vipassana style is the most secular and most Western, and it has the lightest cultural baggage from the East. Many Vipassana teachers, especially those on the West Coast, are also heavily influenced by Western psychological thought and the therapeutic tradition it fostered.

Perched somewhere between the ethnic Buddhism of the Asian immigrants and these three streams of the new Buddhism lies a fascinating Japanese denomination known as Soka Gakkai. The Soka Gakkai traces its origins back to Nichiren, the thirteenth-century Japanese prophet who saw the Lotus Sutra (one of the great religious texts of Mahayana Buddhism) as the apex of Buddhist wisdom and predicted doom for Japan if it did not return to its veneration. The Soka Gakkai was founded in 1930 as a lay affiliate of Nichiren Shoshu—one of the numerous Nichiren sects in Japan. Japan's traumatic defeat in World War II led to the dizzying growth of new religions in the 1950s and 1960s—an era of Japanese history that has sometimes been dubbed the "rush hour of the gods." It was during this period that Soka Gakkai/Nichiren Shoshu saw its most explosive growth, becoming one of Japan's largest faiths, the sponsor of a major political party, and winning many Western converts.

Because most of Soka Gakkai's members in the West are not Asians, it would seem to qualify as an important part of the new Buddhism we are exploring. But unlike those groups, Soka Gakkai remains firmly rooted in mass rather than elite Buddhism. While other groups focus on meditation, the repetition of a chant in praise of the Lotus Sutra (Nam Myoho Renge Kyo) is the central practice of the Soka Gakkai. While other Western Buddhist groups tend to display indifference or even hostility toward the pursuit of material gain, Soka Gakkai believes that diligent chanting produces wealth as well as personal happiness. Whereas most other groups believe that new members will come when they are ready, Soka Gakkai has until fairly recently pursued an aggressive policy of proselytization known by a descriptive Japanese name—shakubuku—which translates as "break and subdue." All in all, Soka Gakkai's practices and beliefs differ from the other Buddhist groups that appeal to Westerners in so many ways that a separate book would be required to do them justice, and I will not attempt that task here.

A Note on Method

When I first started this project, I thought I would focus exclusively on Western Zen. But the deeper I went, the more I realized that there were too many interconnections between the different Buddhist traditions active here in the West, and too many similarities in the adaptations they were making to their new environment to treat any single stream in isolation from the others. I therefore decided to look at this new Buddhism as a whole, examining the history, practices, and problems of all these traditions together, and to explore the differences between them only after laying out their common ground.

Western Buddhist teachers have been prolific writers, and it is easy to look at the bookshelves lined with their works and not realize that very little has been published that takes an objective outside view of the new Buddhism, locating it squarely in its social and historical context. So before we go further, I need to briefly explain where I got my material. First, the foundation of this work is my own experience from over fifteen years of Buddhist meditation, both on my own and in a variety of different groups. Although the literature is patchy and incomplete, there was much to be learned from it, and I read all the books I could get my hands on—general works on Buddhism, the biographies of Western Buddhists, and numerous works by teachers active in the West. I also conducted a long series of formally structured interviews with Buddhist teachers and students that I taped at various Buddhist centers around the country. Just as important as the structured interviews, my visits to those centers also gave me a chance to just hang out and get a feeling for each place and the people who ran it.

Finally, I drew on that ubiquitous sociological tool—the survey. Although surveys are not well suited to plumb the depths of such uncharted seas, they are an unequaled source of hard data for further analysis. In compiling my research, I surveyed the membership of seven different Buddhist centers in North America. From the Zen tradition there were the Berkeley and Rochester Zen Centers. Karma Dzong in Boulder, Colorado, and the Dzogchen Foundation in Boston, Massachusetts, represented the Tibetan tradition, and there were two San Francisco Bay Area Vipassana groups, one led by Gil Fronsdal and the other by James Baraz. Finally, I also included one nonaffiliated Buddhist group—the White Heron Sangha in San Luis Obispo, California. The groups to be sampled were not selected at random but were part of what sociologists call a purposive sample, that is, I intentionally chose groups I thought would best represent the full range of this new Buddhism. I selected two groups from each of the three traditions most active in the West, and one from the smaller number of groups that follow a nonsectarian approach. I also attempted to get broad geographic representation and tried to seek out the groups that seemed to represent the most influential lineages within their tradition.

Altogether, 359 people filled out my four-page survey, which was distributed along with a stamped return envelope at group meetings. I would have preferred to mail the questionnaires directly to the members so that I could send them follow-up mailings to nag them to respond. But the groups were understandably protective of their members' privacy and none of them were willing to give me their mailing lists. The response rate varied from one group to another, depending largely on how strongly their leaders encouraged participation, but as a whole the members of these centers proved quite cooperative. Despite some rather nosy questions, the overall response rate was well above 50 percent, and in one group it ran to over 90 percent. (The Dzogchen Foundation was the only group with a response rate below 50 percent, and I was forced to distribute a second round of surveys to bring up the sample size.) It is difficult to say how those who filled out the questionnaires differed from those who threw them in the trash can, but it is likely that more dedicated and involved members were over represented in my survey, since apathetic members would have been less likely to attend the meetings at which the surveys were distributed.

The New Buddhism

It is 4:45 A.M. A young man with a shaved head and the black robes of a monk has just emerged from the side of a large building that looks like a cross between a country barn and a Japanese pagoda. He's holding a bell mounted on a wooden stick, and it clangs loudly as he begins following a twisted path marked by a series of glowing nightlights.

An unlikely assortment of people begin filing sleepily out of their rooms: a middle-aged man in dark jeans with his long gray hair tightly pulled back into a ponytail; a woman in her late thirties wearing an expensive designer jogging suit; an older woman in a frayed sweater and a pair of well-worn sweatpants; two men and a woman in close-cropped hair and black Buddhist robes; a girl in her late teens or early twenties with punk hair and a mismatched thrift store outfit that seems one size too small; an immaculately dressed man in his early sixties with silver hair and a couple of expensive rings.

One by one they file into a large meditation hall that used to be a barn in earlier days. Each steps in carefully, leading with the foot nearest to the door hinge, arms down against their stomach with their right hand wrapped around the fist of the left. After entering, each bows to the altar bearing a statue of Manjusri, the bodhisattva of wisdom. The raised platform of shiny wood that rings the hall is lined up with rows of large square pads, each with a round meditation cushion resting in the center. Each person goes to the front of one of the black cushions and bows. Turning to their right they bow again, and finally they mount the platform and take their place on their cushions. Wiggling back and forth settling into his seat, one man assumes the classic lotus position. His legs crossed with each foot mounted on the opposite thigh, he has something of the regal bearing of a king. The woman next to him sits with her legs tentatively crossed at the ankles. There is a black pillow propped under each of her knees which stubbornly refuse to reach the floor. Several people have their cushion on edge between their legs and are resting on their knees and the tops of their feet. One woman is sitting on a chair with a straight back, her feet planted firmly on the floor.

There are thirty-five or forty people seated in the hall when a deep bell sounds. By then most of the squirming has stopped, and the meditators sit facing the wall. About five minutes later they hear the rustling of robes as the head priest comes in, circles the hall, and takes her place at the front. After that nothing much seems to happen except for an occasional sneeze or the sound of someone carefully adjusting their posture. Finally, after what seems like days to some and minutes to others, a bell sounds and everyone stands up, straightens their cushions, and begins silently walking in a slow circle around the hall. Five minutes later another bell sounds and they all return to their cushions. And so it goes for most of the next seven days—hour after hour sitting quietly facing the wall or walking in slow circles, punctuated with occasional services of bowing and chanting and a daily talk from the head teacher.

All forms of Buddhism—whether it is the new Western Buddhism, the ethnic Buddhism of the migrant enclaves, or traditional Asian Buddhism—share a common quest: liberation from greed, hatred, and delusion and the suffering they cause. Their paths to that goal, however, often take markedly different directions. As we have seen, in most forms of traditional Buddhism there is sharp distinction between the lay people and the monks, nuns, and priests. At least in theory, the members of those elite groups devote their lives to the quest for liberation; sometimes through the kind of meditation the Buddha recommended for his followers, sometimes through strict moral discipline, sometimes through academic studies, sometimes through the single-minded performance of elaborate rituals. For the vast majority of traditional Buddhists, however, the quest for liberation takes a backseat to the demands of everyday life. The most those average Buddhists can hope for is to accumulate merit by good works or through the grace of a powerful Buddha or bodhisattva and someday win a better rebirth either in a paradise or in a life that offers them the chance to devote themselves to the *Dharma* (truth) and win enlightenment.

In the new Buddhism, this fundamental distinction between monk and layperson is almost wiped away. Although some people live a more monastic lifestyle while others live as householders, the pursuit of liberation is common to them all. The new Buddhism takes the path of liberation that was preserved and refined by countless generations of Asian monks and offers it up to anyone who is interested.

When Asian Buddhists visit the West, they are often confused by Western practitioners they meet. Not really monks but far more involved and dedicated than most laypeople, Western practitioners are hard to classify with the categories their teachers imported from the East. Many Western Buddhist centers have full-time residents who devote most of their time and energy to their Buddhist pursuits, and some of the larger groups maintain isolated retreat facilities for more intensive practice. A few Westerners even shave their heads and take monastic vows, but they remain a distinct minority. And these Western monks never receive the kind of awe and respect that separates the Asian monks from the laity. To most Asians, being a monk means being celibate, but celibacy is a very hard sell in the midst of Western consumer culture. In Western eyes what was traditionally viewed as great moral virtue often becomes a kind of pointless repression. Moreover, the scarcity of isolated monasteries means that the monks are often in much closer contact with the outside world than their Asian counterparts. All in all, the distinction between the monk and the layperson in the new Buddhism is a fuzzy one. Monks are not set off by an aura of holiness and reverence as they are in Asia. Although their practice is usually more highly focused, they are not really doing anything that isn't common among the laity as well. In one sense everyone is a kind of monk, and in another no one is.

If there is a single characteristic that defines the new Buddhism for most of its members, it is the practice of meditation. When I asked the members of the groups in my survey, the overwhelming majority ranked meditation as the single most important activity their group does. But they do more than just talk about it; the survey shows that almost all of these new Buddhists try to carry on a regular meditation practice.

Despite the enormous cultural gulf, the style of meditation they practice is directly derived from the practices and traditions of Asian monastics. Some respondents reported practicing exotic visualizations or working on the unanswerable riddles know as *koans*, but most of their meditation focuses on their breath—either counting breaths one by one or simply following them with close attention.

Most of the time, the members of these groups meditate at home, often before a simple altar adorned perhaps with an incense burner, a statue of the Buddha, or a painting of one of the numerous boddhisattvas who symbolize an important virtue or quality of mind. They also attend group meetings at Buddhist centers or in an ad hoc variety of rented halls and private homes. Although the focus is on meditation, members frequently chant together and perform other rituals and listen to talks from their teachers. These gatherings not only allow the members to encourage each other's practice but they provide the opportunity for social bonding and community building.

In addition to their daily meditation, most of my respondents also attended intensive meditation retreats. These retreats, which usually range from half a day to a couple of weeks in length, offer participants the opportunity to expand and deepen their meditation practice. Each group and each lineage runs its retreats a little differently. Some are rigorous, tightly structured, and highly demanding, whereas others are more relaxed and easygoing. Nonetheless, a common pattern is emerging among all these groups. For one thing, the retreatants are usually expected to maintain silence whenever possible. Many participants report the odd feeling of having attended retreats with the same people over and over again, yet hardly ever having had much of a conversation with them. Retreatants usually rise early and devote long days to alternating periods of sitting and walking meditation. The retreats also provide the opportunity for closer contact with their teachers, who give talks and private interviews to help the retreatants with their practice and with the powerful experiences that often occur during these periods of intense meditation. Many retreats also have work periods where the participants pitch in to help with all the physical demands created by any large gathering of people.

No other transformation is more critical to the creation of Western Buddhism than the way it is redefining gender. In traditional Asian culture, the world of the monastic elite is a male world. Although a few female orders have existed over the centuries, they have always been separate and subordinate to male authority. Some traditional Buddhists have even questioned the ability of women to reach enlightenment at all. In this view, the best a woman can do is to gain merit through good works and by supporting male monastics, so that she can win rebirth as a man in her next life. Such extreme sexism is by no means universal, but women have certainly played second fiddle in Asian Buddhism.

How different are things in the West? Western Buddhist groups have often imported the prejudices of their Asian teachers or assimilated the gender biases of their own culture. At the same time, however, there is clearly a powerful tide pushing the new Buddhism toward gender equality. While Eastern Buddhism picked up its cultural baggage from the ancient patriarchal traditions of Asia, the new Buddhism is taking shape in an age of feminism and a radical rethinking of gender that is rocking even the most staid denominations. Of course, our society remains rife with sexism and patriarchal stereotypes, but the kind of women and men (the women slightly outnumber the men in most Buddhist groups) who are attracted to Western Buddhism also tend to be the same kind of highly educated, left-leaning people who are most likely to believe in gender equality. In almost all the centers in which control has passed from the hands of Asian teachers to their Western students, women and men practice together as equals, sharing the same roles and the same responsibilities in ways unheard-of in most of Asia. Although virtually all Asian and a majority of Western teachers are male, there are a growing number of women in those top positions of respect and authority. Today, no one is surprised to see women leading retreats, giving dharma talks, or running major Buddhist centers. On a more theoretical level, no matter who occupies those positions of power, nearly all Western Buddhist groups recognize the full equality of the sexes and the ability of all persons of either gender to realize their true nature and attain enlightenment.

Of course, we all know that our actual practice often fails to live up to our ideals, and Western Buddhism is no exception. Many women continue to feel a sense of psychological alienation and sometimes social exclusion as well. The Asian teachers are male, the images of the Buddha are male, the leaders of most of the groups are male, and some women complain that the practice itself is still male oriented. On the other hand, however, less than a third of my respondents felt that discrimination against women was a serious problem in Western Buddhism, and most felt that women had an equal chance with men to gain leadership positions in their own group.

The transformation of gender that is evolving in the new Buddhism is not, however, simply a matter of ending discrimination or of women joining a world that used to be reserved for the male Buddhist elite. As more women are becoming full and equal participants in Western Buddhism, their presence is transforming the tradition itself. Numerous changes in attitudes and approaches reflect the experience of women's culture as it mingles with that of their male counterparts, and a new generation of women teachers is bringing a fresh perspective that attracts male and female students alike.

A broad-ranging eclecticism is another characteristic of the new Buddhism that is seldom seen in Asia. In many of the countries of southern Asia, the Theravadin tradition is so dominant that little thought or attention is given to other forms of Buddhism. The Tibetan Vajrayana encompasses a much broader variety of approaches, but all of them are seen from a particular Vajrayana perspective, and there is little knowledge of Zen or the other Buddhist developments of East Asia. Japan probably has more separate and distinct Buddhist sects than any other country but they tend, in typical Japanese style, to stick pretty much to themselves.

Ironically, the real meeting place for the Buddhist traditions from throughout Asia has been in the West. Indeed, the very idea that there is some common thread known as Buddhism that runs through all those traditions is a Western one. Although most of the teachers in new Buddhist groups try to follow one or another Asian tradition, there is a unique willingness to utilize insights from other perspectives as well. It is not at all uncommon for teachers from two different traditions to lead a retreat together or for a teacher to give a dharma talk that not only quotes other Buddhist traditions but Christians, Muslims, and contemporary psychologists as well. Moreover, the important figures who have been active in the West are known to Buddhist teachers from all lineages, and they are coming to form a distinct Western tradition all its own. The "beginner's mind" described by Suzuki Roshi, the "crazy wisdom" of Trungpa Rinpoche, or Jack Kornfield's stories blending ancient wisdom and Western psychology are grist for the lectures and books of Western Buddhists from all traditions.

Not very surprisingly, the most perplexing problems faced by Western Buddhism revolve around those ubiquitous issues of sex and power. Time and again, emerging Buddhist groups have struggled with the contradiction between the almost unquestioned authority, power, and prestige the Asian teachers enjoy in their own traditions and the Western notions of democracy and equality. When the Asians first arrived in the West, they were given an exalted status among their followers, and all the power and authority that accompanies it. But when those teachers abused their power or were succeeded by their Western students, the ideals of egalitarianism quickly reemerged. Today, most Western Buddhist groups remain deeply ambivalent about the role and the authority of their teachers. On one level, it is a clash between Asian traditions of collectivism and Western values of democracy and equality. But the problem goes deeper than a clash of cultures and is unlikely to be resolved simply by shedding the cultural baggage inherited from the East. The tremendous respect and admiration Western Buddhists have for their teachers is not just the result of Eastern cultural influence. The members of these groups want to see their teachers as truly enlightened beings whose depth of understanding and wisdom sets them far apart from ordinary people. And if those teachers are indeed enlightened, it follows that they may make administrative decisions or carry on their personal relationships in ways that other people simply don't understand.

The relationship between students and teachers is a little different in every group. But in general it seems that Western teachers still retain much of the enormous authority and prestige of their Asian predecessors, but it is a *provisional* authority. Teachers whose personal or professional lives violate the expectations of their students often run into serious trouble. Most of the major Buddhist centers in the West have been rocked by some kind of scandal or schism in the last two decades. In some cases the teacher has been removed and replaced with someone else. Other cases have resulted in the creation of new administrative structures and new restraints on the power of the teacher, or a mass exodus of the disaffected who go on to form their own group or just drop out. But however these problems work themselves out, structures and traditions are evolving that define the limits of the teacher's power and what to do when those limits are exceeded.

> The front of the New Age bookstore in upscale Marin County is lined with the usual rows of shelves full of the usual books, magazines, and tapes. But in the back there is a large room whose walls are bursting with a visual riot of Tibetan paintings, Hindu and Buddhist sculptures, incense burners, and Asian art. There are thirty or forty people seated on the floor and in a row of chairs at the back of the room. At the center of all this is a man who looks to be in his forties wearing the robes of a Tibetan lama, but his light skin, curly hair, and slight New York accent leave no doubt that he is as American as anyone in the room. He leads them in an ancient chant: *Om mani padmi hum*. Over and over again. Slowly at first, then picking up speed, he adds new accents and an occasional counter rhythm. When the chant dies away in a long droning note, they sit quietly in meditation for ten or fifteen minutes. Finally, the teacher begins his talk, weaving Buddhist philosophy into an often hilarious story about the acute insecurities he felt as a teenager in high school. Afterward a respectful line of students approaches him with their personal comments and problems, and the others wander off to sip tea together or return to their homes.

Buddhism in Postmodern Society

Much to the chagrin of many of its long-term stalwarts, Buddhism has become rather chic in recent years—a new and exotic religion seemingly free from the dogmatism and intolerance of more familiar faiths. A wide assortment of actors, writers, musicians, artists, and other media figures have publicly proclaimed their affiliation. But aside from the vagaries of fashion and style, Buddhism's influence in the West has grown steadily year by year, decade by decade.

The question of exactly how many Buddhists there are in the West is still difficult to answer. Even the issue of who is or is not a Buddhist is a complex one, if for no other reason than the fact that there is nothing in Western Buddhism that demands exclusivity. As far as the Buddhists are concerned, at least, it is quite possible to be both a Buddhist and a Christian, Muslim, or Jew. (We will examine this issue in more depth in chapter 6.) But when Westerners have tried to estimate the number of Buddhists in their midst that fact has pretty much been ignored. The most common assumption is that someone is a Buddhist if they say they are, but that identification is taken to preclude membership in any other religion at the same time.

The most common estimates put the number of Buddhists in the United States somewhere between 1 and 4 million persons. The general survey of American religion conducted by Barry Kosmin and Seymour Lachman of the City University of New York in 1990 found that about 0.4 percent of the population of the United States called themselves Buddhists. Multiplying that estimate by the current population would lead us to conclude that there are about 1.1 million American Buddhists.[1] There are two reasons to believe that the percentage of Buddhists in the American population has gone up considerably in the decade since that estimate was made, however. First, there has been a lot of immigration from the Buddhist countries of Asia, and, second, the new Buddhist groups we are studying have been growing at an explosive rate. Martin Baumann estimated the number of American Buddhists at 3 to 4 million in his 1997 article in the *Journal of Buddhist Ethics*, and he concluded that 800,000 of them were "Euro-Americans." For Great Britain he puts those figures at 150,000 and 50,000 respectively. If you total up his estimates for all the Western nations you end up with from 5.2 to 6.3 million Buddhists with about 1.2 million coming from Western backgrounds.[2] But when considering such figures it is important to keep in mind that many Westerners who do not identify themselves as Buddhists are nonetheless deeply involved in Buddhist practice.

Whatever the number of people involved in the new Buddhism, there is a general agreement that their numbers have been increasing rapidly. We know, for example, that the number of Buddhist books sold in the West has exploded in recent years. A 1998 article in *Publisher's Weekly* proclaimed that "titles about the 2,500-year-old Buddhist tradition are among the hottest sellers in religion books, attracting readers who once wouldn't have know a lama from a lamp."[3] Perhaps more significantly, the number of Buddhist centers that focus on meditation has also shown explosive growth. The best measure we have of this growth in North America comes from the comprehensive guide to "Buddhist America" compiled by

Don Morreale and his associates. The first edition of this guide, which covered the year 1987, listed 429 meditation-oriented Buddhist centers in North America. Ten years later, the listings in the guide's new edition had more than doubled to 1,062 centers. Moreover, there has been a similar increase in the British Isles. The Buddhist Society, which is head-quartered in London, has been publishing a directory of Buddhist groups in the United Kingdom and Ireland since 1979, and every edition has shown a substantial increase in the number of active groups. In their first directory they listed only seventy-eight Buddhist groups. By 1987, that number had more than doubled to 189 and in 1997 it was 370.

Part of the reason for this remarkable growth is simply the vast im-provements in global communications that have incited all manner of new cultural contacts and have brought ever increasing numbers of West-erners into contact with Asian thought. Another important factor is the kind of adaptations Buddhism is making to the Western environment that we have just been discussing. This new Buddhism is more accessible and less "foreign" than its more traditional siblings. In addition, there is a powerful affinity between methods, goals, and perspectives Buddhism has to offer and the dilemmas of life in the postmodern world.

To understand the nature of this attraction, we need to see who joins these new Buddhist groups and why. A look at the demographics of the new Buddhism certainly produces a fascinating picture. Far from the broadly based mass movement that most of its founders would probably have preferred, the new Buddhism has its strongest appeal to a relatively small slice of the public, but it is nonetheless a slice that is likely to wield a disproportionate influence on the evolution of Western culture in the years ahead. Ethnically, the members of these Buddhist groups are over-whelmingly white—a matter that has been of considerable concern to Buddhist leaders. Members also tend to be from the middle and espe-cially the upper-middle class. But while their income is significantly higher than the national average, the educational level of American Buddhists is right off the charts, and it appears that these Buddhists may well be the most highly educated religious group in the West today. Just as Buddhists are far more highly educated than the average Westerner, they are far more liberal and far more likely to support environmental, antiwar, and human rights causes.

Why do these wealthy, liberal, highly educated Anglos join Buddhist groups? When asked to evaluate various reasons for getting involved in

Buddhism, my respondents emphasized their desire for "spiritual growth" above all other motivations. But what that means isn't exactly clear. Some are certainly attracted by superficial appearance. Buddhism appears mysterious and exotic to many Westerners, and these days more than a little bit cool. Some spiritual seekers believe that Buddhism will give them some kind of special wisdom that will make them better people or set them off from their less-developed fellows. But below such motivations often lies a deeper desire to deal with various kinds of pressing personal and social problems. It is no coincidence that the same kinds of people who are attracted to Buddhism are also the ones most likely to become involved in psychotherapy. Indeed, meditation itself can become a kind of psychotherapy that allows seekers to see their true feelings and face them more directly. At the deepest level, however, the project of Buddhism is not to deal with the various problems of the self but to see through the whole endeavor of self-construction, in other words, to reach enlightenment. And the quest for enlightenment is certainly of the utmost importance to many of these new Buddhists.

Although people often see today's new religious movements as a response to the personal isolation and social alienation so common to contemporary society, the members of groups I surveyed did not assign particularly great importance to building new relationships or a sense of community. More than the quest for community, the social roots of this movement are to be found in the changing sense of self in postmodern society. In traditional societies and in the early epochs of the modern era, our sense of self-identity was far more secure than it is today. Whether a person was at the top or the bottom of the social heap, his or her identity received consistent support and constant reinforcement from the surrounding world. In these societies, virtually everyone we come into contact with knows "who we are" and the social expectations placed on us are usually not only consistent but highly coercive. Most people simply see no alternative to being who society tells them they are. Perhaps the defining characteristic of postmodern society is the fragmentation of that social consensus. There are so many images, so much information, so many conflicting assumptions and expectations that things often don't seem to make much sense. In this environment, self-identity is fundamentally transformed from something we are given to something we must actively construct from a melange of information and opinions. As postmodern men and women struggle with the anxieties attendant upon this project

of self construction, they are inevitably attracted to any tradition or philosophy that offers some hope of relief. And as I will argue in the following
chapters of this book, Buddhism's radical rejection of the independent
reality of the self offers a kind of ultimate solution to this endless, all-
consuming struggle.

Two

✳

ASIAN ROOTS

The Origins of the Buddhist Tradition

The idea that there is a revolutionary new kind of Buddhism growing in the West probably doesn't mean much to most of us, since we know so little about what has gone before. Readers familiar with the sweeping panorama of Buddhist history may want to skip this chapter, but I would urge others to read on. For to really understand this new Buddhism, we must first understand the old by tracing its roots and examining the seeds from which it sprang. That is, however, no easy task. Buddhism is the oldest of the world's universal religions, and much of its early history is clouded by the dust from the more than one hundred generations that have passed since its inception. (Faiths such as Judaism, Shinto, and Hinduism are not considered universal religions because they appeal primarily to the members of a single ethnic group.) Given the metaphysical bent of high Indian culture, it is not surprising that many records still exist of ancient Buddhism's philosophical schools and religious debates. But we are much less informed about the concrete historical events that shaped its growth or the popular Buddhism that flourished away from the monasteries and universities. As Buddhism spread from India into the cultural sphere of the worldly and pragmatic Chinese, the historical record improves substantially, but there are still numerous gaps and omissions.

Though the story may be incomplete, it is a dramatic one boasting all the elements of the best fiction. It contains countless characters in a vast setting that spans twenty-five centuries and numerous different cultures. It tells the triumphant story of the discovery of great transcendent wisdom and the tragedy of slaughtered monks and corrupt religious institutions. The pages of this history are filled with the grand splendor of court religion and the simple austerity of wandering seekers; great patriarchs and charismatic rebels, wild-eyed magicians, simple peasants, brilliant intellectuals, pedantic imitators, self-indulgent pretenders, and furiously dedicated monks and nuns. But underlying all this drama is one unwavering theme: the search for the solution to the riddle of human suffering.

The Beginnings

India already had a long cultural tradition when Siddhartha Gautama was born in the fifth or sixth century B.C.E. But it was an era of social and spiritual ferment that produced a unique cultural flowering not only in India but in Greece and China as well. The Iron Age had dawned in India, and iron-tipped plows created an unprecedented agricultural surplus that could support far larger governmental and religious institutions than ever before. The economy was shifting from local barter to a far-flung network of trade based on monetary exchange. This expansion of commerce and industry led to the growth of a prosperous merchant class that was nonetheless subject to the domination of the priests and nobility, and it was among the merchant classes that the Buddha's new religion was to find its most receptive audience.

Politically, northern India was wracked with conflict. On one side were the kings of the growing empires based on this new economic system. On the other were the tribal republics such as the one Siddartha's father ruled. As in the Greek city-states, the rigid social hierarchy in these republics excluded too many people from political participation to be called democratic by today's standards. But assemblies of local aristocrats did often direct the course of political life and elect their own rulers. These small states were, however, no match for the great empires that were expanding across India, and traditional tribal society was crumbling before the onslaught of change.

The popular religion of the time was based around numerous local cults that were overlaid with an elaborate ritualism led by the hereditary

Brahman priesthood. But this established order was under strong challenge from an ever expanding group known as the *s'ramanas*—wandering ascetics who advocated a host of radical new ideas. These "strivers" gave up family life and their normal livelihood and wandered from village to village. They either lived off the land or by begging, and they often formed loose congregations around a particular master. These teachers advanced an enormous range of different theories and ideals, but there were several common themes. The s'ramanas scornfully rejected the religion led by the Brahmans, ridiculing its rituals, pointing out the contradictions in its sacred texts, and even charging its priests with defrauding the public by charging exorbitant fees for performing useless rites. In the view of the s'ramanas, wisdom was not to be gained from some secret store of revealed truths such as the Brahmans claimed to posses, but from direct examination of one's own personal experience or though such other paths as logical analysis or ascetic discipline. Many s'ramanas practiced celibacy and other ascetic regimes that they believed produced spiritual insight or magical powers, but others were strict materialists and outspoken skeptics.

This era of Indian history provided uniquely rich soil for the growth of new ideas and new religious movements. The constant competition between different teachers and systems of belief and the frequent public debates made it easy for innovative thinkers to gain an audience. Equally important, the prosperity of the times and the Indian custom of donating food and money to spiritual seekers provided an independent economic base from which they were relatively free to challenge the dominant beliefs of their society, a society that was itself in a state of upheaval—a fact that only intensified the quest for spiritual truth that has been so much a part of Indian culture over the centuries.

SIDDHARTHA GAUTAMA: THE BUDDHA Westerners are sometimes confused because the founder of Indian Buddhism is known by many different names. Although in the West he is usually simply called the Buddha, most Buddhists believe that there have been numerous other Buddhas in the past and that more are to come in the future. Aside from his family name, Siddhartha Gautama, he is often called Sakyamuni, which translates as "the sage of the Sakya clan." But he is also referred to as the Tathagata and by numerous other honorific titles such as the World Honored One.

The particulars of Sakyamuni's life are too well-known to require more than a brief summary here. Siddhartha was born a prince in one of the remaining tribal republics in the foothills of the Himalayas—the heir of the man elected king of the Sakya clan and the ruler of their territories. His mother died soon after his birth, and following local custom his father soon married his mother's younger sister. By all accounts Siddartha's early life was one of comfort and ease. Legend has it that a soothsayer told his father that Siddartha would become either a great king or a great saint. Determined that his son would someday rule over the family realm, Siddartha's father tried to hide all suffering from him so he would not be tempted into the religious life. One text attributed to the Buddha himself describes his life this way:

> In my father's house were ponds here and there where they planted red, white, and yellow lotuses and water lilies for my pleasure. I used nothing but fine incense from Kasi. My turbans, robes, underclothes, and outer clothes were of fine, light Kasi silk. Day and night, when I walked through the grounds, someone held a white umbrella over my head to protect me from the heat, the cold, the rain, and falling dust. Three palaces were built for me: one for the hot weather, one for the cold weather, and one for the rainy season. During the four months of the rainy season, I lived in the palace built for such weather, enjoying music played only by beautiful women, and I never went out. In ordinary houses, servants and workers are fed scrap rice and sour gruel, but in my father's house even the servants and workers were given white rice and meat.[1]

As Siddartha grew older, his life of privilege continued, and when he came of age he was married to a beautiful princess, Yasodhara.

Yet no one can be sheltered forever. Legend holds it that one day Siddhartha left his palace for a chariot ride and saw a decrepit old man for the first time. Shocked, he asked the charioteer about the man's condition and was told that it was the fate of all humans. On later trips he saw people sickened by disease, and a dead body. The sensitive Siddartha was profoundly troubled by the suffering he had seen and by the realization that it was an inescapable reality of human life, and he dedicated himself to finding its solution. Siddartha stayed with his family until he fulfilled his obligation to father a son, but soon after that he set out on a new life. Taking one last look at his wife and infant, Siddartha mounted his favorite horse and, accompanied by his charioteer, he rode off toward the great kingdom of Magadha. When he reached the boundary of his tribal lands, he sent his servant back with his horse, exchanged clothes with a passing hunter, and became a wandering s'ramana.

His quest for truth first led him to study under two great meditation masters of the time. Although traditional sources say that Siddhartha quickly mastered their techniques and was soon recognized as their successor, he still felt dissatisfied. Although he could reach states of deep concentration in which nothing could disturb him, the same old problems returned once his concentration was broken. His fundamental questions about the source of human suffering and its solution remained unanswered.

Siddartha next turned to the ascetic practices that were so popular among the s'ramanas of his time, and he spent six long years practicing austerities. He learned to induce a trance by stopping his breath and fasted until he reached the brink of death. A critical turning point in his quest came when he rejected this extreme path and accepted an offering of rice boiled in sweet milk. Henceforth, he became a proponent of what he called the middle way between the indulgent luxury of his youth and the harsh denial of the body he had been practicing.

According to the traditional account, Siddartha had a series of dreams that he was about to become a Buddha. After he regained his strength, he took a seat under a bodhi tree, assumed a meditation posture, and vowed not to leave until he had attained complete perfect enlightenment. Legend has it that the god Mara ("death") was enraged at the prospect of the great bodhisattva's victory and sent an army of fearful demons to assail him. When that failed, Mara himself appeared to challenge Siddartha's right to pursue his path to enlightenment. Finally, Mara sent his three beautiful daughters—Discontent, Delight, and Desire—to tempt Siddartha, but he remained steadfast through it all. By the dawn after the full moon Sakyamuni had attained his goal.

For a time, Sakyamuni wondered whether it was possible to convey the vast insights he had gained to others, and one legend has it that the great Vedic god Brahma personally beseeched him to help alleviate the suffering of humanity. Whatever the reason, his compassion for the suffering of humankind ultimately won out, and Sakyamuni spent the remaining forty-five years of his life as a teacher wandering from town to town spreading the dharma (a term that means many things, including the truth, the teaching, and the nature of things).

It is obvious from the records of his life that the depth of his realization gave Sakyamuni an enormous spiritual charisma, and he soon developed a large body of followers known as the *sangha*. At first, he was simply accompanied by a group of disciples with little in the way of formal structure. As the group expanded, formal rules and initiation ceremonies were created for the monks. Early Buddhist monks lived largely by begging and were expected to have only the barest minimum of personal possessions. Like other s'ramanas, these Buddhist monks lived a wandering life, traveling from place to place spreading the Buddha's teachings. During the summer rainy season, however, they usually settled down and went into retreat together, and it was from this tradition that the first Buddhist monasteries developed.

The sangha was originally organized on the democratic principles of the tribal republic from which Sakyamuni came. Aside from the personal authority of the Buddha, there was no central hierarchy. Leadership in the monasteries was based on the principles of seniority and personal ability, and major decisions required a vote of all the monks. In stark contrast to the orthodox Brahmans, the Buddha accepted followers from all social strata as equal members of the sangha. Sakyamuni also established a monastic order for women, but special rules were eventually created that strictly subordinated the nuns to male authority (see chapter 5 for more on this). In addition to the sangha of monks and nuns, many lay followers were also attracted to the new religion. Although a few exceptions were recognized, the celibate life of a monk or nun was generally considered essential to achieve liberation. Lay Buddhists were encouraged to lead ethical lives and give charity to the monks so that they might create the good karma necessary to be reborn into a future life that offered them opportunity for complete enlightenment.

THE TEACHINGS   Although many scholars have attempted to explain exactly what Sakyamuni realized during his enlightenment, to really have that understanding is itself to be enlightened. Obviously, this is not something that can be achieved by reading a few paragraphs in a book. What we can do is describe Sakyamuni's major teachings—yet even that is no simple task. His teaching career spanned over four decades, and he constantly adjusted his teachings to suit the general level of his audience and the unique needs of the people he was talking to. Another difficulty is that, like Jesus, Sakyamuni's teachings were not set down in writing until long after his death. (Indeed, the Buddha's teaching remained unwritten far longer than Jesus'.) Sakyamuni did, however, tend to give his doctrines in numbered lists, which facilitated memorization. (In fact, it may actually have been the other way around. His teaching may have been reworked by his followers to create lists for easy memorization.) The Four Noble Truths, the Eightfold Path, the Threefold Training, the Four Foods, the Eight Freedoms, the Three Jewels, the Seven Factors of Enlightenment, the Five Skandhas, the Three Poisons, and the Five Precepts are typical of these lists. To the modern reader used to a more discursive presentation, such lists often seem rather stilted. Thus what follows is an attempt to convey the core of Sakyamuni's teachings rather than merely describe these various doctrines.

The first remarkable characteristic of Sakyamuni's teachings is their breadth. While other s'ramanas might expound a particular technique of meditation, metaphysical theory, ethical system, or psychology, Sakyamuni's teachings encompassed them all. But unlike so many other religious leaders, he did not expect his ideas to be accepted on faith. Rather, he called on his listeners to explore their own personal experience to discover directly if they are true or not.

Sakyamuni's teachings can be summarized under three general headings: ethical behavior, meditation, and wisdom. It is clear that he considered all three necessary to enlightenment. Although the Buddha usually stressed compassionate behavior to his least sophisticated audiences, and wisdom can in some sense be seen as the culmination of the quest, these three are not progressive stages but interacting components mutually reinforcing each other. Thus proper behavior facilitates meditation, meditation encourages ethical behavior and leads to wisdom, wisdom encourages proper behavior, and so forth.

The bedrock of the Buddha's ethical teachings was the operation of karma and rebirth—ideas that were widely accepted by Indians of his time. The basic principle is simply that of cause and effect. What happens to us during our life is the result of the karma we create—either in this life or in previous ones. And that karma will in turn determine the kind of lives into which we will be born in the future. Modern-day Buddhists are often told that if they want to know what kind of life they will be reborn into, all they have to do is look at their behavior in this one. The fundamental difference between Sakyamuni Buddha's approach and other common beliefs of the time is that the karma we accumulate is entirely the result of the personal choices we make. Unlike the orthodox Brahman view, rituals and sacrifices are powerless to affect our karma and, unlike the Jain view (the other major new religion to emerge from this fertile period of Indian history), it is the intention, not the result, of our actions that determines our karma. Thus in Buddhism a hateful action that accidentally produces beneficial results will still produce bad karma, while a well-intentioned act will produce good karma regardless of its immediate results. The stark simplicity of this vision has a powerful moral appeal, and it has attracted many average people to Buddhism over the centuries.

Important as ethical behavior was, Buddhism approached it in a far different way from the Western religions. There was no concept of sin or redemption and, as we have seen, the correctness of an action arises from its intention and not from the action itself. The root cause of immorality is ignorance, and its cure is found in wisdom. Sakyamuni did, however, offer some general principles to help guide the behavior of his followers. Laypersons, for example, were expected to strive to live up to five basic precepts, which, in typical Indian style, were expressed entirely in the negative:

1. refrain from taking life
2. refrain from stealing (taking that which is not given)
3. refrain from misusing sexuality
4. refrain from telling lies
5. refrain from taking intoxicants

The expectations for the monks and nuns who committed their entire lives to the pursuit of enlightenment were proportionately greater. Over the years a detailed code of conduct evolved, and violators could be expelled from the order.

The topic of Buddhist meditation is a vast one, and Sakyamuni himself suggested many different techniques to individual students, depending on their level of development and personal circumstances. Many later Buddhist philosophers have attempted to organize these varied meditation techniques into an integrated system in which students start with a basic technique and progress on to more advanced ones. Sakyamuni himself, however, did not seem to follow any fixed pattern but relied on his personal insight into the needs of each student. But whatever the technique, it is clear that Sakyamuni saw meditation as the key to gaining the wisdom necessary for liberation from the suffering of the world. Three of the stages on the Eightfold Path (one of the most central Buddhist doctrines and one that almost certainly came directly from Sakyamuni Buddha) are aspects of meditation. The first is right effort, in which the monk actively attempts to discourage unwholesome states of mind and cultivate positive ones. The second is right mindfulness, that is, bringing every aspect of life into clear conscious awareness. The third is right concentration (*samadhi*), in which monks sit quietly and focus their minds in order to enter into one of several progressively higher meditative states.

The cultivation of wisdom lies at the heart of the Buddha's path and is the key to liberation. But this wisdom is not so much an intellectual understanding as the direct personal realization of the true nature of things. For example, the Buddha's personal attendant, Ananda, was legendary for his knowledge of the Buddha's teachings and his ability to recall them from memory. Yet he is traditionally held to be the last of Sakyamuni's disciples to attain enlightenment.

So what was this wisdom the Buddha was trying to reveal to his followers? The descriptions differ from one source to another with their different languages, different vocabularies, and different cultural perspectives, but it is clear that Sakyamuni saw all existence as a vast interdependent stream of changing phenomena. According to what is called the principle of interdependent causality, everything arises from an infinite chain of past causes and produces effects that have infinite consequences for everything else. Everything is related to and dependent on everything else. Nothing, including ourselves, has any independent being or unchanging essence. We are simply an ever changing stream of experience guided by the karma that we created in the past. There is no separate entity such as a soul or a self to which these experiences happen.

In applying this sweeping vision to human life, the Buddha discovered the Four Noble Truths. The first is that the unenlightened life most of us lead has an unsatisfactory quality about it and is full of suffering. The second is that the cause of this suffering is desire or "thirst." Our desires lead us to long for things we do not have and to become attached to things we do have which sooner or later we always lose. The third truth is that the cause of suffering may be ended. When we stop our clinging, we end suffering and enter the only unconditioned, uncaused state: nirvana. The final truth is the means by which suffering can be ended, that is, the eightfold path involving ethical behavior, meditation, and wisdom.

Volumes have been written trying to explain the nature of nirvana, but ultimately it is beyond the power of our words and concepts to define.

We nonetheless continue to try, usually in terms of what it is not rather than what it is. Nirvana literally means to blow out or extinguish, and it is often said to be the extinction of desire, aversion, and illusion. Some Westerners have mistakenly described nirvana as the extinction of self, but Buddhists hold that there is no self to be extinguished. Another mistaken notion is that nirvana is a kind of nothingness that remains after all things have been eliminated, but Sakyamuni repeatedly described nirvana as beyond the realm both of being and of nonbeing.

Critics of Buddhism have often accused it of being pessimistic and life rejecting, but much of this attitude stems from a misunderstanding of its basic doctrines. The fact that nirvana can best be described in negative terms does not mean it is a negative state. In fact, it is considered a state of the greatest possible bliss. Similarly, Sakyamuni's recognition that life is full of suffering does not mean that he thought that life was all suffering, and the historical record shows that he discussed the many pleasures in life as well. There is, nonetheless, a tendency in early Buddhism, as in much Indian thought of this time, to emphasize the negative side of life and to seek ways to escape from it. The Buddha certainly saw the life of the renunciate who gave up the pleasures of daily life as far superior to that of the householder.

The Evolution of Indian Buddhism

THE EARLY CENTURIES   The death of its charismatic founder is always a time of crisis for a new religion, but early Buddhism probably weathered this crisis more easily than Christianity or Islam. While none of Jesus' disciples could claim to be the "son of God" and no one among Muhammad's followers shared his personal receipt of divine prophecy, Sakyamuni left behind many *arhats* who had traveled the same path he had and experienced many of the same spiritual insights. The Buddha left specific instructions that no one was to be appointed to succeed him and that monks were to work out their own liberation with the dharma as their guide. After his death, the major concern of the sangha was therefore to preserve the Buddha's teachings for future generations. Tradition has it that a general meeting of the sangha was held during the first monsoon after Sakyamuni's death and that great care was taken to preserve and transmit his doctrines—not by writing them down but in what was certainly to become one of the world's most prodigious feats of rote memory. The memorization and repetition of the Buddha's teachings became a kind of spiritual practice in itself, and some monks made the recitation of a particular text their life's vocation. Not surprisingly, however, the followers of the Buddha did not all agree on which renderings of his teachings were accurate, and many conflicting oral traditions continued to be passed along from generation to generation.

Most histories of Buddhism examine the fascinating philosophical disagreements among the different sects in great detail, but these disputes don't really tell us much about what Buddhism meant to most of its followers. Perhaps the best way to get a feel for the day-to-day reality of early Buddhism is to look at the three major groups that made up the Buddhist community: the laity, the average monks and nuns, and the arhats.

The arhats were the living realization of the ideals of early Buddhism (the name literally means "worthy one"), and it was toward the goal of arhatship that every diligent Buddhist strove. The arhat has, in Edward Conze's words, "shed all attachment to I and mine, is secluded, zealous, and earnest, inwardly free, fully controlled, master of himself, self-restrained, dispassionate and austere."[2] Although the monasteries were run on a quasi-democratic basis, the spiritual charisma and prestige of the arhats made them the unquestioned leaders of the Buddhist community.

Around the elite core of arhats was a much larger group of monks and nuns who lived a life of strictly regulated austerity. Upon initiation, the new monk shaved his head, donned a saffron robe, and gave up all his worldly possessions except for his robes and a begging bowl. Originally, the monks were homeless wanderers who settled down together only during the summer. Eventually, large monasteries with a full-time staff developed, but most of the monks still went off to wander and preach during most of the year. Some monks also came to live alone either in huts on the outskirts of a village or deep in the jungles and mountains. Monks were required to follow a strict code of discipline that contained formal procedures for the punishment of violators. Many of the rules, such as the regulations concerning the type of container in which salt might be stored, seem trivial to modern sensibilities. But taken as a whole, the rules had a clear spiritual purpose, especially those prohibiting the taking of life and sexual relations. Monks were also forbidden to work and had to live on charity alone: a requirement that not only encouraged a certain humility but also guaranteed that the monks would have the time to devote to their spiritual quest. There were also many rules that seem oriented toward maintaining a positive image of the order among outsiders.

In addition to the numerous rules that applied to the monks, nuns were subject to eight additional regulations strictly subordinating them to their male counterparts. But women were nonetheless capable of attaining full arhatship. Although the intellectual dueling that was so characteristic of Buddhism throughout the years seems to have been the exclusive province of men, the ranks of the nuns undoubtedly contained many enlightened spiritual masters who have been omitted from the pages of Buddhist history.

Although clearly considered to be of a lower order of spiritual development, the laity must nonetheless have seen themselves as something of a special group. For one thing, after swearing to take refuge in the Three Jewels of Buddha, dharma, and sangha, they were expected to dress in white—a custom that must have helped foster a strong sectarian identification. And despite the fact that the Buddha opened his order to people from all social ranks, most early Buddhists were from the upper strata of society, especially the merchant and noble classes.

To the laity, Buddhism was primarily an ethical religion. The central goal was to acquire merit (good karma), which would then have beneficial effects in this life and in subsequent ones. Although they were not required to follow the stringent monastic code, the layman or laywoman was expected to uphold the five basic precepts. The life of a lay Buddhist was not necessarily one of poverty, but ostentatious personal luxury was to be avoided. The ardent layperson might also pursue a more stringent practice by, for example, fasting four days a month (or more precisely, not eating after the noontime meal as was required of monks) or by practicing complete celibacy. Another important way to gain merit was by supporting the monastic community, for example, by giving food or shelter to wandering monks. Eventually, the idea of the transfer of merit—that the good karma created by one person might be transferred to another—gained great popularity. To this day it is common practice in Buddhist countries for a layperson to pay a monk to recite a *sutra* (religious text) or perform some other holy action in order to transfer the merit to themselves or some deceased relative. Yet despite the important role of the laity, meditation and the study of sophisticated doctrine was left primarily to the monks.

Sakyamuni had a fondness for the sacred places of the villages he encountered in his travels. Although early Buddhists had none of the elaborate rituals of Vedic religion, they continued to venerate these traditional holy places; in time, they constructed many more shrines of their own. The most common were cave temples and *stupas* (a large moundlike structure erected over a holy relic such as some of Sakyamuni's ashes). These places were full of Buddhist symbolism and the faithful would make offerings, bow, circumambulate the shrine, or just stand and reverently remember the sacred presence it symbolized.

Ironically, the establishment of Buddhism as a mass religion that reached beyond the more privileged strata of society was due in no small part to its first great royal patron: King Asoka Maurya of Magadha. King Asoka lived in the third century B.C.E. and is sometimes held to have been the greatest of all Indian rulers. In his early years, he was reputed to be an aggressive and warlike leader, but after his conversion to Buddhism he renounced his militaristic policies and evinced a real concern for the well-being of his people. He not only advanced the cause of Buddhism but began a variety of social programs, encouraged a broad spirit of toleration, and supported all the other major Indian religions as well. Aside from King Asoka's undoubted personal conviction, Buddhism served his political needs as well. For Buddhism is certainly an admirable vehicle to advance the interests of a universal state seeking to incorporate many divergent people under its rule. Not surprisingly, the ideals advocated by Asoka in his numerous surviving edicts were often far removed from the elite Buddhism of the monastery. His pronouncements often spoke of charity, morality, tolerance, and vigor, but he said nothing about meditation or wisdom.

THE RISE OF THE MAHAYANA   As is often the case in Indian history, the record of the growth of the Mahayana is a vague one. It is generally thought to have begun sometime around the first century B.C.E., but there is no consensus about where in India Mahayana Buddhism began, and little or nothing is known about individuals who led these developments. We do know that Indian society and Buddhism itself had undergone some profound changes since Sakyamuni's time. First the tribal republics and then the huge centralized bureaucratic empire of the Mauyras vanished from the scene. Whether in large empires or fragmented principalities, a loose feudal organization based on personal allegiance to local lords predominated for the next thousand years of Indian history. At the same time Indian culture and Buddhism itself were growing increasingly sophisticated. From the original summer camp for wandering ascetics, great Buddhist

monasteries and universities had grown up. The growth of a secular literature, improvements in the techniques of debate and logic, and major advances in the sciences signaled the growing sophistication of elite culture.
A new class of Buddhist scholars with access to rich libraries sprang up,
and they began producing sutras of great philosophical sophistication.

The origins of the Mahayana are usually traced to these new sutras and
the groups that formed around them. The advocates of these sutras saw
enormous "merit" in reading, reciting, understanding, disseminating, and
even ritually venerating them. One contemporary expert called the out-
pouring of these new works "one of the most magnificent outbursts of
creative energy known to human history."[3] Over the years the new sutras
tended to become longer and more complex, and the tone of some grew
increasingly derogatory toward those who followed more traditional
forms of Buddhism. Indeed, the very name Mahayana means the "greater
vehicle," while those who rejected the new approach were dubbed followers of the Hinayana, or "lesser vehicle. " However, most average Buddhists
were not sectarian, and even most monks were probably influenced by
both schools of thought.

One of the most important innovations of the Mahayana was its emphasis on the bodhisattva—an enlightened being on the way to full Buddha-
hood who dedicates him- or herself to help others liberate themselves from
suffering. Although early Buddhism also had the concept of the bodhisattva,
the Mahayana threw open the path to becoming a bodhisattva to anyone
who desired to follow it and created a powerful pantheon of celestial bodhisattvas and cosmic Buddhas who would respond to the pleas of devotees
for their help. The first bodhisattva to become an object of veneration was
Maitreya—the future Buddha who would be born to reignite the flame of
the dharma after it had died out. The Sanskrit root of the word means
benevolent, and to those who worshiped him, Maitreya was a living presence who would help them both with this life and in future ones. One of
the most popular bodhisattvas is Avalokitesvara, the bodhisattva of compassion who listens to all the suffering of the world. In China, Avalokitesvara
metamorphasized into the female deity Kwan-yin. Two other important
bodhisattvas are Manjusri, who symbolizes wisdom, and Samantabhadra,
who represents the spirit of diligent daily practice and application.

In addition to the bodhisattvas, the Mahayanaists conceived a vision of
an inconceivably vast cosmos with entire universes "as numerous as the
sands of the Ganges," some of which are presided over by their own cos-

mic Buddha. These "Buddha lands" are much like the heavens Buddhists believe to be populated by gods except that their inhabitants can practice the way and earn new merit for greater spiritual growth. The most popular of these celestial Buddhas is Amitabha, the Buddha of infinite light, who is one of the most important figures in East Asian Buddhism. Amitabha presides over a pure land, or heaven, and he assists those who have faith in him to be reborn in this wondrous realm. Another celestial Buddha popular in tantric countries is Vairocana, the great illuminator, often seen as Sakyamuni's transcendental counterpart.

The bodhisattva is more than just a supernatural being, however. On a more practical level, the bodhisattva represents an ideal that can be achieved by following a concrete path of Buddhist practice—what is sometimes called the "bodhisattva way." The bodhisattva does not attempt to withdraw from the world or to escape into some blissful state, but lives in the midst of the world's suffering; detached and free, with an unwavering determination to aid those caught up in its delusions. Thus, along with the virtue of wisdom, the Mahayanaists emphasize a second cardinal virtue—compassion. For practitioners, the bodhisattva path begins when they hear the dharma and develop the desire for enlightenment (bodhicitta), and many followers experience a profound conversion experience as they dedicate themselves to this path. The path continues though the practice of the "perfections" known as paramitas—generosity, morality, patience, vigor, meditation, and, the key to them all, wisdom. Another virtue given particular emphasis is skill in means (upaya), that is, the ability to find an effective way to help people out of their suffering.

On a philosophical level, the great Mahayana sutras expounded a doctrine of exquisite subtlety whose apparent contradictions have often baffled the Western student. One of the great yet often puzzling ideas set forth in these sutras is the teaching of emptiness (sunyata). According to the Prajnaparamita Sutras, the perfection of wisdom lies in the direct realization that all dharmas (here meaning the basic unit of existence) are empty. Not only are the events of the material world of life, death, and rebirth empty, but even nirvana itself is empty. Indeed, many Mahayanaists rejected any form of dualism and concluded that nirvana and samsara (the everyday world of suffering and delusion) are actually identical. In the words of the Heart Sutra, "form is emptiness and emptiness is form."

But what does emptiness really mean? Western observers have often equated emptiness with a blank nothingness, but that is a serious mistake.

The sutras frequently warn against this view, reminding their readers that emptiness is beyond both being and nonbeing. Although emptiness is not mere nothingness, neither is it some immutable substance out of which all things are made. Indeed, one of the most fundamental uses of the concept of emptiness is to point to the fact that no such lasting substance exists. The sutras often say that even emptiness is itself empty. In one sense, then, emptiness means empty of independent existence or some immutable essence such as a soul. In another, it means momentary, transitory, impermanent. In a third, it is undifferentiated oneness, the ultimate, the Buddha nature we all have within us. Yet none of these words really captures the real meaning of the term, which can ultimately be grasped only through the direct experience of the state of emptiness itself.

THE TANTRAS   The tantras were the last great development of Indian Buddhism and, at least in the West, the most controversial. The magical elements in tantric belief and the fact that some tantric practitioners intentionally violated traditional Buddhist taboos as part of their spiritual practice (e.g., by eating meat, drinking alcohol, and having sex) led some Western scholars to see tantric practices as a corruption of Buddhism or even to blame them for the fall of Indian Buddhism. But many now recognize the cultural bias in such conclusions. The historical record provides far more support for the view that the growth of tantric practice was part of a revitalization movement that probably helped extend the reign of Indian Buddhism. Indeed, Tantric Buddhism is often called the Vajrayana and is seen as the third major branch of Buddhism, alongside the Hinayana and Mahayana.

As the last of the great Mahayana sutras were being composed in the fourth century c.e., India's second great empire was consolidating its hold on the subcontinent. Although the rulers of the Gupta Empire were not vehement opponents of Buddhism, they were followers of Hinduism and gave most of their patronage to the cult of Vishnu (a major Hindu god). Although Buddhism continued to flourish during this period, it slowly lost ground to a resurgent Hinduism that descended from Vedic religion and was based on fervent devotion to a pantheon of powerful gods. By the seventh century, Chinese travelers such as Hsuan-Tsang and I-Ching reported a considerable decline in Indian Buddhism. While the Buddhist universities continued to be centers of great learning, it appears that they were growing increasingly distant from the mainstream of popular life.

It was during this period that a new type of Buddhist contemplative arose: the tantric *siddha* (adept). These long-haired wanderers were a combination of wizard, saint, and lunatic, and they helped imbue Buddhism with a renewed spirit of vigor and enthusiasm. Living outside the staid monastic communities, the siddhas mocked Buddhism's established institutions and challenged what they saw as its ossified moralism in secret rites that involved everything from eating feces and drinking alcohol to ritual sex. Although some Westerners view them as nothing but corrupt libertines, the true siddha was simply using unorthodox means to achieve the universal goal of all Buddhist sects: liberation. Indian Buddhism had thus come full circle from the arhat retreating from the passions and attachments of the world to the bodhisattva living in detached purity in their midst to the siddhas actively using their passions to liberate themselves from the bonds of illusion.

As often happens with radical religious movements, the techniques and approaches of the siddhas were slowly tamed and integrated into orthodox institutions. Their more scandalous practices were increasingly relegated to a symbolic realm, and the great Buddhist universities that the siddhas had mocked were soon teaching the tantras along with their more traditional curriculum.

Unlike followers of other forms of Buddhism, tantric practitioners have traditionally veiled their most important teachings and practices behind a shroud of secrecy. Part of their motivation was no doubt to conceal their unorthodox activities from prying outsiders, but they also had more spiritual reasons. Tantric practitioners, while considering their path the fastest route to true enlightenment, also thought it the most dangerous one. Many people were considered unsuited for tantric practice, and the guidance of a guru was considered essential. Indeed, absolute faith in a guru, who for some purposes is considered a kind of living deity, is an essential component of tantric practice. Consequently, tantric texts were written in a kind of secret code known as "twilight speech" so that their true meaning could be understood only with the help of a teacher.

One of the distinctive characteristics of this new form of Buddhism was the host of new deities it brought into the Buddhist pantheon. For the first time a significant number of these supernatural figures were female, such as Tara, the "savioress," who became so popular in Tibet. These deities, which can be seen as symbols of various facets of the human psyche, are commonly invoked in ritual or visualized in meditation.

One of the most important tantric practices is the recitation of sacred phrases or syllables known as *mantras*. Indeed, this practice is so fundamental to Tantric Buddhism that it is sometimes referred to as Mantrayana. While Westerners have a tendency to hold vision to be the primary sense ("seeing is believing"), to tantric practitioners sound holds the essence. By reciting the appropriate phrases, the practitioner can ward off evil, evoke the blessings of a supernatural figure, or call it into existence. Repeating a mantra over and over again during meditation is also a powerful device for developing concentration and stilling the mind.

The use of mantras, like many other practices of Tantric Buddhism, is also common in Hinduism, which developed its own tantric tradition during this period. One more distinctively Buddhist device is the *mandala*. The mandala is a kind of sacred space that is packed with symbolic reflections of the seeker's spiritual journey. The mandala often consists of a series of concentric circles with a deity at its center. They are commonly depicted in paintings, but they are also the subject of three-dimensional models, acted out in ritual performances, or just visualized by the tantric yogi during meditation. In one sense, the symbolism of the mandala serves as a spiritual guide for the seeker, but in another sense the whole world can be transformed into a kind of sacred mandala.

The visualization of deities is a third important tantric practice. From the start, the tantric practitioner is usually directed to make a relationship with a particular deity by reciting its mantra, praying, making offerings, and so forth. At more advanced stages, the disciple learns to conjure up a visualization of the deity in fine detail and then dissolve it back into emptiness. Eventually, the disciple actually becomes the deity, which is the object of visualization. At the end of such practice, the practitioner recites a formula reaffirming the fact that the deity is empty and nonexistent, that the world is empty and nonexistent, and that he or she is empty and nonexistent.

The Asian Transmission

The tantras were the last great innovation in Indian Buddhism, and Buddhism eventually died out in the land of its birth. (The last century has, however, seen the reemergence of Buddhism in India among the untouchable castes.) But before the Buddhist flame was extinguished, it had spread thoughout the rest of Asia, where it underwent numerous transformations to meet the changing circumstances it confronted. This subject is a vast one, however, and the focus of the following section will be on the three traditions that have set down the deepest roots in the West, which are most commonly known as Vipassana, Zen, and Tibetan Buddhism.

THE SOUTHERN TRANSMISSION   Sri Lanka and Burma were among the first places outside of India to see the growth of Buddhism, and the ancient Theravadin tradition eventually came to dominate in both countries and in Thailand as well. Doctrinally, Theravadins are the most conservative of the world's Buddhists. As the last remaining sect of the early Buddhism, they are still often skeptical about the innovations of the Mahayana and Tantric traditions. The Theravadin faith is not, however, some kind of unchanging fossil. Although it adheres more closely to the Buddha's original teachings than other Buddhist groups, Theravada has certainly changed over the years. Even the classic form of the Theravadin tradition is not generally considered to have been completed until the work of Buddaghosa, some thousand years after the death of Sakyamuni Buddha.

For most average people in the Theravadin countries, the central objective of religious life is the accumulation of merit or, as it is more commonly termed in the West, good karma. By building up merit, Buddhists believe that their present life will be a happier and more prosperous one and that after death they will have a better rebirth. Many dream of the pleasures of one of the numerous heavens in Buddhist cosmology, but they are equally intent on avoiding one of the Buddhist hells. The principal way to accumulate merit is through proper behavior. On the one hand, good Buddhists try to honor the prohibitions set forth in the five basic precepts and, on the other, they attempt to behave with loving kindness and generosity toward all beings. Of particular importance is generosity toward the monks who depend on public charity for their sustenance. In addition to leading a moral life, the believer can accumulate merit by performing various rituals (e.g., chanting a sacred mantra) by supporting a monk who performs the rituals for them, or by meditation. The goal of accumulating merit is so important in Theravadin countries that many people carry "merit books" in which they keep a careful record of their meritorious activity, which can then be read as they are dying to help ensure a favorable rebirth.

Temples and monasteries, and the monks who inhabit them, are the center of religious life in Theravadin countries, and there is a vital interaction between the monastic sangha and the wider community. The local community provides the economic support necessary to feed and clothe the sangha, and the monks in return carry out many services for the laity. Foremost among these are the performance of rituals that are believed to bestow merit and in some cases even produce direct magical benefits such as bringing rain. The monks also give sermons to the laity and provide other forms of ethical guidance. Like other religious leaders around the world, the monks also preside over various holiday ceremonies and festivals.

Buddhist monks receive enormous respect in Theravadin countries, and they are expected to set an example of right behavior for the community. Pious laypeople might develop a special relationship with a favored monk, taking special care to provide him with the necessities he requires. Many monastic communities do not, however, demand a rigorous schedule of meditation and many monks do little or none of it. It is the so-called forest monks who traditionally lived in remote places away from the cities and villages who are the main bearers of the tradition of meditation in Theravadin countries. But the community does demand ethical behavior of its monks and above all their celibacy.

Although the monks make up an elite religious group, it is a permeable one. In fact, all males in Theravadin countries were traditionally expected to spend a brief period of time as a monk (usually at least one rainy season retreat). Although this practice is less universal than in the past, it is still quite common. Women, on the other hand, are generally excluded from the sangha of monks. In part, this is because menstruation is considered ritually polluting, but the more fundamental cause is the subordinate status of women in traditional culture and the idea that the woman's place is in the home, not the monastery. After menopause, however, an older woman can join special groups of female practitioners that are directly tied to the monasteries or can become a recluse seeking her own liberation.

TIBET   Of all the nations of the world, none has been more shrouded in mystery and wonder than Tibet. Perched in magnificent isolation amid the world's highest mountains, until recently Tibet had little contact with the outside world. But things have changed. The cultural genocide attempted by Tibet's Chinese overlords has left the traditional social system in ruins and helped scatter Tibet's cultural elite to the four corners of the globe. Esoteric teachings that used to be confined to a tiny group of initiates are now being taught to almost anyone with the necessary interest and determination.

Tibet first entered world history in about the seventh century, when its warring clans united under a common sovereign and engaged in a series of conquests that even included some of the outer provinces of the great Chinese empire. As Tibet emerged from its mountainous isolation, it was exposed to Buddhist influences from all sides; from the Buddhist kingdoms of Central Asia, from China, and especially from India. As was the case in much of the rest of Asia, the spread of Buddhism was pushed along by royal patronage especially from the "three religious kings" in the seventh through ninth centuries.

One who stands out among the many powerful religious figures of this era was Padmasambhava—an Indian tantric master who arrived in Tibet in the later part of the eighth century. Legend holds that Padmasambhava had great magical powers and was over a thousand years old when one of the religious kings called him to Tibet to battle the demonic forces that were preventing the completion of Tibet's first Buddhist monastery. Padmasambhava quickly subdued the spirits blocking the monastery's progress and defeated the other magical powers that were blocking the growth of Buddhism in Tibet. Together with his consort, Khadro Yeshe Tshogyal, he traveled trough Tibet performing miracles with his tantric powers and spreading the teachings of Buddhism.

The oldest sect of Tibetan Buddhism, the *Nyingma* (literally, the ancient ones), claims Padmasambhava as its founder and sees him as the spiritual equal of Sakyamuni himself. Compared with the so-called new sects (the earliest of which started around the eleventh century), the Nyingmapa always stayed closer to their Tibetan roots in Bon shamanism (the traditional pre-Buddhist religion of Tibet). Although the Nyingmapa established some of their own monasteries, they remained far more individualistic than other Tibetan Buddhists. Their *lamas* (teachers) were usually married men who operated independently of any central hierarchy. Some specialized in the occult, providing exorcisms, making rain, divining the future, and healing the sick by magical means, while others focused on tantric spiritual practices and gathered an informal group of disciples around them.

With the collapse of the Tibetan monarchy, the country entered a dark age of internal division. Without royal support, Buddhism saw a significant decline in its fortunes. Starting in the eleventh century, the period of the "second transmission" began and Buddhist influence once again began to grow. One of the best-known and most popular figures of this period was Milarepa (1052–1135). Like the other founders of Tibetan Buddhism, his life is shrouded in legend. When he was young Milarepa is said to have taken up black magic to avenge the wrong done to his widowed mother. He not only destroyed his enemies' crops but killed thirty-seven people in his lust for vengeance. When he realized the horrible consequences of what he had done, he turned to the Buddhist dharma to purify himself. He studied with several teachers until he met Marpa Lotsawa, who subjected Milarepa to six years of hard labor, forcing him to repeatedly build and tear down a tall tower. When Marpa finally relented and initiated Milarepa into the tantric mysteries, he soon became a great siddha. Often depicted with a green tinge to his skin from the nettles he had been forced to live on, Milarepa was renowned not only for his miraculous powers but for the beauty of his poetry.

One of the most important sects of Tibetan Buddhism, the *Kagyupa*, traces its lineage from another famous Indian tantric master, Naropa, through Marpa and Milarepa. Like other sects of Tibetan Buddhism, the Kagyupa eventually fragmented into a variety of subsects, the most important of which is the Karma Kagyu. The head of this order is known as the Karmapa. As in several other important lineages this title is passed along through a unique Tibetan system based on reincarnation. When one of these *rinpoches* (previous ones) dies, he usually leaves behind a letter with instructions to guide the hunt for his reincarnation. A search party then looks for a child born at the appropriate time who displays evidence of being the next reincarnation, for example, portentous signs at the time of his birth and the ability to identify objects belonging to the previous rinpoche. Once the correct child is identified, he is usually brought to a monastery and given a special education and upbringing to prepare him to assume his responsibilities. From a sociological standpoint, this unique system not only reduces internal rivalries among those jockeying to be named to high office but produces leaders who have received intense spiritual training from their earliest years. All major Tibetan lineages do not, however, use this system. The leadership of some sects and subsects is transmitted hereditarily through a particular clan. For example, the top position among the *Sakyas*, who were the first Buddhist sect to exercise political control of Tibet, is passed down in the Khon family line.

The last major sect to emerge in Tibet was the *Gelukpas* (partisans of virtue). Their founder, Tsongkhapa, led a movement against the corrupt practices found in some of the older sects and worked tirelessly to revitalize Tibetan Buddhism. He founded several new monasteries, created a rigorous academic curriculum, and demanded that his monks forego sex, liquor, and the practice of worldly magic. Tsongkhapa's nephew later came to be recognized as a reincarnation of Avalokitesvara and the first of a line of incarnating lamas. Like many lamas from the Sakya sect before him, Sodnam Gyatsho, the third lama in this line, went to Mongolia and made many converts to Buddhism. The Mongolians gave him the title Dalai (ocean) Lama, and their support eventually allowed the Gelukpa sect to establish political control throughout Tibet, which lasted until the Communist Chinese crackdown in the late 1950s.

Such a union of religion and secular power was the norm in much of the ancient world. Yet it often seems puzzling to modern-day Westerners, who don't understand the social system in which it was embedded. Tibet is a rugged and sparsely populated land, and most of its people work as either farmers or nomadic pastoralists. The great Tibetan monasteries were not just the religious centers but were the center of all Tibetan civilization. At one time they may have held as much as one-eighth of the entire population of Tibet. The monasteries owned land and serfs, had their own armies, and vied with one another and with outside interlopers for power and influence. They were the centers of Tibetan arts and learning and taught such secular subjects as law and medicine. The class divisions typical of a feudal society were clearly reflected in the monastery. Monks whose families came from the nobility were far more likely to rise to high positions of power and, as we have seen, some monastic posts were passed on through the family line of a powerful clan. Monks were permitted to own private property, and poor monks often worked for the rich ones. Outside this monastic system were the wandering siddhas who also held the title of lama—a group that often served as a source of revitalization and renewal for the more staid institutionalized forms of Buddhism.

Like Buddhists in other parts of Asia, average Tibetans never expected to achieve enlightenment in this lifetime or to engage in meditation or other advanced practices. They turned to religion to help make this life a better one and promote a favorable rebirth in the next one. As in the Theravadin tradition, proper ethical conduct and support for the monkhood were seen as ways of earning the merit to achieve those goals. But popular Tibetan Buddhism also places a particularly strong emphasis on ritual and the magical protection it brings. Perhaps the most important service the monks performed for the laity was the ceremonies that warded off evil forces and enlisted the assistance of the supernatural. Various forms of divination and astrology, as well as the interpretation of dreams and omens, also helped average Tibetans guide their lives. Rituals were performed to win protection against demonic forces, and exorcisms were used to drive them away. To the average Tibetan, the world is full of wrathful spirits that threaten us from all sides, and Buddhism offers a powerful force for supernatural protection.

CHINA   China's first exposure to Buddhism probably did not occur until the first century C.E., and in the beginning it spread slowly. Not only are the Chinese notoriously skeptical of foreign cultural imports, but Buddhism's tendency to reject the world as a realm of suffering and delusion flew directly in the face of the resolute Chinese belief in the importance of life in this world. The Chinese were especially disturbed by Buddhism's shocking indifference to what they saw as the most critical of all social institutions: the family. Over the years, however, Buddhists slowly overcame these barriers by adapting to Chinese cultural expectations and emphasizing the similarities of Buddhism to China's indigenous mystical traditions.

China had a large class of scholars and intellectuals, and they were often fascinated by the contradictions between the various Indian sutras, which were all supposed to have been written by the Buddha. The great scholastic schools of Chinese Buddhism arose from a typically Chinese effort to harmonize these contradictions. The two greatest of these schools—the Hua-yen (Kegon in Japan) and the T'ien T'ai—both saw a particular sutra (the Avatamsaka Sutra for the former and the Lotus Sutra for the latter) as the Buddha's highest teaching. They classified other texts as representing lower level or provisional teachings and then created a philosophic system that integrated all the Buddhist teachings into a hierarchical whole.

The intellectuals were, of course, only a tiny elite class, but Buddhism also had a major impact on the religious lives of the masses of average people. As in other lands, popular Buddhism in China had a strong ethical orientation, and the most popular sects focused primarily on worship and devotion. Like its Indian predecessor, Chinese Pure Land Buddhism was centered around the figure of Amitabha Buddha, who presided over the Western paradise. According to Pure Land belief, Amitabha helps those with a sincere faith in him to be reborn into his paradise. But rather than emphasize meditation on Amitabha as their Indian ancestors did, the Chinese practice focused on chanting the phrase *Namo A-mit'o Fo*—Hail Amida Buddha! Pure Land Buddhism proved to have an enormous appeal to average Chinese. After all, few people had any hope of learning to read or write much less of understanding intricacies of Buddhist philosophy or living a disciplined monastic life. Faith in Amitabha was, on the other hand, something they could and did understand. Indeed, this faith became so popular that as Richard Robinson and Willard Johnson put it, "No native Chinese god has ever commanded the universal worship that Amita has received."[4]

Perhaps the most unique and influential of all schools of Chinese Buddhism was the Ch'an sect. Ch'an is a Chinese corruption of *dhyana*, the Sanskrit term for the states of higher consciousness experienced during meditation; Zen is its Japanese equivalent. Ch'an Buddhists are often described as the sect that centers on meditation rather than sutra study, ethical discipline, or devotionalism, although the matter is a good deal more complex than that.

The credit for the founding of the Ch'an sect is traditionally given to a traveling Indian monk and meditation master named Bodhidharma, who is believed to have arrived in Canton by sea in about 470. Although there are several different versions of the story, tradition has it that Bodhidharma soon met the pious Emperor Wu of Liang. In one version, the emperor described his great generosity to Buddhist causes and asked Bodhidharma how much merit he had gained through his efforts. The Indian monk stunned the emperor with his reply—"none at all"—erasing in one stroke the almost universal Buddhist belief in the accumulation of merit through pious deeds. Another version of this encounter has the emperor asking Bodhidharma about the highest principle of the holy teachings of Buddhism and Bodhidharma responding, "Emptiness: nothing is holy." The shocked emperor then asks, "Who is this man standing before me?" to which Bodhidharma responds "I don't know." In both versions, Bodhidharma either is banished or voluntarily leaves and spends the next nine years staring at the wall of the Shaolin temple—a form of meditation that has since come to be known as "wall-gazing Zen." These tales not only illustrate the iconoclastic tradition of the Ch'an school but provide examples of one of its most important teaching techniques—short and often highly enigmatic stories relating the actions of enlightened masters.

Bodhidharma's Chinese successors in the Ch'an sect soon launched one of history's most remarkable bursts of religious creativity. This "golden age of Zen" occurred during a broad flowering of Chinese culture that took place in the Tang dynasty (roughly from 618 to 907). The Tang emperors unified China after centuries of division and conflict, and the new regime opened up new opportunities for capable men with a system of merit-based examinations that became increasingly important in gaining high bureaucratic office. The government of the Tang was, nonetheless, dominated by a small aristocracy of landed families, and it exercised vast powers over every aspect of its citizens' lives. The central government was the official owner of all land in China and had the power to redistribute it upon the death of any tenant. It controlled the price of food through an "ever-normal" granary system and operated regulated monopolies for other essential goods such as iron and salt. The prosperity of this era made the cities of the Tang the most wealthy and cosmopolitan to be found anywhere in the world, and they bustled with creativity in scholarship and the arts.

The great religious revolution of the Ch'an masters, nonetheless, occurred in remote rural monasteries and temples far from the burgeoning cultural centers. Although the affluence of the time allowed generous imperial patronage for Buddhism, that patronage also brought with it strict state controls and a sense of complacency that sapped the spiritual vigor of the established sects. The creators of this new style of Ch'an Buddhism, like the Indian siddhas before them, were revolutionaries challenging the religious establishment and the restraints of conventional society. In contrast to the staid self-control of the traditional sects, the adherents of this new Buddhism acted with a radical disregard for social custom that must have made them seem like madmen to many of their contemporaries. In the words of Heinrich Dumoulin, they would "burn Buddha images and sutras, laugh in the face of inquirers or suddenly shout at them, and indulge in a thousand follies."[5]

The beginnings of this new approach are reflected in the Platform Sutra which is traditionally attributed to the sixth patriarch of Ch'an, Hui-neng. This sutra attacked the goal-oriented style of meditation that sought to attain a pure or quiet state of mind through self-controlled effort. One of the pivotal figures in the Ch'an revolution was the great Ma-tsu (709–788), who developed a host of new techniques to shock his students out of their attachment to their habitual patterns of thought and into the direct realization of their true nature. Sometimes it was a completely unexpected answer to a student's question, an earsplitting shout, or even a physical assault. The key was not so much in the technique but the timing of the strike to cut the ground out from under the student. One favored device was to ask a student an unanswerable question and then shout suddenly in his ear while he was struggling for an answer. Another was to unexpectedly call out a student's name after he had just turned to leave and then demand, "What is it?" Ma-tsu's students were likely to be pummeled with blows at the most unexpected moments. He is even credited with enlightening one student by painfully twisting his nose. Such a man as this certainly had few predecessors in a faith that traditionally saw nonviolence and peaceful equanimity as cardinal virtues.

Another towering figure of the era was Lin-chi (known as Rinzai in Japanese). Like Ma-tsu, Lin-chi was rough and aggressive with his students. Famous for his thundering shout and shocking words, he tried to spur his students into a direct realization of their own insight, not a counterfeit copy based on the words of others:

> Followers of the Way, if you want insight into dharma, just don't be taken in by the deluded views of others. Whatever you encounter, either within or without, slay it at once: on meeting a Buddha, kill the Buddha; on meeting a patriarch, kill the patriarch; on meeting an arhat, kill the arhat.... By not cleaving to things you freely pass though.

Many historians see the Tang period as the apex of Chinese Buddhism. Buddhism's spiritual influence was a major force among people of all social ranks, and thousands of flourishing temples and monasteries were scattered thoughout the empire. The Buddhist sangha and its institutions became increasingly involved in caring for the old and sick, helping the poor, sheltering orphans, and providing public education. The major temples and monasteries grew into powerful financial centers that often operated their own businesses, such as mills or craft workshops, and lent money and provided other banking services. Through gifts from wealthy donors and generous imperial patronage, they built up large tax-exempt landholdings. Since only the Ch'an monks did manual labor, the temples and monasteries used their own slaves and serfs to work their land.

This worldly prosperity came crashing down during the great persecution of 842–845. Thousands of monasteries and temples were destroyed and hundreds of thousands of monks, nuns, serfs, and slaves were returned to the laity. This devastating blow spelled the end of many of the flourishing schools of Chinese Buddhism. Fifty years or so after the end of the persecution, the Tang dynasty collapsed. By the time China was reunified under the Sung dynasty (960–1279), Chinese Buddhism was dominated by two schools—the popular Pure Land school and the more elite Ch'an school, which was itself divided into two camps best known by their Japanese names, Rinzai and Soto.

The Sung dynasty saw the maturity of many social trends that had begun over a thousand years before. Scholar-bureaucrats under imperial control finally displaced the feudal aristocracy of great families, and a newly developed neo-Confucianism swept Buddhism from its dominant position among the scholars and intellectuals. Although the number of Ch'an monks increased remarkably during this era, they were never able to equal the extraordinary creativity of the Tang. In an effort to restore the vigor of earlier times, the masters of the Rinzai tradition developed a technique known as koan practice. Literally translated, a koan is a "public case." The original koans were stories, either real or imagined, about the great masters of the Tang era. On the surface, these stories present a seemingly impenetrable wall of paradox, but at their core they embody the profound religious insight of the great masters. Students in the Rinzai sect were often assigned a particular koan and were expected to work on it in their meditation and throughout their day. Students were then called on to demonstrate their understanding in regularly scheduled interviews with their teacher who might respond with everything from warm praise to a blow on the head. Once a student had "passed" a particular koan (i.e., satisfied his teacher that he had mastered it), he was generally assigned one after another until he had completed an entire series of koans designed to cultivate mature realization. Although koans are often pictured as a kind of illogical puzzle that the student had to solve, the objective is not some verbal understanding but the direct experience of the true nature of things.

In later dynasties, several Buddhist-influenced cults, such as the Maitreya Society and the White Lotus Society, played a major political role in fomenting popular rebellions against corrupt and repressive governments. But the technique of systematic koan practice was the last great religious innovation of Chinese Buddhism. In the later years of Chinese Buddhism, the Ch'an and Pure Land sects became increasingly interwoven, and popular Chinese religion came to center on an eclectic mix of Buddhist, Taoist, and Confucian elements known as the Three Doctrines (san-chio).

THE SPREAD OF CHINESE BUDDHISM Like India, China was also a cultural wellspring that profoundly influenced the development of its less sophisticated neighbors. Korea, Vietnam, and Japan all bear a strong imprint of

Chinese influence, and they all adopted the Chinese style of Buddhism. In Vietnam, the Ch'an Buddhists (*Thien* in Vietnamese) eventually came to dominate, but the Thien tradition intentionally avoided sectarianism by incorporating many Pure Land practices as well. As in China, the Ch'an style of practice predominated in the monasteries and the Pure Land among the common villagers.

Like Vietnam, Korea has always felt the strong influence of its huge Chinese neighbor. Buddhism was first introduced to Korea by Chinese missionaries in the fourth century, and it played an important political role as a unifying national force and eventually an official state religion. However, during the Yi dynasty (1392–1910) Buddhism was ousted from its official position in the Korean state and replaced by the neo-Confucianism imported from China. Buddhism experienced several periods of intense repression under the Yi. As in China, the doctrinal schools were the ones to suffer most while a *Son* (the Korean term for the Ch'an sect) oriented practice continued in the rural monasteries and the Pure Land faith flourished among the masses.

The Japanese colonization of Korea in the early part of this century encouraged something of a revival of Buddhism. But it also fostered deep divisions in the sangha between those who adopted a more Japanese style of practice and those who adhered more closely to Korean tradition. The question of whether or not priests should marry as they do in Japan eventually became one of the central issues in this conflict. Today, the status of Buddhism under the repressive communist regime in North Korea is somewhat unclear. But in the South, although faced with a strong Christian challenge from evangelical Protestants, Buddhism remains a vital religious force.

The history of Japanese Buddhism is a complex one. On the one hand, the Japanese imported their Buddhism lock, stock, and barrel from China and actually preserved it more faithfully than the Chinese themselves. But the Japanese were not the mindless copyists they are sometimes made out to be. Not only did they modify the Chinese imports to fit their own cultural demands, but they made major innovations in the Pure Land faith. Moreover, the followers of the Japanese monk Nichiren created a distinctively Japanese form of Buddhism different from anything found in China or anywhere else in the Buddhist world.

Tradition has it that Buddhism was first introduced to Japan by a delegation from Korea in 538 C.E. Over the ensuing years, a growing number of monks and religious delegations came to Japan from China as the Tang dynasty exerted an increasingly powerful cultural influence throughout East Asia. During this era, Japan's warring clans were slowly being unified under imperial control, and its rulers struggled to establish a Chinese-style centralized state. As in Korea, Buddhism came to be seen not only as a useful ideological tool to legitimize the new state but a source of powerful magic to help protect the emperor and his court. In its early centuries, Japanese Buddhism was largely restricted to the social elite, who preferred the various scholastic schools of Chinese Buddhism. But eventually a Buddhist movement developed outside of traditional state-controlled institutions. A new style of holy man (*hijiri*), who tended to ignore the traditional regulations for monks, brought relatively simple teachings directly to the common people. As in China, it was the chanting of Amida Buddha's name and other Pure Land practices that proved most popular.

During the Kamakura period (1185–1333), a group of samurai wrested power away from the imperial aristocracy. This newly dominant class of provincial landholders and warriors was not attracted by the elegant ritualism of the more established sects, and Kamakura Buddhism took on a much more popular and down-to-earth style. Belief in the salvation offered by Amida Buddha continued to spread among all strata of society, and a Japanese prophet, Nichiren (1222–1282), created a unique and revolutionary new form of Buddhism. The son of a fisherman, Nichiren was trained as a Buddhist monk. But he eventually came to see all the established Buddhist sects, and Japan itself, as hopelessly corrupt. Instead of looking to Amida Buddha for salvation, Nichiren turned to the Lotus Sutra—not as an object of study but as an object of worship. The central practice of his new faith was to chant *Nam myoho renge kyo* ("Hail to the Lotus Sutra") before a shrine known as a *honzon*. Nichiren himself adopted an aggressive religious style more like the Hebraic prophets than the traditionally tolerant Buddhists. He condemned all the other Buddhist sects and predicted disaster for Japan if it did not convert to the true faith of the Lotus Sutra. He even demanded that the government ban all other creeds and establish his faith as the state religion. For his trouble, he was exiled on two different occasions, at one point narrowly escaping execution.

While the Nichiren and the Pure Land sects gained an increasing number of followers among the common people, it was Ch'an Buddhism that established itself as the religion of the samurai class. One of the towering figures in the entire history of Japanese Zen is Eihei Dogen (1200–1253).

The son of an aristocrat who lost his parents at an early age, Dogen is often considered one of the greatest thinkers Japan has ever produced. After studying in China, Dogen returned home and founded what is now Japan's largest Zen school, the Soto. Not only did Dogen accept students from all walks of life, but he saw women and men as equally capable of enlightenment. Whereas the Rinzai (Lin-chi) Zen sect placed a heavy emphasis on koan practice, for Dogen the heart of Buddhist practice was *shikan taza* ("just sitting"). Dogen made it clear, however, that *zazen* (sitting meditation) is not a means of achieving enlightenment. Rather, practice and enlightenment were one and the same thing. The practice of zazen was simply a natural expression of our true nature.

Dogen's Soto school was the most popular form of Zen among the common people (its opponents sometimes derisively called it "farmer Zen"), but it was the Rinzai school that won over the samurai. And there is no one among the ranks of Rinzai teachers more influential than the monk Hakuin (1685–1768), who helped shake the sect from the spiritual lethargy fostered by the patronage and control of the Tokugawa shoguns. A man of shining personal brilliance, Hakuin was not only the most accomplished Zen master of his time but also a writer, composer, poet, and painter. Hakuin felt that all the Buddhist sects of his time had fallen into decay and corruption. He aimed stinging criticism against his fellow Zen practitioners both for pursuing lifeless quietistic meditation and for the formalistic question-and-answer game into which much koan practice had deteriorated. Hakuin's greatest contribution to Japanese Zen was probably to revitalize koan meditation and return it to the center of Rinzai practice. Despite the uncompromising demands he placed on his own students, Hakuin was also active in promoting ethics and spiritual practice among the masses. He even composed popular songs to convey his spiritual message. His "Song of the Weeds," for example, urges farmers to cut off their passions at the roots as if they were weeds.

The vast panorama of Buddhist history is apt to leave most people a bit dizzy. But there are a few fundamental themes that can help set the growth of Western Buddhism in context. Throughout the years, the marrow of Buddhism remains in the great enlightenment Siddartha Gautama experienced under the bodhi tree. The original path laid out by the Buddha showed his followers how to escape their suffering by withdrawing from the mundane world and cultivating ethical behavior, meditation, and transcendent wisdom. Over the years, it split into two broad camps. A small monastic elite withdrew from the world and continued on Sakyamuni's quest, while new forms of popular Buddhism sprang up that were more concerned with earning an auspicious rebirth by accumulating merit by faith or by chanting magic formulas. While the quest for enlightenment was never the central concern of popular Buddhism, even elite Buddhism was soon divided between those who pursued that goal and those who focused on worldly affairs, academic study, or formal ritualism. As we will see in later chapters, Western Buddhism has drawn its primary inspiration from a relatively narrow spectrum of Asian Buddhism: the meditation-oriented elite Buddhists who do not see monastic renunciation as an essential component of the path to enlightenment.

Wherever it was introduced, Buddhism's initial appeal was always to the social elite. The merchants, nobility, intellectuals, and even the warriors were the first to adopt Buddhism, and over the years it usually filtered down to the masses. To the rulers, Buddhism provided an ideological prop to legitimize their regime; to the courtiers it provided elegant rituals; to the superstitious it was magical power; to the spiritual seeker it was a path of awakening; and to the common man or woman a source of solace and ethical guidance. From the time of Asoka on, noble patronage provided a vital support for many Buddhist institutions. But such largesse has often carried a high price. Worldly status, wealth, and political power often undermined the spiritual vitality of the Buddhist community, distracting its leaders from their religious objectives and attracting those more concerned with worldly rewards than spiritual pursuits. When institutionalized Buddhism became weakened or corrupt, radical reform movements often sprang up to challenge the old order of things—thus producing a periodic cycle of decay and revitalization. Western Buddhism is far too young to have experienced such cycles yet, but it certainly has far more affinity with radicals and reformers than old-line establishmentarians. Indeed, Western Buddhism seems to be posing the same kind of radical challenge to the Western religious establishment that the Ch'an masters of the Tang or the Indian siddhas posed to the religious establishment of their societies.

Three

❋

WESTERN FLOWER
The Growth of the New Buddhism

Perhaps the most remarkable thing about the early history of Buddhism in
the West is how little of it there is. A few Greek philosophers were apparently influenced by Buddhist thought, but until the tide of European
colonialism reached the shores of Asia, that huge continent's most popular and influential religion was largely unknown in the West.

The Word Spreads

Most of the early European accounts of Buddhism came from Christian
missionaries who were usually more concerned to debunk it than to understand it. Reminiscent of Buddhism's spread through Asia centuries before, the earliest real Western interest in Buddhism began among
intellectuals. But it was still not until the nineteenth century that Euro-
peans began a serious study of Buddhist texts, and even then it took generations of scholarship to penetrate the subtleties of their doctrine.
Although the early Western interpretations of Buddhist thought were
often sketchy and inaccurate, some influential European philosophers, including Schopenhauer and Nietzsche, incorporated their understanding
of Eastern thought into their own work, as did such American writers as
Emerson, Thoreau, and Whitman.

The nineteenth-century missionaries and travelers who brought back the first accounts of Buddhism portrayed it as just another "heathen" religion—full of exotic ceremonies and strange gods. By the middle of the nineteenth century, European scholars had begun to form another picture of this distinctive Eastern faith. In this view, Buddhism was almost entirely a negative religion. It rejected the idea of God and the salvation of the individual soul and held the highest good to be total annihilation of the individual (their interpretation of nirvana). One Unitarian minister described the Buddhist viewpoint this way: "God is nothing; man is nothing, life is nothing, eternity is nothing. Hence the profound sadness of Buddhism."[1] Clearly Buddhism differed radically from Christianity and, for that matter, any of the world's other major religions. Shocked Western Christians were left to puzzle over the question of how half the world's people could have been converted to such a life-denying faith.

Things began to change in 1879 with the publication of Sir Edwin Arnold's epic poem about the life of the Buddha, *The Light of Asia*. This highly sympathetic account emphasized the parallels between the lives of Jesus and the Buddha, and it was a smashing success—eventually going through eighty editions and selling between half a million and a million copies.

This new perspective on Buddhism arrived at a time when mainline American Protestantism was in something of an intellectual crisis, challenged by both growing scientific skepticism and the social dislocations caused by the industrial revolution and the urbanization it spawned. Darwin's theory of evolution was shaking the cosmological foundations of Christian faith, while the academic study of comparative religion and critical biblical scholarship eroded Christianity's claim to being the one true religion. Some disaffected intellectuals began to see Buddhism as an alternative to Christianity that was both more compatible with the scientific worldview and more tolerant of divergent opinions and viewpoints.

For others, an interest in Buddhism grew out of the new wave of occultism that was sweeping through the West. Although most seekers were satisfied to focus their attention on local spirits and Western occult traditions, some turned to the exotic East for inspiration. One of the most important developments of this era was the spread of a new religion known as Theosophy. Led by Madame Helena Petrova Blavatsky and Colonel Henry Steel Olcott, the Theosophical Society was inspired by Madame Blavatsky's accounts of her contacts with powerful occult masters she believed to be secretly guiding the future of the world. The goal of the

Theosophical Society was to help spread the ancient wisdom of these masters, which they saw hidden in all the world's great religions.

Originally inspired by occult sources from Egypt and India, Theosophists turned increasingly to Buddhism—the contemporary religion they saw as most faithful to the wisdom of the ancients. Not only did the Theosophical Society win great popularity in its time, establishing numerous branches in North America, Europe, and Asia, but Colonel Olcott actually played an important role in stimulating a renewal of Buddhism in its ancient home of Sri Lanka. The Theosophists' mixture of Western occultism and Eastern mysticism is a long way from any sort of mainstream Buddhism. But it did play an important role in spreading the idea that the Orient in general, and Buddhism in particular, held a treasure trove of mysterious wisdom that might bring about a profound personal transformation in the sincere seeker.

At the height of this first wave, there were perhaps two or three thousand "Euro-Buddhists" in the United States, while several times that number probably held some sympathy for the tradition. But this first flirtation with Buddhism cooled off after World War I, and even at its height, it never got beyond the stage of love letters and longing glances. Westerners studied Buddhism and tried on its worldview, but they never consummated the relationship with actual Buddhist practice or established much of an ongoing institutional structure. According to Thomas Tweed, the leading scholarly authority on early Buddhist influence in the United States, disaffected Americans were surprisingly willing to give up the idea of a creator God and an immortal soul, but the criticisms of Buddhism as cosmologically negative and socially passive were more troubling. Any new faith must have clear differences from the established religions to gain a significant following. But the Buddhist worldview as seen through the lens of late Victorian culture proved too divergent from the pragmatic optimism of American culture to gain much of a foothold in a society still dominated by a single Anglo-European perspective.

Arriving in the West

While information and misinformation about Buddhism had arrived much earlier, the introduction of the first of the traditional Buddhist denominations to the West is usually traced to the World Parliament of Religions, which was held as an adjunct to the Chicago World's Fair of 1893.

The organizers of the parliament sent out more than ten thousand letters to religious groups around the world. The final result was an unprecedented gathering of religious leaders that helped crack open the doors of American religious life to Eastern faiths.

The most popular Buddhist at the parliament proved to be a Sri Lankan, Anagarika Dharmapala. He was a close associate of Olcott and Blavatsky's, and his flowing hair and fiery rhetoric made him an immediate hit. The Japanese Rinzai master Soyen Shaku attracted less notice, but he and his students were to have far greater influence on the development of American Buddhism in the years ahead. Soyen Shaku's role in the Parliament of Religions was limited by his inability to speak English, but his credentials were nonetheless impressive. Before his voyage to America, he had studied Buddhism in India and Sri Lanka and had been appointed to the abbotship of a major Japanese monastery. The most important contact Soyen made at the World Parliament of Religions was probably Paul Carus, an influential editor and publisher. Carus soon asked him to help translate a new series of oriental works. Although Soyen declined, he suggested one of his students for the job. That student was D. T. Suzuki, the man Rick Fields later described as the "first patriarch of American Zen."

The son of a samurai family of limited means, Suzuki was a dedicated Zen student. His ability to speak English made him a natural choice for the job, which included helping Carus with his translations and, as it turned out, serving as his servant and houseboy. Suzuki probably did more than any other single individual to introduce Zen Buddhism to the West. Yet like many of the early leaders of Western Zen, he seems a rather paradoxical figure for such a role. Shortly before he left for the United States, Suzuki had a profound *satori* (enlightenment experience) while meditating on the classic koan Mu (see chapter 5 for discussion of this koan). But he never received the official seal of dharma transmission and was not a Zen teacher in the traditional sense. Rather, he was an intellectual and a philosopher in the most anti-intellectual of all Buddhist traditions.

Suzuki was a prolific writer, and his works gave the West its first picture of the Zen tradition from someone who spoke from the depths of direct experience. But Suzuki's influence came as much from his own personal example as his writings. A man of greatest humility and simplicity (his Buddhist name, Daisetz Teitaro, actually means great simplicity); the Christian mystic Thomas Merton once described the experience of drinking a cup of tea with him as "like finally arriving at one's own home."

Suzuki's writings and his persona had an enormous impact on the Western intelligentsia in the postwar period. Psychologists Erich Fromm and Karen Horney, avant-garde composer John Cage, writers and poets like Alan Ginsberg and Jack Kerouac, as well as leading students of Buddhism, including Edward Conze, Christmas Humphreys, and Alan Watts were all deeply influenced by Suzuki. In his later years, he even became something of a media figure. He was interviewed on television, profiled in the *New Yorker*, and even featured in *Vogue* magazine. With the enthusiasm typical of his admirers, the poet Gary Snyder once described Suzuki as "Japan's greatest cultural contribution to the world so far."[2]

In contrast to Suzuki's unsought celebrity, another of Soyen Shaku's students, Nyogen Senzaki, made his pioneering contribution to American Zen in almost complete obscurity. Right from the start, Nyogen Senzaki was someone who never fit into the conventional mold. An orphan of mixed parentage in racist Japanese society, Senzaki was raised by monks who began his Buddhist education early. After completing five years of study with Soyen Shaku at the Engakuji monastery, Senzaki's career took an unusual turn. Instead of serving as a village priest or staying on as a monk, he left the monastery for the remote island of Hokkaido to start an unorthodox nursery school he called the Mentorgarten. Senzaki became increasingly critical of the Buddhist establishment, comparing its priests to businessmen and their temples to chain stores. He also spoke out against the virulent nationalism that culminated in the Russo-Japanese War and the complicity of the Zen establishment in the war effort. Obviously disaffected with Japanese society, Senzaki came to the United States in 1905 working as a houseboy in the home of a wealthy couple Soyen knew.

When Senzaki decided to stay in the United States, his teacher gave him strict instructions to wait seventeen years before teaching the dharma. Senzaki followed those instructions to the letter. For the next seventeen years, he worked a variety of menial jobs. When his waiting period was up, he promptly rented a hall and gave his first lecture on Buddhism. He set up what he called his "floating zendo" in many places over the years and eventually created a zendo in the modest rooms he rented in Los Angeles. Although his students sat on folding chairs and not in the traditional crossed-legged position, Senzaki provided Westerners with a taste of real Buddhist meditation. Senzaki himself always remained an outsider for whom material possessions and public recognition seemed to hold little meaning. Senzaki often compared himself to a mushroom—no roots, no seeds, and no flowers—but his life of simplicity and commitment left a lasting impression on American Buddhism.

Although white America's first encounter with organized Buddhism was with Japanese Rinzai Zen, early British Buddhism had much more of a Theravadin flavor—hardly a surprise since the British Empire ruled two of the world's most prominent Theravadin countries, Sri Lanka (then known as Ceylon) and Burma. Britain's most important Theravadin organization was the Maha Bodhi Society, which was brought to England in 1925 by Anagarika Dharmapala—the same Sri Lankan monk who had been such a hit at the World Parliament of Religions three decades before. The Maha Bodhi Society's original goal was to restore the site at Bodhi-Gaya where the Buddha had attained enlightenment to serve as a shrine for all the world's Buddhists, but its Regent's Park headquarters also housed a more-or-less permanent contingent of English-speaking Sri Lankan monks.

Dharmapala's contribution notwithstanding, for over half a century the leading figure in British Buddhism would be a barrister for the Old Bailey (London's criminal court), Travers Christmas Humphreys. Although his Buddhism had a rather unorthodox Theosophical slant, Christmas Humphreys was a tireless organizer, speaker, and writer who made an enormous contribution to the growth of British Buddhism. He founded an organization known as the Buddhist Lodge in 1924, which was originally affiliated with the Theosophical Society. Some years after it had parted company with the Theosophists, it was renamed the Buddhist Society and became, along with the Maha Bodhi society, one of the twin pillars of British Buddhism. As in so many other nations, Buddhism in Britain was most attractive to the comfortable and well educated, and London's Buddhist Society had, according to John Snelling, "very much the aura of a gentleman's club."[3]

Beat Zen

By the end of World War II, Buddhism had made only the shallowest penetration of Western culture. A few intellectuals knew something of Buddhist philosophy, but it was often misunderstood or interpreted with one sort of odd twist or another. Real Buddhist practice was even more rare. There were only a handful of qualified teachers, and even those few had to water down their practice or risk driving off the students they had managed to attract. While many Westerners were drawn to the "mysteries of the East," there was little appetite for the years of hard practice necessary to follow the Buddhist path to its fruition.

After the war, however, things began to change. First in the United States and then throughout the Western world, widening gaps appeared in the foundations of the old cultural order. In one sense, the 1950s and early 1960s were the culmination of the America Dream. Not only did the United States occupy a position of almost unprecedented political and economic hegemony in the postwar world, it was a time when the dream of wealth and comfort seemed within reach for all Americans—or at least for all white Americans. But the combination of triumphant consumer capitalism with the stream of radical individualism that had long run through American culture proved a corrosive and unstable mix. For one thing, the materialist values of consumer culture are rife with psychological contradictions. The struggle for personal gain may be satisfying to those working their way up the status ladder. Those who fall short, however, are left jealous and dispirited, and even the successful find that material prosperity seldom lives up to their expectations. As more and more Americans achieved their dreams of material success, they often came face-to-face with a powerful, albeit ill-defined, discontent.

At the same time, the cultural hegemony of Anglo-Protestantism was in serious decline. On one side was the continuing onslaught of scientific rationalism. On the other were the decades of immigration that had left the United States a much more diverse place than it had been in the nineteenth century. Anglo-Protestantism could still lay claim to being the dominant American faith, but it was no longer as easy to dismiss its challengers as foreign aberrations.

Another important factor was economic prosperity itself. Always a nation that idealized individualism, America's ever growing material abundance served to ease the economic restraints that provided one of its strongest barriers to nonconformity. This abundance also helped make higher education available to a far wider audience than ever before in history. Working in tandem, these two developments soon helped expose a generation of young Americans to a broad new horizon of possibilities.

Although many traditionalists were also skeptical of America's new culture of consumption, it was the movement of young writers, artists, musicians, and bohemian hangers-on known as the Beat Generation that presented its first organized challenge. The Beats' vehement rejection of conventional American culture opened the door to new perspectives on life, and it was among this group that Buddhism found its first broad appeal in the West.

The beginnings of the Beats' new interest in Buddhism are sometimes traced to the series of lectures D. T. Suzuki gave at Columbia University in the early 1950s, but its real origins had far deeper roots. The most influential figures in what came to be know as Beat Zen—Alan Ginsberg, Gary Snyder, and Jack Kerouac among others—first encountered Buddhism in the library, not the lecture hall (although Suzuki's books were inevitably on their menu of readings). Wherever they found it, there was something in those early descriptions of Zen that struck a deep chord among those young rebels. For one thing, there was the spontaneity. Even more than the jazz musicians the Beats idolized, the masters of Zen seemed to make their everyday lives a kind of improvised performance, acting out their realization in the most surprising and unpredictable ways. Then there was the freedom. Not only did the heroes in the Zen stories the Beats read seem to stand completely outside the restraints of traditional morality, Zen itself provided an absolute perspective from which the standards of consumer society could only be judged meaningless, arbitrary, and unreal. Zen soon became a powerful philosophical ally in the Beats' attack on the conformism of conventional society. Finally, as Epicureans and far more than casual dabblers in drugs and alcohol, the Beats were drawn to the ecstatic descriptions of Zen *satori,* which seemed to them a kind of ultimate high.

Japhy Ryder, a character in Jack Kerouac's novel *The Dharma Bums* (who was based on the poet Gary Snyder), gave voice to the Beats' vision of Zen spontaneity:

> I see a vision of . . . thousands or even millions of young Americans wandering around with rucksacks, going up to mountains to pray, making children laugh and old men glad, making young girls happy, and old girls happier, all of 'em Zen lunatics who go about writing poems that happen to appear in their heads for no reason, and also by being kind, and also by strange unexpected acts keep giving visions of eternal freedom to everybody. . . . We'll have a floating zendo, a series of monasteries for people to go and monastate and meditate in . . . wild gangs of pure holy men getting together to drink and talk and pray."[4]

Beat Zen didn't include much in the way of discipline or systematic meditation, but the tendency to dismiss the Beats as dilettantes who found Buddhism an easy rationalization for their personal excesses reveals more about the critics and their values than about the Beats. Anyone who doubts the sincerity of their spiritual quest should read Alan Ginsberg's epic poem *Howl* or Jack Kerouac's Beat "sutra" *The Scripture of Golden Eternity*. The Beats' rejection of conventional social mores in their quest for some better path actually has many Buddhist precedents, not only among the great Zen masters of the Tang but in the tantric siddhas as well, and it remains a powerful undercurrent in Western Buddhism to this day.

Alan Watts: The Way of the Writer

Ironically, the most influential figure to come out of the era of Beat Zen was not a Beat at all. Although Alan Watts traveled in many of the same circles as the San Francisco Beats, he was never really one of them. As Watts put it, he was "*in* this milieu rather than *of* it."[5] In one of his most influential essays, "Beat Zen, Square Zen, and Zen," Watts challenged both the "Beat Zen" of the bohemians and the "square Zen" of those who copied the elaborate forms of the Japanese religious establishment: "Zen is above all the liberation of the mind from conventional thought, and this is something utterly different from rebellion against convention, on the one hand, or adapting foreign conventions, on the other."[6] But despite his criticisms of Beat Zen, Watts's own philosophy and way of life, if not his personal style, followed very much in the same path.

Born in England and educated in Eastern thought under the tutelage of Christmas Humphreys and the other members of the London Buddhist scene, Watts affected a bit too much sophistication and elegance to really fit in with the Beats. He once described them as "aggressively dowdy and slovenly" and said they "went about in shaggy blue-jeans with their feet bare and grimy and . . . overuse of marijuana made them withdrawn and morose."[7] Watts was, nonetheless, personal friends with most of the leading figures of the San Francisco Beat world. More important, his voluminous writings were a major force in popularizing the same kind of approach to Buddhism that had such an appeal to the Beats. Although D. T. Suzuki provided many Westerners with their first introduction to Zen, Alan Watts was read far more widely. Not only did Watts's work strike a much more popular note than Suzuki's, he was a better writer who could present esoteric Eastern ideas in a way that was interesting and understandable to Western readers.

Like most of the Beats, Watts's Buddhism was mainly intellectual. His writings on Zen and the other Eastern ways of liberation never placed much emphasis on the disciplined meditation that is so much a part of those traditions. Influenced by the great Indian philosopher Krishnamurti, Watts argued that a determined struggle to achieve enlightenment was more likely to encourage an "ego-trip" than to break it down. Watts did meditate occasionally but not, he said, with the idea of attaining any goal, but only for the "joy of being quiet."

Another attitude Watts shared with the Beats was a healthy skepticism about all organized religion—including Buddhism. He once described the majority of Japanese monks as "bored and sleepy young men, mostly sons of priests, attending the Japanese equivalent of an ecclesiastical boys' boarding school."[8] Another area of common ground was what Watts called his "unrepentant sensualism" when it came to matters of sex.

The most popular of Watts's twenty books was probably *The Way of Zen*, but most of his other numerous works also helped acquaint Western readers with the riches of the Buddhist and Taoist traditions. Through all his writings, Watts emphasized one major theme again and again: the Western idea of a separate "skin encapsulated" ego is an illusion, and, in fact, we are all interconnected with everyone and everything else. As he put it in his autobiography, "the ego named Alan Watts is an illusion, a social institution, a fabrication of words and symbols without the slightest substantial reality. . . . Nevertheless . . . this temporary pattern, this process, is a function . . . of all that is . . . I simply, and even humbly, know that I am The Eternal."[9] Writing about his life, Watts commented, "I am not controlling it voluntarily any more than I am controlling my autonomic nervous system, and at the same time it is not befalling or happening to any separate me as its observant victim. There is simply the whole process happening of itself, spontaneously, and with every pair of eyes it takes a fresh look at itself."[10]

The Zen Boom and the New Bohemians

New York's Greenwich Village and San Francisco's North Beach were the centers of the Beat revolution. But during the 1960s, San Francisco would see a major shift in its cultural balance that was to reverberate across the industrialized world. The North Beach Beats found themselves displaced by a new style of bohemian community that was evolving across town in the Haight Ashbury district. Soon to be far more numerous than the Beats, these new rebels the press dubbed the "hippies" shared their predecessors' rejection of the consumer culture. Their personal style, however, was radically different. The Beats emulated the cool reserve of the African American jazz musicians they idealized, favored dark-colored clothes, and displayed a good deal of existential angst. The hippies, on the other hand, wore every color of the rainbow and valued above all the openness and emotional expression reflected in their famous slogan "Peace and Love." While the Beats saw themselves as a collection of individualistic artists and bohemians struggling for survival in conformist America, the hippies believed they were on the cutting edge of a new ethos of sharing and communal living that would remake the world. The Beats preferred poetry and the introverted sounds of cool jazz, while the Haight Ashbury counterculture centered on the celebration and rebellion expressed in its flamboyant rock music.

In many ways, the Beat subculture provided a more sympathetic environment for the spread of Buddhism. Unlike the Beats, the hippies had few intellectual pretensions, and as we have seen Buddhism has often had its strongest appeal among the intelligentsia. Moreover, the reserved style of the Beats certainly fit far better with the traditions of Japanese Zen (which was the only form of Buddhism with which Americans had any familiarity) than the more emotional and expressive hippies. There was, however, one facet of this new subculture that helped open up the hippies to Buddhism as well as to countless other "exotic" beliefs. That, of course, was the use of LSD and the other psychedelic drugs that the members of this new counterculture experimented with on a scale never before seen in Western society.

LSD was first synthesized in the laboratories of the Sandoz corporation in the 1930s. After a chemist accidentally discovered its psychedelic effects, Sandoz sent out samples to numerous scientists and researchers hoping they would discover some profitable medical use for the drug. The CIA even got into the act, secretly funding studies of what they hoped would be a weapon to disorient enemy soldiers and civilian populations. The body of scientific research on the drug increased steadily during the 1950s, but it wasn't until the 1960s that LSD exploded on the drug scene—probably reaching its peak in the middle to late 1960s and then slowly declining in popularity along with the hippie movement itself.

To this day, the argument continues about whether or not some LSD users undergo an experience equivalent to Zen satori. But there is no question at all that the drug is capable of producing a profound alteration of consciousness. The effects of the drug vary enormously from individual to individual, and even from one "trip" to another by the same person. Users report everything from the most overwhelming sense of fear to ecstatic bliss. But whether pleasant or unpleasant, large doses produce fundamental changes in the way the user thinks, feels, and sees the world. For many users, LSD literally shook their faith in reality, at least as it was conventionally defined by the consumer culture. Consider, for example, how Albert Hofmann (the chemist who first synthesized LSD) described what was probably the first intentional LSD trip:

> The faces of those present appeared like grotesque colored masks. . . . I lost all control of time; space and time became more and more disorganized and I was overcome with fears that I was going crazy. . . . Occasionally I felt as being outside my body. I thought I had died. My "ego" was suspended somewhere in space and I saw my body lying dead on the sofa. I observed and registered clearly that my "alter ego" was moving around the room.[11]

However one judges the spiritual qualities of such experiences (a task I certainly do not have the temerity to undertake), it is easy to see how they led someone to look beyond the conventional confines of Western culture for some kind of explanation. The psychedelic counterculture seemed to have a natural affinity for the almost hallucinatory gods of the Hindu and Tibetan Buddhist pantheons, and images of Shiva and Krishna soon became staples of psychedelic art. Two apostate Harvard psychologists even published a version of the *Tibetan Book of the Dead* (*Bardo Thodol*) under the title *The Psychedelic Experience,* which was designed to serve as a guide for LSD trippers. When the veterans of the psychedelic world began looking for something more stable than their chemically induced trips, many turned to the disciplined world of Zen. The late 1960s and early 1970s saw what became know as the "Zen boom" as newly created American zendos filled up with refugees from the psychedelic counterculture. To many of these new converts, meditation was just another kind of high, and most didn't keep their practice going very long. But some did stick it out, and they became the backbone of the Zen centers that were springing up around the country.

The first seeds of the new Buddhism that was proving so attractive to the psychedelic counterculture came from the Beat Zen of the bohemian intellectuals. But there was another important source as well: the conservative ethnic Buddhism that Asian immigrants had brought with them to their new home. Typical of most popular Buddhism, North America's ethnic Buddhists didn't place much emphasis on meditation or the kinds of esoteric doctrines that attracted the Beats. Their main focus was, and still is, the psychological and social needs of their community. These traditional Buddhist organizations did, however, give American Buddhism new respectability in the eyes of the public. More importantly, they provided a link between the great practice centers of Asia, where the more sophisticated forms of Buddhism were centered, and North Americans searching for some kind of meaning in those chaotic times.

As we have seen, North America's first contacts with Japanese Buddhism were with the aristocratic Rinzai sect. Soto Zen, however, had always had more adherents in Japan, and in the 1960s Soto-style practice began spreading out from the ethnic enclaves of Japanese Americans into the general population. Two of the most pivotal figures in the history of American Zen, Shunryu Suzuki and Taizan Maezumi, both came to the United States to work in the Soto temples that served California's Japanese American community.

Although both men were the sons of Soto priests, Suzuki Roshi adhered more closely to the traditional Soto style. Maezumi Roshi, on the other hand, was trained in the Harada-Yasutani lineage, which freely combined elements of both Japanese Zen traditions. Unlike most Soto teachers, Harada Roshi, the founder of this lineage, placed great emphasis on the attainment of *kensho* (satori) and the use of koan study to achieve it. His *sesshins* (meditation retreats) were know for their intensity and their single-minded push toward kensho. Harada Roshi also made a strong effort to reach out to lay students. In contrast to the traditional approach, which provided precious little guidance for the new student, Harada Roshi gave detailed instruction in the right techniques of Zen practice. The direct approach of the Harada-Yasutani lineage proved to be well suited to the American environment. Not only did Maezumi Roshi attract a large number of students in the United States, but several other teachers in this lineage were also highly successful in the West.

The new Buddhism had a third seed, which was planted by Western students who went to Asia to study and then returned home to teach what they had learned. Because the Harada-Yasutani lineage not only had a reputation for rigor but was among the most willing to work with Westerners, it also attracted some of the most dedicated foreign students. Foremost among them were Philip Kapleau, who founded the Rochester Zen Center, and Robert Aitken, who still heads Diamond Sangha in Hawaii.

Of all the foreigners to make the pilgrimage to Japan to study Zen during these years, perhaps the most remarkable story was that of Peggy (Jiyu) Kennett. The product of a "very snooty, very expensive" English boarding school, Kennet says she might well have ended up a Christian priest if that calling had not been barred to women in the Church of England. After becoming involved with Buddhist groups in Britain, she happened to meet the Abbot of Sojiji Temple (one of the two principal training centers of the Soto sect) and was invited to go to Japan to study— a rare honor for a foreigner and virtually unheard of for a woman. When she took up his offer, she became the first woman to study at Sojiji since the fourteenth century. In 1969, after completing a rigorous training program, she returned to the West and founded the Shasta Abbey monastery, which now has numerous affiliates in California and the Pacific Northwest. Unlike some Zen teachers active in the West, Kennett Roshi received official "dharma transmission" and the authorization to teach from her Asian mentors, and she was even the abbott of a Japanese temple for a time. Yet the path she hewed after leaving Japan was a very unorthodox one even by Western standards. Her efforts to adapt Soto traditions to Western culture have given Shasta Abbey and its affiliates something of the flavor of the Church of England. Their priests are referred to as Reverend, traditional Buddhist texts have been set to music based on Gregorian chants, and Christian terminology, including some explicitly theistic language, is often used to illustrate Buddhist concepts.

While showing decidedly more Christian influence than most other teachers, such westernization of traditional forms is hardly unusual among the Zen groups we are studying. A far more fundamental change in direction occurred in 1976, when Kennett's physician told her that she had only three months to live. She immediately entered into a meditation retreat and had a series of visionary experiences that reflected various aspects of Buddhist teachings. She relived a series of past lives, seeing herself as both male and female and, among other things, as a Buddhist and a Christian monk. She had a vision of Shakyamuni Buddha, who was then absorbed into "the great golden Cosmic Buddha," and another of a radiant ball of light through which passed a red ribbon manifesting all manner of beings while nonetheless remaining continually unstained and immaculate. Many other Zen practitioners have, of course, had such visions, but they are traditionally viewed as *makyo*—illusions—that are transitory and unreliable. Yet until her death in November 1996, Kennett Roshi continued to see these experiences as a profound kensho (enlightenment experience). She even had illustrations of some of her visions painted on the windows of the ceremony hall at Mount Shasta.

Zen is not, of course, confined to Japan, and as the Zen boom continued teachers from other Asian nations also made their way to the West. But in Korea, Vietnam, and China, Zen had not maintained the sectarian distance from other Buddhist denominations that it had in Japan. When Zen teachers arrived from those lands, their message often had a more eclectic flavor. This is true, for example, of the great Vietnamese Zen master, Thich Nhat Hanh, who despite living in France has still been a major force on the American scene. Similarly, Sueng Sahn, the most influential Korean Zen master in the West, belongs to the Chogye Order, which arose out of a movement to unify the various Buddhist denominations of Korea and incorporates elements from many different Buddhist traditions. After their long period of colonial domination by Japan, modern-day Koreans often bridle at comparisons with their island neighbor. Nonetheless, Sueng Sahn's forceful no-holds-bared style certainly bears strong similarities to Japanese Rinzai Zen, both in his emphasis on koan study as well as their common Chinese ancestors. But the Korean style of Zen practice tends to be more informal than the Japanese, and more than other Zen masters in the United States, Soen Sa Nim (Sueng Sahn's Buddhist name) has emphasized the Chinese tradition of probing verbal encounters sometimes known as "dharma combat."

Shunryu Suzuki: Just Sit

Perhaps it was because Shunryu Suzuki's Zen was so different from what most Americans imagined Zen to be, or perhaps it was just the unique quality of the man, but there is probably no other figure who has had as great an influence on the growth of American Buddhism. Born in 1904, Suzuki's father was a Zen priest, so in one sense he was simply following his family tradition. A diligent student, he assumed responsibility for a major Japanese temple when he was only thirty years old, and unlike most of the Japanese Zen establishment, Suzuki Roshi was an outspoken critic of Japanese militarism during World War II.

Suzuki had long desired to go to the United States to teach Zen, and in 1959 he was finally sent to San Francisco to serve as a priest for the Soto Zen Mission's temple. There were already a few Americans of European descent practicing at Sokoji (the San Francisco Temple), and Suzuki's presence gradually attracted more and more. Suzuki Roshi was deeply impressed with his Western students' openness and the sincerity of their aspirations, and he was soon devoting himself almost entirely to their needs. In 1961, his students founded America's first Zen Center, and in 1967 the San Francisco Zen Center purchased Tassajara Hot Springs in a remote part of central California and set about creating America's first Buddhist monastery. Suzuki Roshi died in 1971, only twelve years after his arrival in the United States, but he left behind America's fastest growing Buddhist lineage.

Like all Zen masters, Suzuki Roshi taught as much with his example as his words. Jacob Needleman captured some of the character of the man in his 1970 book, *The New Religions:*

> Short and slight, he appears to be in his early sixties; his head is shaved, and he wears the robes of a priest. One's overwhelming first impression is of openness and warmth. He laughs often, noiselessly—and when I was with him, trying to discuss "profound questions," I found myself laughing with him throughout the interview. Beneath the lightness and the gentleness, however, one feels as well his tremendous rigor; more than one student has called him "awesome."[12]

Trudy Dixon, one of his long-time students, gave this description:

> The flow of his consciousness is not the fixed repetitive patterns of our usual self-centered consciousness, but rather arises spontaneously and naturally from the actual circumstances of the present . . . His whole being testifies to what it means to live in the reality of the present. . . . without anything said or done, just the impact of meeting a personality so developed can be enough to change another's whole way of life.[13]

In addition to setting such a powerful example for his students, Suzuki Roshi seemed to have the knack of seeing people as they really were and, even more importantly, of making them feel he accepted and respected them.

Suzuki Roshi's teachings were radically different from the Zen of the other famous Suzuki or of the Beats he so profoundly influenced. To D. T. Suzuki, the great breakthrough to satori was the heart of the Zen experience, but Suzuki Roshi hardly mentioned it at all. To this new Suzuki, the heart of Zen was just to sit in meditation. It was clear that he loved it, and his students and successors have spent countless hours just sitting facing the *zendo* (meditation hall) walls.

There was no particular goal to his *zazen* (sitting meditation); no special state of mind to attain. One simply sat down and paid attention to the breath, body, and mind. Suzuki Roshi was, however, particular about meditation posture, and he would constantly wander around the zendo, making small changes in the way his students sat. But once someone settled into a good sitting posture, there was nothing else to achieve. As he put it, "Enlightenment is not some good feeling or some particular state of mind. The state of mind that exists when you sit in the right posture is, itself, enlightenment."[14]

This was obviously an unsettling idea to students who often didn't feel very enlightened when they were doing zazen. But time and again, Suzuki Roshi would point out that it was not their zazen that was the problem. It was their attachment to the idea that they should get something out of it; that there was some particular way their zazen should make them feel. "Our zazen is just to be ourselves. We should not expect anything—just be ourselves and continue this practice forever."[15]

Aside from the long hours of zazen, Suzuki Roshi made the very structure of the Zen center into a teaching tool. He established a strict schedule and introduced countless formal rules that regulated everything from how to eat to which foot should be used to step into the zendo. Students were required to bow to him, to each other, even to their meditation cushions. Bowing was, according to Suzuki Roshi, "very serious practice" that was especially important for individualistic Americans. Entering the Zen center and running into all those rules and all that traditional etiquette must certainly have been a profound shock to the kind of countercultural "free spirits" it often attracted. But those who stayed came to realize that the rules were not ends in themselves but a device to push students to exercise constant mindfulness of their behavior and to discover the freedom within the forms. "It is not a matter of good or bad, convenient or inconvenient," Suzuki Roshi said. "You just do it without question. That way your mind is free."[16]

The Tibetan Diaspora Reaches the West

Spanning the heart of the world's highest mountain range, Tibet has long been considered one of the most remote and mysterious countries on earth—an air of mystery that was no doubt heightened by the tendency of Vajrayana Buddhism to shroud its highest teachings in a cloak of secrecy. But all that was profoundly changed in the 1950s as the communist Chinese asserted their claim to Tibet and launched a ruthless campaign of repression that eventually killed or drove into exile a third of the entire Tibetan population. As the traditional rulers of Tibet and a symbol of feudalism in the Chinese mind, the Buddhist establishment was a particular target of communist rage. Countless monasteries were destroyed and many influential teachers from the Dalai Lama on down were forced to flee. Large refugee communities grew up in India, and with them new monasteries and religious centers.

The harsh realities of their new circumstances forced a radical reorientation among many Tibetan teachers who feared that their ancient tradition was in danger of being lost. After generations of isolationism, Tibetan teachers began to make a concerted effort to pass their tradition on to people from other cultures. Some of those teachers inevitably made their way to the West, where they exerted a powerful influence on the new Buddhism developing there.

Although some Tibetan scholars had preceded him, it was not until 1969, when Tarthang Tulku established the Tibetan Nyingma Meditation Center in Berkeley, California, that an organized effort was begun to reach Western students. Tarthang Tulku, an incarnate lama who was the son of an incarnate lama, belonged to the royal family of Sogpa in eastern Tibet. He escaped Tibet at the height of the Chinese invasion in 1959 and spent several years as a professor of Buddhist philosophy in India until the leaders of the Nyingma order sent him to the West to spread the dharma. He arrived in the United States with virtually nothing but some rare Tibetan texts and a pregnant wife. Despite the language problem and some very high expectations, he had no trouble attracting a group of eager students. Like most traditional Tibetan teachers, he expected his students to begin with an arduous series of preparatory practices that included hundreds of thousands of prostrations, vows, and visualizations. Tarthang's students were also expected to attend a traditional three-year, three-month, and three-day retreat when he thought they were ready. In addition to this curriculum, he created the Human Development Training Program designed for psychologists, physicians, and therapists, which offered instruction in Buddhist psychology as well as basic meditation techniques. Tarthang Tulku also started the Nyingma Institute as a place for education and study, as well as his own publishing house.

As it turned out, however, the first three-year retreat for Westerners was not offered by Tarthang Tulku but by a renowned Tibetan yogi, Kalu Rinpoche. At age twenty-five, Kalu Rinpoche began a twelve-year solitary retreat, wandering possessionless in the mountains of Tibet, that only ended when his guru told him to come back and begin teaching. He made the first of his many trips to the West at the Dalai Lama's request in 1971. He established his principal North American center in Vancouver, Canada, but that first three-year retreat was held in France on land donated for that purpose. One student who participated in that retreat described it as a virtual "college of contemplative techniques."[17] Before his death, Kalu Rinpoche went on to establish a permanent retreat center on an island near Vancouver and another near Woodstock, New York.

Trungpa Rinpoche: Crazy Wisdom

Despite the success of Tarthang Tulku and Kalu Rinpoche, it was Chogyam Trungpa, more than any other single individual, who shaped the face of Tibetan Buddhism in the West. Even though he arrived in the United States long after the end of the Beat movement, Trungpa Rinpoche was far more the inheritor of the countercultural mantle of "'Beat Zen'" than any of the other Tibetan teachers in the West—or for that matter any of the Zen masters. It is no coincidence that Alan Ginsberg, the quintessential Beat poet, became one of Trungpa's students and would teach at Trungpa's Naropa Institute until his own death in 1997.

A brilliant and innovative teacher, Trungpa Rinpoche was unique among his generation of Tibetans in his understanding of Western culture and his ability to adapt traditional teachings to the needs and experiences of his Western students. Trungpa established an international network of practice centers that is still far larger than any other Tibetan organization in the West. He promoted a variety of "contemplative arts" from flower arranging to horseback riding. He founded the Naropa Institute, which now offers bachelor's and master's degrees in Buddhist studies and psychology, among other subjects. He even created a more secularized path to spiritual awakening known as Shambhala training, with a separate organizational structure parallel to his Buddhist centers.

Despite his enormous success and his unquestionable spiritual power, Trungpa Rinpoche remains a controversial figure. A husband and father, Trungpa openly had sex with his students, smoked, and drank heavily enough to be characterized as an alcoholic by many who knew him. To most of his students, Trungpa's unconventional behavior was as much a part of his teachings as his dharma talks—a way of showing that enlightenment is to be found in even the most profane activities. But for others with more traditional Western expectations about the way a spiritual leader should behave, Trungpa remains a puzzle that is unlikely to ever be unraveled.

Born in a small village in northeastern Tibet in 1939, he was discovered and enthroned as the eleventh Trungpa Tulku at the age of only thirteen months. The Trungpa line of reincarnation was an important one in the Tibetan hierarchy, and the enthronement ceremonies that installed him in the abbotship of the Surmang monasteries were attended by thirteen thousand monks and laypeople. After a rigorous education and training with some of Tibet's most important gurus, the Chinese invasion forced the young Trungpa to flee his home. In 1959, he led a party of about three hundred refugees in a dramatic escape to India. After continuing his studies among the Tibetan refugee community in India, Trungpa moved to England to attend Oxford University, where he perfected his English and studied Western culture, religion, and society. Trungpa also had a lively interest in the arts and took classes in art history and painting as well as lessons in Japanese flower arranging.

Trungpa soon established a meditation center in Britain, but he was not completely satisfied with it, since it seemed to him that many of the participants were "slightly missing the point."[18] Social obligations forced Trungpa to go to India for a short stay, and upon his return to Britain a pivotal event in his life occurred. At that time, Trungpa was still wearing the robes of a monk but was not leading the celibate life that implies. In

May 1969, while driving with one of his girlfriends, Trungpa missed a turn and crashed headlong into, of all things, an English joke shop. His companion was not seriously injured, but Trungpa was left paralyzed on the left side of his body. To Trungpa, "it was a direct message. . . . The accident not only brought me more completely in touch with wisdom again but it also finally cut through the seduction of materialism. Keeping the image of monk in order to handle situations was an imbalance of skillful means."[19] "With a sense of further involving myself with the sangha, I determined to give up my monastic vows. More than ever I felt myself given over to serving the cause of Buddhism."[20] From this point on, Trungpa took off his robes and continued his Buddhist teachings as a layman.

Trungpa Rinpoche came to North America in 1970. He settled in Boulder, Colorado, but continued to pay periodic visits to the many other Buddhist centers that looked to him for guidance. Many of his earliest Boulder students came from a hippie commune known as the Pygmies, and his teachings had a particularly strong appeal to artists and bohemians of all kinds. His growing band of followers soon developed a reputation for wild parties that stood in stark contrast to the puritanical image of many other Buddhist groups. Along with the partying, Trungpa introduced an ever increasing emphasis on meditation and disciplined Buddhist practice.

Trungpa started off his new American students with a stern warning about the dangers and pitfalls of the spiritual path, and especially about what he called *spiritual materialism*—a term that soon became a part of the vocabulary of Western Buddhists from all traditions:

> Walking the spiritual path properly is a very subtle process; it is not something to jump into naively. There are numerous sidetracks which lead to a distorted, ego-centered version of spirituality; we can deceive ourselves into thinking we are developing spiritually when instead we are strengthening our egocentricity through spiritual techniques. This fundamental distortion may be referred to as *spiritual materialism*.[21]

Tibetan teachers such as Kalu Rinpoche or Tarthang Tulku required most of their Western students to follow tradition and perform years of preparatory practices before receiving meditation instruction. But Trungpa, probably influenced by his contacts with Suzuki Roshi in San Francisco, started beginning students right off with *shamatha* meditation practice, which in fact was not so different from the zazen Suzuki himself taught. After his students were grounded in meditation, they were urged to attend an intensive "seminary," where they were usually given *tonglen* practice—a kind of compassion meditation in which one takes on the suffering of the world and gives back joy and happiness. Finally, after years of preparing his sangha, Trungpa introduced his most qualified students to the high tantric practices traditionally held secret in Tibet.

As the teachings deepened, the style of the sangha changed as well. After the 1974 visit of the Karmapa (the head of the Kagyu lineage), the meditation hall kept the more formal air it took on during his visit, and Trungpa began encouraging his students to wear suits, ties, and polished shoes—a radical change from their original countercultural style. Indeed, making sudden and often uncomfortable changes was very much a part of Trungpa's teaching style—a manifestation of the "crazy wisdom" he often discussed. In the early 1980s, for example, Trungpa shook the Boulder community out of its complacency when he unexpectedly decided to move his center of operations to isolated Nova Scotia.

In 1977, Trungpa introduced Shambhala training as a kind of secular alternative to Buddhism. Although there is no question that it was deeply influenced by Buddhism as well as by Tibet's original Bon religion, the exact origins of Shambhala training are still a matter of debate. Some believe it was Trungpa's own creation. Others hold that it reflects some little-known Tibetan tradition, possibly handed down in the Nyingma lineage. Still others believe it is a *terma*—a secret teaching hidden by an early master to be discovered by later generations when the conditions are right to receive it.

Although disciplined meditation is as important to the Shambhala path as it is in Buddhism, the ideal is not that of a monk or yogi but of the warrior who remains passionately involved in the world. In Trungpa's teachings, however, the real warriors are not the violent killers we usually picture but the ones who are brave enough to face their own tender heart. The goal of Shambhala training is to discover the basic goodness that lies at the root of human experience. But in a unique and insightful twist, Trungpa also emphasized awakening to the "the heart of genuine sadness" that is an inevitable part of the joy of a truly open life. As Trungpa put it, "Experiencing the upliftedness of the world is a joyous situation. But it also brings sadness. It is like falling in love. When you are in love, being with your lover is both delightful and very painful. You feel both joy and sorrow. This is not a problem, in fact it is wonderful. It is the ideal human emotion."[22]

Trungpa Rinpoche died in 1987 before he reached the age of fifty, and his years of heavy drinking are widely believed to be the principal cause. Very much in the Tibetan tradition, Rinpoche's death was reported to have been accompanied by a host of magical events. Several of his students have said that their clocks stopped at the moment of his death, and, as he had predicted years before, a miraculous display of rainbows appeared at his cremation ceremony. Steven T. Butterfield, one of the most skeptical and outspokenly critical of Trungpa's students, gave this description of the event:

> Everyone who stayed long enough at Trungpa's cremation saw the rainbows. . . . The sky . . . was thickly overcast on the morning of the cremation ceremony, but then turned bright blue around our hill when the lamas torched his body and conducted their rituals. Strangely, it continued to be overcast elsewhere. Many people had already left before the rainbows began, a little after lunch. I looked up and saw brilliant colored rings around the sun. I looked to the side and saw arches of color in the distance. Several conventional rainbows appeared one after the other. Then a cirrus cloud grew long bony fingers and went through a brilliant sequence of colors: gold, rose, turquoise, and pink.[23]

Vipassana: New Insight from an Ancient Tradition

Theravada is the most ancient of all the Buddhist traditions, but far from being enfeebled with old age, organized Buddhism is probably a greater political and social force in the Theravadin countries than anywhere else on earth. Why then was Theravada the last of the major Buddhist traditions to arrive in North America? Part of the explanation may be that the Theravadin countries never had the military and political involvement with the United States that the Japanese and Koreans did. (Sri Lanka and Burma did, however, have a long colonial tie to Britain, and the Theravadin tradition was among the first to take root in Europe.) Moreover, the very political strength of Theravadin Buddhism may also have been a factor. Unlike the Tibetans or the Vietnamese, Theravadin Buddhists never experienced government persecution, so they had less of an impetus to strike out and spread the dharma in other lands.

Many Asian Theravadin teachers have come to North America over the years, but few actually took up residence here. So Vipassana (the approach to the tradition most popular in the West) was spread mostly by Westerners who went to Asia and brought it back. As a result, Vipassana centers tend to be more westernized in their cultural forms and less inclined toward elaborate symbolism and ritual than Zen or Tibetan centers. Moreover, the Asian Vipassana teacher who has been the most successful at establishing a base in North America, S. N. Goenka, has a surprisingly "Western" style himself. Not only is he a layman, not a monk, but he himself ignores most of the traditional Buddhist symbols and rituals. He refuses to allow himself or his students to accept any kind of payment for their teachings.

The three central figures in American Vipassana, Sharon Salzberg, Joseph Goldstein, and Jack Kornfield, have remarkably similar backgrounds, strikingly so in the case of Goldstein and Kornfield. Both came from upper-middle-class Jewish homes on the East Coast, both attended Ivy League colleges in hopes of starting a professional career, and both came into first-hand contact with Buddhism while volunteering in the Peace Corps in Asia. Goldstein and Kornfield did not actually meet, however, until both were invited to teach Vipassana meditation at Trungpa's Naropa Institute in 1974. They soon developed a close friendship, and together with Sharon Salzburg they founded the Insight Meditation Center (IMC) in Barre, Massachussetts, in a mansion-like red-brick building that once served as a Catholic seminary. Right from the start, Vipassana struck a responsive cord among Westerners, and the IMC quickly grew into a major retreat center.

In 1984, Jack Kornfield left IMC and was instrumental in founding a similar organization on the West Coast. The Insight Meditation Center and the Spirit Rock Meditation Center (as the West Coast organization is known) now form the twin axes of Vipassana practice in North America. Unlike most other Western Buddhist centers, which were formed under the leadership of a single dominant teacher, both Vipassana centers are organized around a community of teachers with collective decision making and a very Western sense of egalitarianism. But despite their organizational similarities and the underlying continuity in the Vipassana practice itself, the two centers have taken distinctively different directions. Under the leadership of Goldstein and Salzberg, the Barre center has stuck close to traditional Vipassana practice, whereas Kornfield and his associates have led Spirit Rock to incorporate the insights and perspectives of Western psychology and other spiritual traditions into its practice.

Jack Kornfield: American Dharma

Some say that Jack Kornfield has a voice like chocolate pudding. When he gives his dharma talks, he projects a kind of childlike innocence and sincerity that has helped make him one of the most influential of all American Buddhist teachers. He has, moreover, been a major force urging America Buddhism to openly confront the problems of abuse and misconduct created by a few of its most respected teachers.

Kornfield grew up in what he described as a "scientific and intellectual household." His father was a biophysicist who worked on artificial organs and space medicine. The atmosphere in his family was a tense one and there was lots of conflict between Kornfield's parents. After high school, he went to Dartmouth College and planned on becoming a physician. Like someone in one of the stories Kornfield is so good at telling, he was inspired by a wise old professor of Chinese philosophy to switch his major to Asian studies. He grew his hair long and dropped out of school for a year. He spent four months in the capital of hippie culture, Haight Ashbury, and experimented with LSD. After graduating, he joined the Peace Corps and was sent to Thailand where he began his Buddhist practice under the "forest monk," Achaan Chah.

Kornfield ultimately became a monk himself and underwent years of rigorous training, including a year-long silent retreat with twenty hours a day of sitting and walking meditation. Describing this period of his life, Kornfield writes:

I developed concentration and *samadhi* (deep levels of mental absorption), and many kinds of insights came. I had visions, revelations, and a variety of deep awakenings. The whole way I understood myself in the world was turned upside down as my practice developed and I saw things in a new and wiser way.

But then he goes on to add:

Alas, when I returned to the U.S. as a monk all of that fell apart. Although I had arrived back from the monastery clear, spacious and high, in short order I discovered . . . that my dedication had helped me very little with my human relationships. I was still emotionally immature, acting out the same painful patterns of blame and fear, acceptance and rejection that I

had before my Buddhist training. . . . I had used the strength of my meditation to suppress painful feelings, and all too often I didn't even recognize that I was angry, sad, grieving, or frustrated until a long time later.[24]

Like many other Westerners who return home after years of spiritual
practice in Asia, Kornfield realized that he had still not faced his deepest
personal problems. So he turned the tools he learned in his Buddhist practice to the more mundane psychological level: "I began a long and difficult
process of reclaiming my emotions, of bringing awareness and understanding to my pattern of relationships, of learning how to feel my feelings, and what to do with the powerful forces of human connection."
Seeking to integrate the Eastern and Western approaches, Kornfield en-
rolled in a graduate program in clinical psychology and eventually earned
a Ph.D. He not only worked as a therapist but underwent therapy himself.

After helping found the Insight Meditation Center in 1976, Kornfield
became one of its three principal teachers along with Salzburg and Goldstein. Over the years, however, his teaching and practice took a divergent
course. Salzberg and Goldstein were increasingly influenced by U Pandita, a charismatic Burmese teacher who placed strong emphasis on the
traditional Theravadin quest to uproot the defilements of greed, hate, and
delusion. According to Kornfield, "Joseph and Sharon's Dharma talks
began to focus more and more on the defilements. I was more interested
in teaching Dharma from the heart, engaging feelings, and applying experience to every day life."[25] Unlike Salzberg and Goldstein, Kornfield
married and started a family. In 1984, he left the Insight Meditation Center and moved to the West Coast. After years of Buddhist teaching and
work as a therapist, Kornfield and a group of Bay Area Vipassana teachers
founded the Spirit Rock Meditation Center in Marin Country, which is
now one of the fastest-growing Buddhist organizations in the West.

Today, Jack Kornfield continues to use classic Vipassana meditation
techniques as the heart of his teachings, but he combines them with an
eclectic mix drawn from Western psychology and the wisdom of other
Eastern traditions. "To open deeply," Kornfield writes,

we need tremendous courage and strength, a kind of warrior spirit. . . .
We need energy, commitment, and courage not to run from our life nor
to cover it over with any philosophy—material or spiritual. We need a
warrior's heart that lets us face our lives directly, our pains and limita-

tions, our joys and possibilities. This courage allows us to include every aspect of life in our spiritual practice: our bodies, our families, our society, politics, the earth's ecology, art, education. Only then can spirituality be truly integrated into our lives."[26]

New Approaches Emerge

Most of the first generation of Western teachers had a firm tie to one of the three major Asian traditions, but it wasn't long before Buddhism's encounter with Western individualism led to the emergence of new approaches and new allegiances. As time went on, a growing number of teachers came to be trained in more than one tradition, something that seldom happened among the more traditional Asians. This new style of Western teacher freely mixed the insights and approaches of all the Asian Buddhist traditions, often combined with a healthy dose of such things as Sufism, Taoism, the nondualistic schools of Hinduism, and Western psychology. For the most part, these teachers continued to see themselves as Buddhists, albeit with a broadly based nonsectarian approach. But for some, even a general identification as a Buddhist was still a type of clinging that needed to be transcended, and they carried on their teaching without labels or affiliation.

One of the most influential of all these Western innovators was Dennis Lingwood, an Englishman now known as Sangharakshita. Born to a working-class family in southwest London in 1925, he eventually came to head an international network of over one hundred independent Buddhist centers, retreat facilities, residential communities, "right livelihood" businesses, and educational, health, and art programs.

His first exposure to Eastern thought came in 1940, when he read a book by Mme. Blavasky of the Theosophical Society. After reading some Buddhist sutras, he made contact with the Buddhist Society in London and took the precepts. He was drafted into the British army during World War II, and it provided his passage to India. At the end of the war, however, he went AWOL and began almost twenty years of Buddhist studies in India. Although he never worked closely enough with any teacher to be recognized as a dharma heir, he had a wide variety of Buddhist contacts. In the early years, he was most strongly influenced by the Theravadin tradition. In fact, it was a Burmese monk who gave him ordination and the name Sangharakshita. Later he came under the influence of a German student of the Tibetan tradition known as Lama Govinda, who helped expand Sangharakshita's already broad Buddhist horizons. His last important influence was the Indian leader of the untouchable classes, Bhimrao Ramji Ambedkar, who led a mass Buddhist conversion of untouchables who had, of course, so long been stigmatized by Hindu belief.

Sangharakshita had both a penetrating intellect and tremendous organizational skills. He founded his own Buddhist organization at age twenty-four and just two months later he started publishing a journal. In 1957, he published a wide-ranging study of the Buddhist tradition, *A Survey of Buddhism,* which has received broad recognition even though he knew only rudimentary Pali and Sanskrit, and no Tibetan at all. Sangharakshita did not return to Britain until 1964, when the English Sangha Trust invited him to settle at the Hampstead Buddhist Vihara. He stayed there two years, but his unorthodox views and lifestyle eventually led to a falling out. He found that his view of Buddhism didn't fit with either the genteel approach of London's Buddhist Society or the traditional Theravadin monasticism favored by the Sangha Trust. His solution was to found his own organization, the Friends of the Western Buddhist Order (FWBO). Only a year after it was formed in 1967, he ordained nine men and three women as the nucleus of the Western Buddhist Order.

The FWBO grew rapidly in the following years, focusing not just on Buddhist practice but on building a broadly based Buddhist community that included local centers where members could meet for services and meditation, retreat centers where they could go for intensive practice, residential centers where they could live, and businesses where they could work. The ultimate goal of the FWBO is nothing less than a radical transformation of society. As Sangharakshita's second in command, Dharmachari Subhuti, put it: "The creation of a New Society is the purpose of the FWBO." Its aim is "not to find a corner for Buddhists in the midst of the old society. . . . It wishes to change the old society into the new."[27] Although the FWBO certainly has wide-ranging doctrinal roots, even including some Theosophical influences, it differs from the other broadly based Buddhist organizations in that its centers are largely closed to teachers from outside their group. Perhaps because of its orientation toward community building, the FWBO is, in the words of Stephen Batchelor, "often perceived by other Western Buddhists as a self-enclosed organization, that . . . has limited interaction with the wider Buddhist community."[28]

Toni Packer: Beyond Buddhism?

The Springwater Center in upstate New York is no longer called a Zen center. It has no official ties to organized Buddhism, no Buddhist icons, no bowing, no chanting. They don't even burn incense anymore. Yet somehow you can't help feeling that the heart of Buddhism is still flourishing there. Certainly anyone familiar with Western Zen would feel quite at home at Springwater. During retreats, they have the same schedule of sitting and walking meditation you would find at any Zen center. Although Toni Packer doesn't call herself a teacher anymore, she still gives a daily talk during retreats and gives a long series of private interviews, just as a Zen master would. The meditation room (it's no longer called a zendo) has the same polished wood floors with the same square pads and round meditation cushions. The cooks even use the same vegetarian menu they used at the Rochester Zen Center before Packer's group split off. Toni (that's what everyone calls her) usually ends the retreats with a series of readings that might include the Chinese Zen master Huang Po along with the likes of Krishnamurti and the Hindu sage Nisargadatta. But most importantly, Toni's single-minded focus on simply paying full attention to the present moment here and now—without the images, thoughts, and ideas that lead us to distraction—reflects the essence of Buddhist realization. The Springwater Center seems to practice a kind of bare-bones Buddhism stripped down to its most basic essentials. So stripped down that even the term Buddhism has been ejected.

Anyone who is familiar with her background would not find it surprising that Toni Packer was drawn to years of intense Zen practice, nor that she had a deep discomfort with the structure of power, authority, and tradition she found in organized Buddhism. Raised in Nazi Germany with a Jewish mother and a gentile father, she and her family lived in constant fear that even her father's status as a successful scientist and their acceptance of Christianity wouldn't protect them from the stormtroopers. When one interviewer asked her what started her relentless search for the meaning of it all, she replied:

> The traumatic happenings during the years of my childhood in Germany: the persecution of Jews, the War; the disappearance of people I knew, and those who did not come back from the front; the air raids; the incessant news of destruction and killing; fear for one's own life, either through

being taken to a concentration camp or being burned in an air raid shelter. [There was] . . . a deep questioning of what the sense of it all was.[29]

After the war, she met a young American student, Kyle Packer. They were married in 1950 and moved to the United States the next year. She attended the University of Buffalo, where she first encountered Buddhism through the works of Alan Watts. Later Kyle gave her a copy of Kapleau Roshi's *Three Pillars of Zen,* and she soon began a meditation practice at home. Toni eventually sought Kapleau out and spent years as his student at the Rochester Zen Center. She threw herself into her koan study and was eventually recognized by the Roshi as his leading student and successor. She was given full charge of the Rochester center while the Roshi was taking a year off, yet she found herself more and more doubtful about how the center was operated and about whether or not she still saw herself as a Buddhist. Around this time she encountered the work of Krishnamurti and "realized that while I thought a certain degree of freedom and insight had been attained, one really was attached—hung up on a system, a method, and spiritual advancement."[30] Toni wondered about all the rituals at the Zen center. "I know the teaching that things leading up to enlightenment are worth doing: practices like rituals, bowing, and incense burning. But these things don't lead to truth. They comfort us. . . . These practices have nothing to do with understanding."[31] But most of all she questioned the whole structure of power that was embedded in Zen practice at Rochester: "In Zen teaching I was told the teacher sits in the Buddha's place. When I started teaching, I was told, 'You are sitting in the Buddha's place.' Can you imagine what happens to the mind when one is being told that, and then the students start coming and prostrating to the teacher?"[32]

At the end of 1981, Toni left Kapleau Roshi's center, and she and her students started the Genesee Valley Zen Center. A few years later they bought a beautiful three-hundred-acre parcel of land near Springwater, New York, and built a new center, where she still teaches and holds retreats.

Toni calls her work meditative inquiry, and instead of teaching doctrines, techniques, or ideas, she questions. She urges people to inquire into the nature of their experience with an open mind, free from preconceived thoughts and beliefs. If people want to meditate the structure is there, but if they just want to walk in the beautiful woods at Springwater it seems to make no difference to Toni. Again and again she points directly to this present moment—to the sounds of the birds, the way the sunlight falls across the floor, or to the confusion in the minds of so many of her questioners. Is what she is doing teaching Buddhism? Toni wouldn't admit that she is doing anything. As she puts it, "Every moment life is teaching. . . . There can be learning every moment because every moment is new. The Buddha's last words were, 'Be a lamp unto yourself.' See for yourself, find out for yourself."[33]

Crisis and Renewal

The 1970s were, as we have seen, a period of booming growth in Western Buddhism. As numerous practice centers sprang up, the focus of Western Buddhism shifted from free-spirited bohemian intellectuals to organized centers based on disciplined meditation. Not quite monasteries but far different from traditional Asian temples, those practice centers were something entirely new in the history of Buddhism. The centers usually formed around a charismatic teacher—sometimes a Westerner but more often an Asian—and at their heart was a group of dedicated practitioners who usually lived in the center or nearby. Unlike the great Asian monasteries, women and men usually practiced and lived together without vows of celibacy or much isolation from the outside world. Over the years, the social dynamics of these centers came to share much in common with those of a large extended family. Even the discipline of Buddhist practice and a dominating authority figure couldn't prevent the buildup of the tensions typical in such families, and during the 1980s one center after another underwent a painful upheaval.

One problem lay in the very success of Western Buddhism. Centers had sprung up so rapidly that some growing pains were inevitable, especially since Western Buddhism was so new and so different from its antecedents that there were few traditional models to follow. Because their Asian teachers were often considered enlightened beings whose actions were virtually beyond question, unvoiced frustrations and discontents often built up among students. For one thing, Westerners trained to believe in democracy from their earliest years often had great trouble with the Asian tradition of obedience and reverence for authority. Resentments about what appeared to be favoritism and the arbitrary exercise of power often festered in silence. Asian teachers also brought many traditional patriarchal attitudes with them that didn't set well with the liberal, highly educated women these centers attracted.

Another common problem was that as the centers grew, students often saw less and less of their teacher, and in some places that became a major source of resentment. In the older centers, many long-time students came to feel that they were at a dead end with no clear career path ahead of them. Though this volatile mix of rapid growth, unmet expectations, and culture conflict provided the fuel, it was often sex that set off the explosion.

The first major upheaval of the 1980s was at the Rochester Zen Center, which Philip Kapleau had founded almost a decade and a half before. The trouble began when Kapleau Roshi's protégé Toni Packer began a painful reevaluation of her practice that eventually led her to start her own center. The result was something very much like a divorce in a large, close-knit family. The Rochester Center split down the middle, with those who supported Kapleau on one side and those who supported Packer on the other. Accusations flew and the center's membership plummeted—both because many of Packer's students left to join her new center and because others became disillusioned with both sides and simply dropped out.

This same kind of family drama was soon replayed at the nation's largest Zen center in San Francisco, only this time the divisions were deeper and the emotional wounds more lasting. The crisis centered around Richard Baker, who was Suzuki Roshi's dharma heir and the one selected to take over after the Roshi's death in 1971. During the next decade, Baker Roshi lead the Zen center through a period of rapid expansion in terms of both its membership and its physical facilities. But at the same time, members were becoming increasingly alienated by Baker's grand lifestyle and his inaccessibility to his students. In 1983, the Zen center exploded when it was discovered that Baker (who was married) was having an affair with one of his students who was the wife of another prominent member of the Zen center. For Baker, at least, this was no casual affair, since he still describes her as the "love of my life." The community was instantly polarized by revelations of the affair and was soon awash in a sea of anger and grief. Although certainly a charismatic figure, Baker was still a Westerner and lacked that air of mystery and infallibility that many foreign teachers enjoyed.

The ultimate result was that for the first time in the short history of Western Buddhism, the head of a major center was forced by its members to resign. As in Rochester, these events shook the community to its foundations; membership dropped and those who stayed entered a period of reevaluation and healing. Although neither of them was forced to resign, very similar scenarios played themselves out when the Asian founders of the Zen Center of Los Angeles and the Kwan Um Zen School were found to have been having their own long-term affairs with female students. Soon other teachers around the country were facing similar accusations.

Although Trungpa Rinpoche drank heavily and led a wide-open sex life, he never tried to keep his activities secret, and they never precipitated a crisis among his students. One simply accepted Rinpoche as he was or went elsewhere for spiritual guidance. However, Trungpa's American successor, Osel Tendzin, was the focus of what was probably American Buddhism's biggest crisis so far. Like his guru, Tendzin openly had sex with his students. But unlike Trungpa, he contracted AIDS, and not only kept it secret from the sangha but even from his lovers. Although no one can be certain if Tendzin was the source, one young man he had sex with later contracted the disease and died. When the news finally broke in 1988, the community was washed by a wave of recriminations aimed both at Tendzin and those in his inner circle who helped keep his condition secret. Despite the Tibetan tradition of absolute allegiance to the guru, Tendzin was eventually forced to leave the center and go into retreat, where he died in 1991. Trungpa Rinpoche's son was appointed as Tendzin's successor and has been working diligently to rebuild the sangha since then.

After the turmoil and confusion of the 1980s, things settled down in the 1990s and membership in North America's Buddhist centers is once again growing rapidly. For many students, that time of troubles was a kind of coming of age when they saw through their idealistic expectations and realized that their teachers had human flaws just as they did. Organized Buddhism has also been struggling to learn the lessons those events had to teach. The San Francisco Zen Center now elects the members of its governing board, many centers have adopted specific codes of conduct governing behavior between students and teachers, and many other centers are focusing more attention on traditional Buddhist precepts as a guide to behavior. The celibate Vietnamese teacher Thich Nhat Hanh has been a particularly important figure in this movement, encouraging both reconciliation and devotion to the precepts. But equally important has been the growing willingness to examine the problems posed by the interplay of sexuality and power in the Buddhist community. One turning point in this process of healing occurred during a historic conference at the Spirit Rock Center in 1993 that brought a large number of Western Buddhist teachers from all traditions together for the first time ever. The official topic was the art of teaching, but the focus of attention unexpectedly turned to sexual abuse after several female teachers gave heartfelt accounts of the pain and confusion they had experienced after having sex with their teachers. Although the teachers took no common action or even reached any kind of consensus, American Buddhists were finally talking about what Allen Ginsberg called the "elephant in the meditation hall."

Thich Nhat Hanh: Engaged Buddhism

Thich Nhat Hanh, a gentle Vietnamese monk, often speaks about the need for inner peace and for peace in our families, communities, and nations. But more than just talking about peace, he seems to *be* peace. Those who have meet him or just heard him talk often comment on the powerful aura of tranquillity and compassion he seems to radiate.

At the age of sixteen, Thich Nhat Hanh became a monk in the Lieu Quan school of Vietnamese Zen. The year was 1942, and his country was in the midst of a convulsion of blood and destruction that was to last for decades: the Japanese invasion of World War II, followed by the communist-led independence movement and the war against the French colonialists and their American proxies. After he completed his training, Nhat Hanh opened the first Buddhist high school in Vietnam and helped found the Van Hanh Buddhist University in Saigon. Always a prolific writer, he became a spokesman for an "engaged Buddhism" that sought to dispel the hatred and division and to bring his tortured country back together again. He tells the powerful story of sitting in a meditation hall with his fellow monks when bombs started dropping around them. Realizing that he couldn't just sit there, he made up his mind to put his meditation into action and do something to relieve the suffering and fear.

In the early 1960s, Nhat Hanh spent three years in the United States studying comparative religion and teaching Buddhism at Columbia University. Upon his return in 1964, he was drawn inextricably back into Vietnam's political chaos. As a leading advocate for peace and reconciliation, he was a target of both sides. The dictators of South Vietnam denounced his "neutralist" writings and branded him a communist, while the communist government in the North declared that he had been bought by "the Pentagon and the White House."[34] Narrowly escaping an assassination attempt, Nhat Hanh came to the West in May 1966 and worked to spread the word about the suffering of his people. He was instrumental in persuading Martin Luther King to come out against the war, and he was later nominated by King for the Nobel Peace Prize. Thich Nhat Hanh continued to work for peace in his country, but when the peace accords were finally signed in 1973, the government refused to allow him back to his homeland.

Nhat Hanh settled in a small rural community named Sweet Potatoes that he started south of Paris. In 1976 and 1977, a crackdown on ethnic Chinese living in Vietnam filled the Gulf of Siam with "boat people" fleeing its repressive government. Nhat Hanh flew to Singapore and organized a rescue operation. The governments of the surrounding nations refused the refugees permission to land, so Nhat Hanh and his colleagues used three boats to bring food and water to the refugees at sea and helped smuggle some of them ashore during the night. The operation was soon raided by the police, and the peace workers were forced to abandon more than seven hundred people they were caring for at sea. In reaction to that failure, Thich Nhat Hanh stayed in retreat at Sweet Potato for the next five years, meditating, reading and writing, and gardening. In 1982, he visited New York and later that year established a larger retreat center in southern France known as Plum Village. Since then, he has traveled to North America every two years or so to lecture and lead retreats.

In the wake of the crises and confusion that plagued many Buddhist centers in the 1980s, Thich Nhat Hanh has been a powerful influence pushing Western Buddhism away from the "crazy wisdom" of the Beat era and the 1960s and 1970s, and toward more conservative ethical standards. Nhat Hanh gave strong emphasis to the importance of the Buddhist precepts that he now calls the "five mindfulness trainings" and the ceremony that symbolizes the commitment to try to live up to them. Working with his Western students, Thich Nhat Hanh rewrote the traditional precepts to better fit contemporary society, in the process making them considerably more detailed and specific than those used by other teachers in the West. The third precept, for example, is usually phrased in terms of avoiding "sexual misconduct," but Nhat Hanh's version specifically spells that out in terms of a commitment "not to engage in sexual relations without love and a long-term commitment" as well as respecting "my commitments and the commitments of others," protecting children from sexual abuse and "preventing couples and families from being broken by sexual misconduct." Similarly, the fifth precept that traditionally prohibits the consumption of intoxicants is expanded to include "foods or other items that contain toxins such as certain TV programs, magazines, books, films, and conversations," and even to encourage eating a "proper diet."[35]

Thich Nhat Hanh has been as instrumental in promoting politically engaged Buddhism in the West as he was in his own country. He made several tours of the United States during the 1980s that gave a needed boost to the Buddhist Peace Fellowship—the organization of politically involved Buddhists founded by Aitken Roshi of Hawaii's Diamond Sangha among others—and his lectures and writings often touch on social issues. Rejecting the tendency of some Buddhists to see social involvement as an obstacle to enlightenment, Nhat Hanh writes that "meditation is not an escape from society. Meditation is to equip oneself with the capacity to reintegrate into society." At the same time, however, he always makes it clear that outer peace begins with, and depends upon, inner peace. "It is not by going out for a demonstration against nuclear missiles that we can bring about peace. It is with our capacity of smiling, breathing, and being peace that we can make peace."[36]

One of Thich Nhat Hanh's greatest teachings is just his presence, and the tremendous sense of peace he projects. In his books and lectures, he repeatedly emphasizes the importance of mindfulness—whether it is eating a tangerine, washing the dishes, or taking a walk. He has also developed a number of specialized techniques to help promote mindfulness amid the bustle of everyday life. In Thich Nhat Hanh's hands, even the telephone can be a mindfulness bell. Instead of picking the phone up as soon as it rings, he recommends that the listener repeat this phrase while breathing mindfully: "Listen, listen. This wonderful sound brings me back to my true self." His meditation instructions usually focus on the awareness of breathing. Among the various techniques he suggests to his students are counting their breaths and reciting a phrase with each in-breath and out-breath, for example, "I breathe in I calm my body, I breathe out I smile. Dwelling in the present moment, I know this is a wonderful moment!" He is also famous for what he sometimes humorously calls his "mouth yoga"—doing walking or sitting meditation with a half smile on his face.

Four
❋

AT THE MARROW
Practice and Belief

The San Francisco Zen Center's Green Gulch Farm lies in a lush coastal valley in Marin County just north of the city. Most of its numerous buildings have the sturdy, unpretentious feel of a cabin in the redwoods. But its spacious meditation hall has an altogether more formal atmosphere. Its walls are ringed with a smoothly polished wood platform that is usually covered with neat rows of black meditation cushions, each sitting on its own black pad. In the center there is an altar at which the priests make prostrations and offer incense to a large statue of Manjushri, the bodhisattva of wisdom. When entering for a period of meditation, everyone is expected to follow an elaborate code of etiquette. You step into the zendo with the foot nearest the door, your right hand clasped over the left about waist high. You stop and bow to the statue and then proceed to your assigned place. You bow to your cushion, turn 180 degrees to your right, bow again, and mount your cushion with your back to the wall. Finally, you turn another half circle to face the wall, straighten your back, balance you head, and place you hands in the "cosmic mudra"—an oval with your thumbs touching lightly at the middle. A series of bells marks the beginning and the end of the meditation period and, except for emergencies, no one is expected to leave until it is done nor even to wiggle around too much. The head priest is the last to enter and the first to leave—a process that for most involves rerunning the same steps in reverse.

Only ten or fifteen miles north lies the Spirit Rock Meditation Center in another beautiful expanse of rolling California hills. Spirit Rock has its own large room for meditation, but the feeling is entirely different. Members amble in at their own pace, pick a spot on the carpeted floor, and put down whatever kind of cushions that seem to work for them. Many just sit in a chair. Some even bring in a cup of tea or a bottle of water to sip while they sit. There are bells to mark the beginning and the end of the meditation sessions, but little in the way of ritual and imagery.

The bustling city of San Rafael, a few more miles southeast, provides still more Buddhist contrasts. Lama Surya Das holds occasional retreats in a meeting room in the back of a downtown bookstore that aptly symbolizes the approach of his own Tibetan tradition. Although smaller than the gathering places at Spirit Rock or Green Gulch, it is a riot of color and symbolism. The floors are covered with bright oriental rugs and the walls are jammed with Tibetan *thangkas*, statues, incense burners, and ritual instruments. Within walking distance of the bookstore is the Dominican College, where Toni Packer's group rents a former convent for their California retreats. Not only is the room they use for meditation and lectures bare of any Buddhist images or oriental trimmings, but the courtyard that many retreatents use for walking meditation still has a prominent statue of the Virgin Mary and other symbols of the Christian faith.

The peaceful affluence of Marin County has proven to be especially fertile ground for the growth of Western Buddhism, but the contrasting approaches found there are unusual only in their close proximity. The new Buddhism contains a cornucopia of ideas, practices, techniques, and styles, yet underlying all this there is a common core that defines it as a distinct religious movement. In the pages that follow, we will begin by focusing on the differences among the three major branches of Western Buddhism and then turn our attention to the common ground they share.

Although it is possible to make many useful generalizations about Zen practice or Vipassana practice or Tibetan practice, it is important to keep in mind that Buddhism isn't structured like the Western religions most readers are familiar with. There is no central hierarchy or official doctrine. There is no way to punish "heretics," or for that matter any idea that there is such a thing. In some ways, it is better to think of the branches of the Buddhist tree as a group of lineages descending from some common

ancestors. Each Western lineage not only has its own distinctive characteristics, but each individual teacher is free to change things in any way he
or she sees fit. Indeed, it is not unusual for a teacher to completely reject
key aspects of his or her own teacher's approach and strike out in a completely new direction. Although there is a good chance that other disciples in the same lineage will frown on such behavior, it isn't likely to have
much effect as long as the teachers can continue to attract students and financial support. So the generalizations that follow about Zen or Vajrayana
or Vipassana practice are just that—generalizations. I hope they express
the typical middle ground in each of these three traditions, but there are
far too many individual lineages and styles to examine them all here.

Zen

Zen was the first style of Asian Buddhism to take root in North America
and, not surprisingly, it is still its largest. While there are no reliable data
on the total number of people affiliated with the different Buddhist lineages, there is a comprehensive listing of Buddhist groups in North America that "focus on meditation." Using this definition, Don Morreale,
editor of *The Complete Guide to Buddhist America,* and his associates excluded Buddhist groups that do not emphasize meditation, such as the
Soka Gakkai and Jodo Shinshu, and thus they come pretty close to our
definition of the "new Buddhism." In 1997, they counted 423 Buddhist
groups in the United States and Canada that were affiliated with the Zen
tradition—about 40 percent of all the groups listed. Of all the traditions
they surveyed, only the nondenominational groups grew faster in the last
decade. All in all, the number of Zen groups increased by 260 percent
during the ten years between the publication of the first edition of Morreale's book and the second.[1]

The Japanese immigrants who were so critical in bringing Zen to
North America were never much of a presence in Great Britain, and Zen
is not as commonly practiced there. The British equivalent of Morreale's
book, *The Buddhist Directory,* was first published by London's Buddhist
Society in 1979 and is now in its seventh edition. Thus it actually provides
a bit longer view. About 17 percent of the groups listed in the latest directory are in the Zen tradition, and although the percentage has varied
somewhat from edition to edition, that is a fairly typical figure. This

British data, however, is not strictly equivalent to the U.S. statistics because the *Buddhist Directory* attempts to list all the Buddhist groups in the British Isles, not just the ones that have a meditation orientation. While the percentage of Zen groups in Britain has remained fairly stable, the total number of groups has nonetheless been growing rapidly. The 1983 edition of the *Buddhist Directory* listed only twelve groups; fourteen years later there were fifty-seven.

Although few Westerners realize it, several different Zen traditions are active here, and each includes numerous different lineages. To complicate matters further, particular teachers are sometimes affiliated with more than one tradition. The first Zen Buddhists in the West came from Japan, and we usually apply the Japanese word to the Ch'an Buddhist of China, the Son Buddhists of Korea, and the Thien Buddhism of Vietnam. But each Zen has its own distinctive characteristics. Japanese Zen has two different branches that both made their way to the West. The Rinzai sect is the more aristocratic of the two, and its long association with the warrior nobility of Japan has earned it the nickname "samurai Zen." As befits a warrior religion, the way of Rinzai Zen is to launch a frontal assault on the barriers to liberation and demand the highest levels of discipline and commitment. This decidedly masculine tone is clearly reflected in its membership. Of the seven Buddhist groups I surveyed, the one most strongly influenced by Rinzai Zen (the Rochester Zen Center) was also the only one in which the majority of the members were men. The larger of the two Japanese Zens, however, is the Soto sect. Less aristocratic and somewhat softer in tone, groups in the Soto tradition generally place more emphasis on ritual and ceremony than their Rinzai counterparts.

Buddhism has been much more eclectic in Korea than Japan. The Chogye Order that dominates Korean Buddhism encompasses not only the Son approach with its focus on meditation but also academic sutra study and the popular devotionalism of the Pure Land sects. Nonetheless, Seung Sahn and the other Korean teachers who have come to the West place a heavy emphasis on meditation and trace their lineage back to some of the same Chinese teachers as Japanese Rinzai Zen. The differences between Japanese and Korean Zen in the West are therefore mostly in matters of cultural style. In contrast to the formality of the Japanese, Korean groups have a more casual feel. There are also numerous differences in terminology, rituals, and ascetics. The influence of Vietnamese Buddhism on the West has come primarily from one man, Thich Nhat

Hanh, and his approach differs sharply from the Korean and Japanese Zen teachers who have been active here. Although Nhat Hanh is also part of a Zen lineage that traces its lineage back to the great Chinese teacher, Lin Chi, his style is much softer and more eclectic than the Korean or Japanese Zen masters or for that matter Lin Chi himself. In fact, many Western Buddhists don't even think of Thich Nhat Hanh's groups as a branch of Zen despite the importance they place on meditation and mindfulness in daily life.

ZEN STYLE   Like the other styles of Buddhism, Zen has undergone enormous changes as it has adapted to its new Western environment. Since there is little in the way of an overarching hierarchy, every group and every teacher is free to develop its own approach. What makes a real Zen group is not a particular doctrine or practice, but its participation in the Zen tradition, which has been handed down from teacher to student over the generations. Even though few generalizations fit all Zen groups in the West neatly, it is possible to say something about the Zen style in contrast to the Vipassana or Tibetan approach.

A visitor doesn't have to stay long to see that the air in most Zen centers is thick with strenuous effort. As a whole, Zen students are a disciplined, serious, and self-controlled lot (even though Zen as much as any Buddhist tradition firmly rejects the reality of the personal self). Compared to the groups founded by the extroverted Tibetans, most Zen groups tend to be rather uncomfortable with the expression of strong emotions, and residents and long-term students are generally expected to fit in and follow the program as it is set up. Perhaps the most famous symbol of this discipline is the *kyosaku*—the "encouragement stick"—which has been used by generations of Zen masters to hit students on the back and shoulders in order, among other things, to rouse them from their lethargy during long periods of meditation. Although most recipients see these blows as a useful stimulus to their practice, the symbolism is difficult in the Western culture. Most centers in the West now administer the *kyosaku's* blows only to students who request it by making a bow at the appropriate moment.

Zen is famous for the elegant simplicity of its aesthetic style, and that feeling is very much in evidence in the larger Zen centers of North America. The newer buildings tend to show a strong East Asian influence and many Asian touches are inevitably added to existing structures when a Zen group moves in. Groups from Japanese lineages tend to favor dark colors, especially black, which is often the only color permitted for meditation cushions and pads. The Koreans on the other hand tend to use more gray. Somber isn't the right word, but I think it would be fair to say that most Zen centers are serious and rather austere places.

By American standards, most Zen centers are very formal places. Daily life is regulated by a seemingly endless profusion of rules, and it is easy to get the feeling that you aren't quite doing things right. Casual visitors are also inevitably struck by all the bowing that everyone seems to be doing, and they often interpret what is meant as a social courtesy as a sign of deference or obedience. There is, nonetheless, a good deal of real hierarchy in evidence as well. For one thing, just knowing all the rules and expectations immediately sets off the old hands from the newcomers, and the hierarchy becomes even more obvious as soon as you step into the meditation halls that are the heart of these centers. Although there are numerous variations between the different centers, the head priest tends to occupy a central location in the *zendo* and is flanked by a few of his or her highest ranking students. As in so many other social settings, clothes are also marks of social status. While some groups require that everyone in the zendo wear robes, it is common for outsiders and new students to come in wearing street clothes while only more committed members, residents, and monks wear robes. All robes, moreover, are not equal. Priests generally wear more elaborate regalia than the laity, and the head priests, who have received official "dharma transmission," often wear robes of a special color or style. Another important symbol is a kind of roughly sewn bib worn around the neck, known as a *kesa* in Japanese. In some groups it indicates that the wearer has "taken the precepts" and declared his or her commitment to Buddhism, while in others it is worn only by those who have successfully passed their first koan. Even hairstyle has its significance, for monks and priests usually shave their heads or wear their hair extremely short.

Yet outward appearances can be misleading, for underneath its formal hierarchy Zen still places great value on honest simplicity. My first experience with organized Zen was as a "guest student" at the San Francisco Zen Center's Green Gulch Farm. It was harvest time and one of our work assignments was to dig up the little gourmet potatoes Green Gulch sold to local restaurants. Unaccustomed to stoop labor, I made some casual comment to a coworker, who gently said that it worked best if we remained silent and focused on what we were doing. It wasn't until later that I found out that the man digging potatoes next to me was Norman Fischer, the Zen master who directed Green Gulch and who later became the abbott of the entire Zen center.

ZEN PRACTICE   Like most religions, Zen Buddhism, especially its Japanese varieties, has a host of rituals and ceremonies, but their objectives are often quite different from the Western religions. In the theistic religions one central goal of ritual is to glorify and exalt the deity, but Zen of course lacks an all-powerful deity to exalt. Western Buddhists don't perform rituals such as chanting or bowing to a statue because the Buddha wants them to but because of the ritual's own intrinsic value. The meticulous performance of rituals and ceremonies is seen as a meditative practice in its own right. It encourages the participants to be fully aware of what they are doing in the present moment, and it allows them to express and strengthen their feelings of gratitude and devotion. Even the elaborate rules that govern so many aspects of behavior in many Zen centers are seen as a tool to force students to wake up and pay attention to what they are doing.

All effective rituals, nonetheless, serve to promote some of the same ends, such as bonding the participants together and evoking strong shared emotions such as a sense of awe, wonder, or commitment. A common objective of many religious rituals, both Eastern and Western, is to gain some supernatural benefit such as the absolution of sin or merit for a better rebirth. It must be noted, however, that while such magical notions are not entirely absent in Western Buddhism, they are far less influential than in most Asian traditions.

The norms that govern behavior in the zendo turn even the simple process of entering and leaving into a kind of ritual. Inside, many of the most powerful rituals involve some kind of group chanting. Passages from sutras or other traditional chants are recited in translation or in the original Asian languages. Most centers distribute a kind of chant book with a written text as a guide, but the chanting still often proceeds at a breakneck pace that is difficult for beginners to follow. The idea is not to understand what the words mean but to lose one's self in the chanting. Indeed, one common type of chant is the *dharani*—a string of syllables that has no literal meaning in any language.

One of the most misunderstood of all Buddhist practices is bowing. To many Westerners and especially to Americans, bowing to another person is a symbol of a kind of blind feudalistic obedience that has no place in a free, democratic society. In Asia, on the other hand, it is seen as nothing more sinister than shaking hands. But beyond that, bowing is often seen as a powerful tool to loosen one's deep-seated egotism. As Suzuki Roshi put it:

> Bowing is a very serious practice. You should be prepared to bow, even in your last moment. Even though it is impossible to get rid of our self centered desires, we have to do it. Our true nature wants us to. After zazen we bow to the floor nine times. By bowing we are giving up ourselves. To give up ourselves means to give up our dualistic ideas. So there is no difference between zazen practice and bowing.[2]

Zen groups also hold ceremonies to commemorate great events, such as Buddha's enlightenment, to honor particular individuals, or to mark important transitions in their members' lives. One of the most important of these is known in Japanese as *jukai,* which literally means to receive the precepts. "Taking the precepts" is a very significant step for most participants, for it is seen as the ceremonial initiation into Buddhism. Although the exact vows vary from group to group, the initiates generally commit themselves to take refuge in the Buddha, the dharma (truth), and the sangha (the Buddhist community), to attempt to follow the basic Buddhist precepts for ethical behavior, to avoid evil, to do good, and to work for the liberation of all beings. In some traditions, the initiates sew a kesa from small scraps of cloth, which they wear as a sign that they have taken the precepts.

Another Zen tradition is that of physical work as meditation practice. In ancient India, monks begged for their food, but that kind of behavior was frowned upon in China. Chinese Zen monasteries turned necessity into virtue, and developed a strong emphasis on absorption in physical labor as a meditative practice. Raking leaves, working in the fields, cleaning and cooking all came to be seen as important spiritual disciplines. For example, Dogen Zenji, the founder of Soto Zen in Japan, wrote a detailed set of "instructions to the cook," which on one level serve as a guide for monastery chefs but on another level are a guide to the whole process of liberation. Although Western Zen centers differ vastly from Asian monasteries, the tradition of work practice continues. Most Zen centers intersperse work periods and meditation periods in their daily schedule.

One Zen priest, Edward Espe Brown, has written a series of popular cookbooks that in Dogen's tradition are as much guides to spiritual practice as cooking.

Some of the larger Zen centers even started their own businesses, such as bakeries and restaurants, to provide training grounds for their students and revenue to support their organization. The results, however, have not always proven satisfactory. Many of the students complained that the demand for profitability inherent in a capitalist enterprise was not compatible with the kind of mindful equanimity cultivated by meditative practice. A waiter who walked slowly and mindfully to each table, placed each knife, fork, and spoon in exactly the right relationship to the plate, and meticulously served each individual dish would never be able to serve the number of customers required of a profitable business. Some students inevitably ended up feeling that the Zen center was more interested in low-wage labor than personal growth.

Another common practice, not only in Zen but in Western Buddhism in general, is walking meditation. During retreats most Zen groups sandwich short periods of walking meditation (around five minutes or so) between longer periods of formal sitting meditation (usually around half an hour). Practiced in this way, walking meditation serves to loosen up the tight muscles and sore backs that come from long periods of sitting meditation without breaking the participant's meditative concentration. During formal meditation the time for walking (*kinhin* in Japanese) is signaled by a gong or bell. Participants get up, bow to their cushions, and walk together in a large circle around the meditation hall. Groups in the Rinzai tradition tend to walk at a vigorous clip, while Soto groups favor a deliberate pace far slower than normal walking speed.

The idea of walking meditation is to focus your entire attention on the process of walking. The lifting of the foot, the moving of the foot, and the return of the foot to the floor, as well as the breathing that accompanies them, are all brought into mindful awareness. Students are sometimes told to synchronize their breathing with their steps or to synchronize their steps with those of the person in front of them. Many teachers also recommend walking meditation as an important practice in its own right; ideally suited for lunch breaks at the office or a bright sunny day. Thich Nhat Hanh's groups place particular emphasis on this style of meditation, and some of them have established beautiful outdoor walking trails. In Nhat Hanh's words:

Walking meditation can be very enjoyable. Walk slowly alone or with friends, if possible in some beautiful place. Walking meditation is really to enjoy the waking—walking not in order to arrive, but just to walk. The purpose is to be in the present moment and, aware of our breathing and our walking, to enjoy each step. Therefore we have to shake off all worries and anxieties, not thinking of the future, not thinking of the past, just enjoying the present moment. . . . When we do walking meditation outside, we walk a little slower than our normal pace, and we coordinate our breathing with our steps. . . . Be aware of the contact between your feet and the Earth. Walk as if you are kissing the Earth with your feet. We have caused a lot of damage to the Earth. Now it is time for us to take good care of her. We bring our peace and calm to the surface of the Earth and share the lesson of love. We walk in that spirit. [3]

Finally, there is no practice closer to the heart of Zen Buddhism than sitting meditation (*zazen* in Japanese). All the large Zen centers keep a regular schedule of zazen and hold periodic retreats for intense meditation practice. Indeed, sitting meditation is so important that the smaller Zen groups that have formed in many cities and towns are often known as "sitting groups."

Zen Buddhism places particular emphasis on posture, and the first instructions a beginning student receives are often on how to sit while meditating. While that may seem like a trivial point, it isn't. Good posture helps the student maintain alertness, avoid the distractions caused by a shifting unstable stance, and minimizes the physical discomfort that can come while practicing long periods of meditation.

The preferred position for the legs is the famous lotus position in which the meditator sits on a cushion and places the foot of the right leg on the left thigh and the foot of the left leg on the right thigh with both knees resting firmly on the floor. The intertwined legs in this "full lotus" position provide the most stable possible base for the sitter, but Westerners who have spent their whole lives sitting in chairs often find it impossible to assume this position, and there are numerous alternatives. Among the most common are the "half lotus" in which one foot is on top and the other underneath the opposing thigh, the "Burmese posture" in which the legs are crossed but both feet rest on the floor rather than the thighs, and a variation of the traditional Japanese sitting posture in which a cushion is placed between the legs, and the tops of the feet and knees rest on the floor. Others use a special meditation bench or even a regular chair. Whatever the position of the legs, the pelvis is tilted forward, the head is erect, and the spine is in its normal s-shaped curve.

Once in their meditation posture, beginning students are usually told to start off by counting their breaths from one to ten and then starting over. This may seem like a ridiculously easy task, but it is actually quite a challenge for most people, whose minds are used to darting endlessly from one subject to another. Distracting thoughts inevitably arise to take the meditators' attention away from their breath, but instead of trying to repress all the thoughts the instruction is merely to avoid being caught up in them. When meditators are swept up in a chain of thought (which is a very frequent occurrence), they are supposed to simply recognize that it has occurred and return their attention to the breath. After the students' powers of concentration have improved, they usually drop the counting and simply follow their breath. Merely sitting and paying attention to one's breathing sounds like a big waste of time to most Westerners, but it is an enormously enriching practice and many students continue it for years on end. There is, however, a higher stage known in Japanese as *shikantaza,* in which students even stop trying to focus on their breath and just sit with full awareness. Such practices are sometimes described as formless meditation, since no effort is made to direct the mind to any object or create any particular state of mind.

A unique technique of Zen meditation that exists in no other tradition is known as koan practice. A koan (*kung-an* in Chinese, *kong-an* in Korean)—literally a public case—is usually a short, paradoxical account of the sayings, actions, or dialogues of a Zen master. Most koans pose a question that challenges the student's understanding yet allows no logical answer. Only the flash of clear direct insight will resolve the mystery. In formal koan practice, a student is usually given one of the 1,700 or so traditional koans and is periodically required to present his or her understanding to the teacher. Most students have to work for months or years before they are finally "passed" by their teacher, and many never succeed. There are several traditional koan collections and once the first breakthrough is achieved, students are given one koan after another in order to deepen and solidify their understanding.

The most common koan given beginning students is known as Joshu's Mu, and it can be stated in a single sentence: "A monk asked Joshu, 'Has a dog Buddha nature?' and Joshu replied, 'Mu.'" Literally, Mu means no, but that is not the answer to the question. Mumon's famous commentary poses the dilemma like this:

> To master Zen you must pass through the barrier of the masters, and cut off the way of thinking. If you do not pass this barrier you are nothing but a ghost clinging to the underbrush. Now what is the barrier of the masters? Why, it is this single word "Mu." It is called the barrier locking the door of Zen. If you pass through it you will meet Joshu face to face and see with the same eyes and ears as the masters. Wouldn't that be wonderful?
>
> You must summon up a spirit of great doubt and concentrate on this word Mu. Carry it continuously day and night. Do not understand it as nothingness, do not understand it as the absence of something. It is as if you had swallowed a red hot iron ball that you cannot spit out no matter how hard you try.
>
> Suddenly, all your deluded thoughts will disappear and inside and out will become as one. But like a mute who has had a dream, you know about it but cannot tell. An explosion will occur that will astonish the heavens and shake the earth. It will be as if you have snatched the sword of the great General Kuan. When you meet the Buddha, you kill the Buddha, when meeting the Zen masters you kill them too. On the brink of life and death you command perfect freedom, and enter the world as if it were your own playground.
>
> How will you attain this realization? Just devote every ounce of your energy to Mu. If you don't falter, then it is done! A single spark and the candle is lit.[4]

There is nothing quite like the Zen koan in any other religious tradition, Buddhist or non-Buddhist, and countless Zen students have wrestled with them over the years.

The apogee of Zen practice is the intensive meditation retreat known as a *sesshin* in Japanese. Although retreats vary in length, seven days is probably the most common. A typical retreat day starts early in the morning and runs till late at night with alternating periods of sitting and walking meditation, chanting and ceremonies, and meals (groups in the Soto tradition often take their meals in the meditation hall in the ritualized *oryoki* style). Some retreats include a work period as well. All participants are expected to follow a demanding schedule that allows no time for anything which would detract from the focused intensity of the retreat. The head teacher usually gives a daily talk, and there are periodic personal interviews that are often run according to a highly formalized tradition. Students doing koan practice are usually required to present their understanding to the teacher once or twice a day, while in other cases students request an interview only when they have a particular question to discuss with the teacher. The atmosphere of a Zen sesshin is one of intense struggle. Knees get sore, backs hurt, and effort is strained to the breaking point. Even experienced participants see it as challenge to their practice and their determination.

Vajrayana

After centuries of isolation in the snowy wilds of the Himalayas, the ope-nening of Tibetan Buddhism to the rest of the world was one of the great cultural events of the twentieth century. Virtually unknown in the West until the 1960s, there were 180 recognized Vajrayana groups in North America by 1987, and that number doubled in the next ten years. Today, roughly a third of the Buddhist meditation centers in North America follow some kind of Tibetan tradition, and many of those who practice in other traditions have come to see the Tibetan Dalai Lama as the living symbol of the Buddhist faith. Similar growth has also taken place in Britain and Ireland. The *Buddhist Directory* listed only fifteen Tibetan groups in 1979, but that number grew to sixty-five in 1997—about 19 percent of the total.

THE SPIRIT OF TIBETAN BUDDHISM   Among all the world's major religions, there is nothing that compares to Tibetan Buddhism. Many traditions can boast of colorful costumes and exotic rituals, but no other denomination selects its leaders because of their past lives and goes on to train them from earliest childhood. Where else would you find temple walls adorned with images of deities graphically depicted in the throes of sexual intercourse or a shrine decorated with a huge set of eyes staring out at the world?

Even the Western groups that follow the Tibetan tradition maintain an air of the exotic and mysterious that is not found in Zen or Vipassana. Of course, someone who has never been exposed to the Eastern wisdom traditions or had much contact with Asian culture is likely to find any meditation group a bit strange at first. Once the newness wears off, however, it is easy to see that both Zen and Vipassana emphasize a pragmatic, down-to-earth approach to life. The mysteries of Vajrayana, on the other hand, only deepen after the initial contact.

The bright colors and profusion of imagery and symbolism found in most Vajrayana groups stands in stark contrast to the reserved simplicity of so many other Buddhist centers. If the tone of Zen and Vipassana can be said to be cool, then Vajrayana is hot. The same applies when it comes to their emotional style. The passionate expressiveness of the *tantrikas* (practitioners of the tantras) contrasts with the calm distance cultivated by most other Buddhists.

Vajrayana groups practice many complex and intricate rituals, but in contrast to the formality of most Zen practice their approach seems far more casual. Yet Zen groups have taken on an increasingly Western feel as their leadership has passed to a new generation of native-born teachers, and the Vipassana movement imported far less Asian cultural baggage right from its beginnings. Since the majority of the most influential Vajrayana teachers in the West are still Tibetans, the Asian influence remains strongest in those groups. While Western egalitarianism has slowly reduced the social distance between native-born Zen and Vipassana teachers and their students, the very foreignness of the Tibetan teachers helps maintain their charisma and the sense that they are something special and unique. The fact that visiting dignitaries from the Tibetan hierarchy are often driven around in chauffeured limousines, waited on by teams of servants, and deliver their lectures from a gilded throne has certainly done nothing to reduce this social distance.

THE PRACTICE OF VAJRAYANA   Any casual visitor to a Vajrayana center cannot help but be impressed by the complex symbolism on display, and that complexity carries over into the practice itself. Tibetan Buddhism contains more practices, more meditation techniques, and studies more different schools of Buddhist philosophy, than any of the other Buddhist traditions. Although the Vajrayana encompasses all the myriad of different approaches and perspectives that evolved in over a thousand years of Indian Buddhism, it imparts a distinctive stamp to its understanding of them all.

Aside from this complexity, the casual student is soon confronted by another unique barrier—secrecy. Although things have changed since the Chinese invasion that forced the Tibetan hierarchy into exile, there is a long-standing tradition that the highest teaching of Vajrayana Buddhism should be kept secret—not to hoard the "wisdom of the East" but to prevent the serious harm that is believed to result when the unprepared and the poorly guided experiment with powerful tantric practices. In the past, very few people in other lands even knew of the highest Tibetan teachings, but these days translations of key tantric texts are easily available in the West (even if a huge amount of material remains untranslated). These texts, however, contain numerous symbolic codes that require personal instruction from a qualified teacher to interpret, and beyond that the teachings are considered "self-secret" in the sense that they cannot really be grasped without face-to-face oral transmission from a qualified teacher.

Another unique focus of Tantric Buddhism is guru devotion. Of course, any Buddhist teacher is likely to enjoy enormous respect and authority in his or her own community, but students in Tibetan Buddhism are expected to worship their guru as a higher being. Students even take special vows of obedience to the teacher known as the *samayas*. While this may be seen as a holdover from Tibetan feudalism, the idea is that students are to ignore whatever faults the teachers may have and visualize them as a living Buddha so that they can get a direct taste of their enlightened mind. Needless to say, this tradition has created numerous problems in the West, from its obvious violation of our social values to the way it may facilitate the kinds of abuses that are examined in the next chapter.

Obviously, only a very few people are worthy of such devotion, and in recent years the death of many of the great Tibetan teachers who helped bring Buddhism to the West has created another kind of problem. The passing of the Gyalwang Karmapa, Trungpa Rinpoche, Kalu Rinpoche, Dudjon Rinpoche, and Dilgo Khyentse Rinpoche, among many others, has meant that their numerous Western students must either find another guru or fend for themselves until the reincarnations of their original teachers are discovered and reach their maturity. To further complicate matters, some believe that the younger generation of Tibetan teachers, reared in exile in industrializing India, are simply not the equals of their elders raised in the isolation of feudal Tibet.

Although Vajrayana Buddhism encompasses most of the practices and techniques used in other traditions, its higher practices have a unique quality of their own. (Few Tibetans have much knowledge about Zen, however, and they do not use koans.) All the symbols, the rituals, and even the idealization the guru are part of a unique process of visualization in which the practitioners imagine themselves as a Buddha or deity and the world as a sacred mandala. As Robert A.F. Thurman puts it:

> Tantric initiation is an opening of imaginative space where you have a vision of potential perfection. You may still feel like a "schmo," but that's the dynamic tension. Your habitual imagination of yourself as an unenlightened schmo is brought into tension with an artificially constructed imagination of yourself as a perfected being.[5]

Again and again, the tantrikas conjure up a sacred world in which they are enlightened beings and then dissolve it into nothingness—until their ordinary ego-centered self seems as unreal and as transitory as their visions.

There is a saying in Tibet that "every valley has a different lama," and each of those lamas has their own way of teaching. Most Tibetan teachers see the practice path as a progression through a long series of stages involving one technique after another, but they often use those techniques in different orders. Trungpa Rinpoche was a very unorthodox teacher who made several radical departures from usual Tibetan practice, but his lineage has more adherents than that of any other Tibetan teacher in the West and that fact alone testifies to his exceptional understanding of the needs of his Western students. Group meditation is not a common practice in Tibet, and "formless" practices such as meditation on the breath or "just sitting" are thought to be beyond the abilities of all but the most advanced students. Yet after seeing the success Suzuki Roshi had with this approach at the San Francisco Zen Center, Trungpa began starting his students off with a kind of formless meditation practiced in groups. Trungpa invented a square meditation cushion he called a "gomden," which seemed to be more comfortable for Westerners than the traditional cushion.

Trungpa instructed his students to get into a comfortable upright posture, sit, and "see what happens." When thoughts arise, they should be labeled as such and then attention should be returned to the sitting. The meditators are told to pay attention to their breathing but not to make it an exclusive focus of concentration. Beginning students in Trungpa's lineage are also encouraged to go to weekly classes that explore the principles of Hinayana and Mahayana Buddhism and to attend an occasional weekend workshop. Inspired by the Zen sesshin, Trungpa created the *dathun,* which is a month-long retreat for intensive meditation. After a few years students may have completed one or two dathuns and perhaps a solitary retreat on their own and are ready for the next step, when they formally become Buddhists by taking refuge in the Three Jewels (the Buddha, dharma, and sangha) and reciting the bodhisattva vows. After they finish this Tibetan equivalent of the jukai ceremony, they undertake a new set of meditation practices that focuses on the six paramitas (perfections).

Direct exposure to tantric practices finally comes after students have attended a three-month group retreat called the seminary. Only then are they considered ready to begin the grueling preliminary practices known as the *ngondro* (preliminary in the sense that traditionally they were the first practices a beginner was given). The ngondro begins with 100,000 full prostrations before a tantric shrine. The practitioners throw their bodies face down and climb up again and again while repeating a tantric prayer. After those arduous prostrations, practitioners go on to repeat a hundred-syllable mantra 100,000 times, make a formal offering of 100,000 mandalas made of colored rice, and repeat a short supplication to their guru 1 million times. The whole process can be done in two years if the practitioner can include several months of solitary or group retreats, but those with more outside commitments may take considerably longer. After completing the ngondro, students are finally ready to receive the *abhisheka,* or empowerments, that authorize them to engage in high visualization practices. It can take an entire year to learn the complexities of their first visualization, and after that a succession of different visualizations are given to the students to meet their individual needs, and they are likely to attend many specialized retreats over the following years.

The whole idea of visualizing oneself as some sort of a god is completely alien to most Westerners. But the following description of one Western practitioner's first successful attempt at a tantric visualization gives us some feel for this practice:

> In this visualization, we first transform into the sparkling light-body of the Goddess, red and transparent, holding drum and skinning knife (to skin the ego), dancing in the advancing posture with a great haughty demeanor, sexually magnetic, disciplining the beings. A big problem for me has been imagining myself as a female. But this time—maybe because the

Goddess seemed so powerful—I succeeded! Glancing up with my single eye I saw the Guru above me and he was Rinpoche. I began to spin the root mantra in my heart. . . . He looked at me with compassion and just like it is supposed to happen, a rain of nectar began to fall on me. . . . Suddenly I was transfixed; I mean really lifted. The profound final mantra of all the Buddhas poured forth like thunder: OM GUHYAJNANA BOD-HISITTA MAHA SUKHA RULU RULU HUNG JHO HUNG! Joy flooded my heart and I could hardly keep back the tears.[6]

Kalu Rinpoche, who ran a system of Vajrayana training centers in North America until his recent death, used to start off his beginning students with a simple visualization practice in which they identified with the bodhisattva of compassion. Although technically a tantric practice, this visualization is considered safe even for beginning students. As students advanced, they performed the same kind of ngondro practices described above. Committed students were then encouraged to attend a long retreat in which they took monastic vows and commited themselves to practice day and night for three years, three months, and three days. This three-year retreat is, according to Ken McLeod, "primarily a program of training in meditation. It is virtually a college of contemplative techniques. There is a considerable amount of material to assimilate, both theoretical and practical. And it is an important step into a contemplative life, a life of retreat and practice."[7] A commitment to attend a three-year retreat obviously requires enormous dedication; participants are even expected to sleep upright in a "meditation box." Yet many, including McLeod himself, turn right around and do another three years.

Other Tibetan teachers are more focused on academic studies, and many Tibetan centers, especially those from the Gelug and Sakya sects, have developed a program of graded instruction in Mahayana Buddhism. Particularly important in these programs are the teachings on the philosophy of emptiness known as the *Madhyamaka,* or middle way. While studying the nature of emptiness, the students are introduced to simple tantric practices. As their understanding deepens, they are given more difficult and complex visualization practices.

The teachers of *dzogchen* take the most Western approach of any of the Tibetans. Dzogchen, which translates as "great perfection," is a type of open formless meditation with similarities to Zen's *shikantaza* as well as to the *mahamudra* meditation practiced by the Kagyu and Gelug sects of

Tibetan Buddhism. Dzogchen is traditionally considered the highest teaching of the Nyingma sect and, like mahamudra and shikantaza in Rinzai Zen, it was only practiced by the most adept yogis. In the West, however, it is playing an entirely different role. Teachers such as Lama Surya Das, who is himself a Westerner, now give dzogchen instructions to anyone who is interested. No long years of preliminary practices or other special preparations are required. Surya Das feels that although students "need a lot of preparation, one surprise is that people are a lot more prepared than one thinks. Westerners are sophisticated psychologically, but illiterate nomads (as in Tibet) are not." Nonetheless, dzogchen has proven particularly popular among Western students who have had a good deal of experience with other traditions of meditation. Along with formless meditation techniques, dzogchen students are also given various chanting and breathing exercises and a foundation in Buddhist philosophy. In Surya Das's view, dzogchen is the Tibetan approach most compatible with contemporary Western culture, and "this is the time of dzogchen."[8]

Vipassana

Vipassana was something of a latecomer to the Buddhist scene in North America, and it got started without much help from the kind of charismatic Asian teachers who were so important in founding the other Western lineages. There are fewer Vipassana than Zen or Tibetan groups, but the Vipassana movement is still growing rapidly and bubbling with creative energy. The 1988 edition of *Buddhist America* listed only 72 Vipassana groups, but in the 1998 edition that number had more than doubled to 152. The Theravadin tradition from which the Vipassana movement sprang is much stronger in Britain than North America, probably because staunchly Theravadin Burma and Sri Lanka were both part of the British empire. Today, Theravadin groups make up 26 percent of the entries in the British *Buddhist Directory*—more than any other tradition. However, many of these groups appeal more to traditionally oriented ethnic Asians than the new Buddhists who are the focus of our concern here.

THE SPIRIT OF VIPASSANA   The Vipassana movement presents us with a strange paradox. Its roots are in the Theravada Buddhism of Southern Asia, which is by far the world's most conservative branch of Buddhism—

in both its steadfast adherence to the Buddha's original teachings and its strong emphasis on the importance of celibate monasticism. Yet Vipassana is more westernized and less traditional than either Zen or Vajrayana. While the Theravadin path is one of withdrawal and renunciation, few Vipassana practitioners are monastics and the focus is clearly on attaining spiritual realization in the midst of everyday life. To Theravada Buddhism, the objective of Buddhist practice is to uproot the desires and defilements in order to attain *nibbana* (nirvana in Sanskrit) and win liberation from the otherwise endless round of death and rebirth. But few Western Vipassana teachers pay much attention to the more metaphysical aspects of such concepts as rebirth and nibbana, and of course very few of their students are celibate monks. Their focus is mainly on meditation practice and a kind of down-to-earth psychological wisdom. "As a result," one respected Vipassana teacher writes, "many more Americans of European descent refer to themselves as Vipassana students rather than as students of Theravada Buddhism."[9]

Anyone familiar with Zen or Tibetan practice is bound to be struck by the casual atmosphere of most Vipassana groups and the kind of secular spirit they exude. There are usually no robes and few images and symbols. The participants wear the same kind of clothes they would anywhere else. (Although warm shawls do seem very much in style at Vipassana retreats.) During retreats, the students are more likely to be spread out in a chaotic jumble than arranged in the neatly aligned rows you'd find at a Zen center. Although there is some chanting and singing, religious ceremony and ritual are kept to a minimum. The approach of most Vipassana students is more like a client visiting a psychotherapist than a parishioner at a church service. It is no coincidence that six of the eleven regular teachers at the Spirit Rock Center (the West Coast's largest Vipassana center) are trained psychotherapists, and Vipassana teachers regularly address such psychological issues as "feelings of unworthiness," "guilt," "jealousy," and "anger."

Another striking feature of the Vipassana movement is its egalitarianism. The teachers don't wear special clothes or assume special titles such as *roshi* or *rinpoche*. In fact, they are usually just called by their first names. The ideal of the teacher is that of a "spiritual friend" rather than an authority figure or a surrogate parent, and Vipassana teachers share their responsibility to a far greater degree than is common in other groups. The Spirit Rock Center, for example, has no abbot or head teacher. A committee of experienced teachers provides its spiritual direction, and larger retreats are usually led by several senior teachers utilizing a kind of "team teaching" approach. This spirit of egalitarianism is also reflected among the members of the Vipassana groups, which tend to have a vaguer sense of boundaries and less of an "in group–out group" mentality than Zen or Vajrayana.

THE PRACTICE OF VIPASSANA   Because ritual and ceremony are deemphasized, meditation takes an even bigger place in Vipassana groups than in most other Western groups. The techniques of mediation given by Vipassana teachers fall into two broad categories—concentrative techniques that seek to stabilize and calm the mind by focusing on a particular object of attention and insight meditation (Vipassana actually means insight in Pali) in which the meditator tries to develop an open awareness of the events unfolding in the present moment. An informational brochure from the Spirit Rock Center gives this description of their approach:

> In Insight Meditation we pay clear attention to whatever exists naturally in this present moment. The specific focus of our awareness can vary from bodily sensation to sights to thoughts and feelings. We often begin by paying attention to the sensations of breathing. We sit still, either cross-legged on the floor or upright in a chair, and allow our eyes to close gently. Then we turn our attention to the breath and simply experience, in as continuous a way as possible, the physical sensation of breathing in and breathing out.[10]

In contrast to Zen practice, in which students are often given basic instructions and left on their own, Vipassana teachers provide much more guidance and direction. During a group meditation the teacher might, for example, tell the assembled students to focus their attention on one particular part of the body after another or give other spoken directions, and teachers often give detailed specific advice to individual students about their meditation practice. One Vipassana teacher has even developed a hi-tech approach to meditation in which he and a number of his students wear headsets and microphones, so he can give rotating interviews and advice during a meditation session.

The most common technique of concentrative meditation used by Vipassana teachers is known as *metta*, which means "loving-kindness" in Pali. The idea is to focus the energies of the mind to cultivate a feeling of loving-kindness toward the world. Metta practice can easily be done alone, but it is often carried on as a "guided meditation" in which a leader gives oral instructions to a group of meditators, guiding them through the various stages of the meditation together. Metta practice is begun by sitting comfortably and calmly. The first object of the meditators' loving-kindness is themselves, which often turns out be a surprisingly difficult task for people in our highly judgmental society. To help get the process going, the meditators might be instructed to call to mind something they have done out of the goodness of their heart to help someone else. Then they would be told to repeat a series of phrases silently to themselves in order to reinforce those feelings. Sharon Salzberg, one of the leading proponents of this technique, defines the classic formula as follows: "May I live in safety. May I have mental happiness (peace, joy). May I have physical happiness (health, freedom from pain). May I live with ease (may the elements of daily life—work, family—go easily, not be a struggle)."[11] However, the meditators are encouraged to create their own phrases if they seem to work better. After spending some time on this first phase, the next step is to call to mind a benefactor—someone who has helped in some way or another—and then direct the same phrases toward them as well. After a while, the meditator includes a good friend or friends in the field of metta and repeats the same phrases. Eventually the meditation is expanded to include someone the meditator has no strong feelings about. Then the loving-kindness is directed toward someone the meditator dislikes or has had conflict with, and finally it is offered boundlessly to all beings everywhere. All in all, metta practice has considerable similarities with the Tibetan practice of *tonglen,* in which the meditators imagine themselves breathing in all the suffering of the world and breathing out peace and contentment.

Walking meditation also holds a very important place in Vipassana's arsenal of meditative techniques. Although its practice is similar to that described in the previous section on Zen, Vipassana retreats tend to have much longer walking periods. While five minutes is a fairly typical period of *kinhin* (Japanese for walking meditation), forty-five-minute walking periods are not unusual at Vipassana retreats. But the biggest difference between the Zen and Vipassana styles of walking meditation reflects their fundamental difference in approach. At a Zen retreat, everyone walks together in an orderly circle around the zendo at the same consistent pace. They are even expected to keep their hands in the same position near their navel with one in a fist and the other wrapped around it. Vipassana on the other hand reflects the full chaos of Western individualism. Meditators simply walk where they want at the pace they want. Of course, as in the larger society, there is always a potential for collisions, and part of the meditation is to remain aware of the people near you and adjust your trajectory accordingly.

Group retreats are another important part of the Vipassana practice. As in Zen, the retreats typically run from around 5:00 or 5:30 in the morning until 9:30 or so at night. Alternating periods of sitting and walking meditation are broken up only by meals and a dharma talk. The following schedule, taken from Joseph Goldstein's book *The Experience of Insight*, is fairly typical:

4:30	Awakening
5:00–6:30	Walk and sit
6:30–7:30	Breakfast
7:30–8:00	Walking
8:00–9:00	Group sitting
9:00–9:45	Walking
9:45–10:45	Group sitting
10:45–11:30	Walking
11:30–1:15	Lunch and rest
1:15–2:00	Group sitting
2:00–2:45	Walking
2:45–3:45	Group sitting
3:45–5:00	Walk and sit
5:00–4:30	Tea
5:30–6:00	Walking
6:00–7:00	Group sitting
7:00–8:00	Talk
8:00–8:45	Walking
8:45–9:45	Group sitting
9:45–10:00	Tea
10:00	Further practice or sleep[12]

In addition to longer periods of walking meditation, the other major difference from Zen retreats is the absence of periods for services (chanting, bowing, and other rituals).

It is a fairly straightforward task to describe the Zen, Vipassana, and Vajrayana approaches to Buddhism, but the nonsectarian groups examined in this section are an altogether different matter. Because these groups are not affiliated with any single tradition, they show far more diversity in their practices and beliefs, and even in their underlying objectives. Although the nonsectarian groups have fewer members than the other types of groups, they are growing much faster. The 1988 edition of *Buddhist America* listed only fourteen nonsectarian groups, but the 1998 edition listed 135—an increase of nearly 1,000 percent. If we exclude the Friends of the Western Buddhist Order, which has a huge presence in the British Isles but as we will see is rather different than most other nonsectarian organizations, about 13 percent of the groups listed in the British *Buddhist Directory* are not affiliated with a specific tradition—just about the same percentage as in the United States.

The most common nonsectarian groups are probably local "sitting groups" that are not led by any particular teacher. These groups are usually loose associations of people who come together to share an interest in meditation (sitting) and Buddhist thought. The members of these groups tend to have a wide variety of different experiences and affiliations with organized Buddhism. Some are likely to be newcomers, while others may have had extensive experience with Zen, Tibetan, or Vajrayana groups. This nonsectarian approach is obviously the best way to reach a "critical mass" of local practitioners large enough to create a real sense of community and generate some mutual support. Moreover, the idea of learning from all Buddhist (and even non-Buddhist) traditions often seems more attractive than following a single approach.

Because they do not have an official teacher, these groups are also the most egalitarian and most democratic. One individual usually steps forward to be the contact person or coordinator, but decisions are most often made by consensus, and there is seldom much in the way of formal hierarchy. The smaller groups usually meet in the homes of the members, while larger groups often rent out some public place to get together.

As you would expect, the style of practice varies considerably from one group to another. A few groups meet daily, but most meet weekly or monthly. Typical group meetings are centered around a period of shared meditation. Although members all meditate together, they do not necessarily have a common style or approach. Many groups listen to tapes or watch videos of talks given by various teachers, or they may discuss some common readings. Although this style of nonsectarian group is usually light on rituals and ceremonies, members may recite a common chant or carry on some similar activity. Many groups hold their own short retreats without a teacher, and larger groups may bring in teachers from a variety of different traditions to give talks and lead retreats.

Another type of nonsectarian group is that organized around a particular constituency. Examples include San Francisco's Gay Buddhist Fellowship, the Pentagon Meditation Club in Washington, D.C., Amherst's Buddhism, Meditation, and Psychotherapy Group (intended for psychotherapists), and the numerous Buddhist groups formed around the students and faculty at different colleges or by the inmates at different prisons. Like local sitting groups, these constituency-oriented groups also attract people with affiliations to many different Buddhist traditions. They also tend to carry on the same kind of meditation and group activities but with a focus on the special needs of their particular community.

There are a growing number of nonsectarian groups that are led by a teacher. In some cases, like that of Toni Packer, the teacher was trained in a particular tradition but came to reject some of its basic practices and beliefs. In others, the teacher was trained in more than one tradition or was just self-taught. (Most traditional Buddhists are highly skeptical of such self-proclaimed teachers, but Buddhism has no central body authorized to decide who is and is not qualified to teach.) Whatever the case, teachers in nonsectarian groups tend to be an eclectic lot, bringing in practices and teachings from whatever source seems appropriate. And as these rebels and innovators have trained teachers in their own style, new nonsectarian Buddhist lineages have emerged.

By far the biggest of these is the Friends of the Western Buddhist Order, an international network of over one hundred independent Buddhist centers, retreat facilities, residential communities, "right livelihood" businesses, and educational, health, and art programs. The FWBO has a particularly strong presence in the British Isles, where its affiliates make up one in every five of the groups listed in the *Buddhist Directory*. The FWBO was founded by an Englishman who is now known as Urgyen Sangharakshita. Although not the direct dharma heir of any Asian teacher, he spent twenty years studying and practicing in India. Sangharakshita eventually created a tightly structured blend of traditional Buddhist elements but without, as far as possible, the Asian cultural baggage that so often accompanied Buddhism to the West. One of the FWBO's teachers described their practice this way:

> There are meditation practices, chanting, and study of the Pali texts—activities associated with the Theravada. Yet, there is also puja in which the *bodhisattvas* are mentioned and the *Heart Sutra* [a text central to the Mahayana tradition] is recited. The study and lectures are frequently based on one of the great Mahayana scriptures, or on what is clearly a Mahayana doctrine. Yet again, we meet Milarepa, Padamsambhava, *dakinis* [feminine deities], gurus and the four foundation practices of the Vajrayana. Chinese meditation texts, Japanese poems, a modified tea ceremony, and Zen stories all may appear during the course of a retreat. . . . this is not simply a ragbag of Buddhist practices, but a developing Western tradition that owes its allegiance to the Three Jewels, and not to any particular school of Buddhism.[13]

Organizationally, the FWBO is light years apart from most of the nonsectarian groups. Not only is it far larger than any of the others, but more importantly, the FWBO is tightly organized around a clear "spiritual hierarchy," while most nonsectarian groups tend to be loose-knit egalitarian affairs. Those participating in the FWBO are grouped in one of three hierarchical levels, and they must get official approval before being allowed to move up. The broadest group, the Friends of the Western Buddhist Order, includes anyone who has shown interest in or support for the group. The next level, the mitras, must have demonstrated their commitment to the Buddhist path and have met such criteria as maintaining a regular meditation practice and a commitment to Buddhist ethics, as well as pursuing a "right livelihood" that contributes to the overall well-being of their fellows. Finally, there is the Western Buddhist Order itself. According to the 1997 edition of the *Buddhist Directory,* there are about 660 members in the order. To join one must have demonstrated a long-term commitment to the Buddhist path, must win approval from several different organizational layers within the group, and must be formally ordained. The most influential members of the order are the preceptors, who are individually selected by Sangharakshita, and must approve any new candidates for the order. The head of the entire organization is Sangharakshita himself. Recently, however, he has begun withdrawing from his day-to-day administrative duties in order to encourage the organization to prepare for the day when he is no longer around.

One of the most interesting things about the FWBO is its emphasis on community building. The FWBO encourages (although it certainly does not require) those interested in following its path to live together in some form of communal housing. Very often this means nothing more than several people with common interests getting together to share an apartment or a house, but the FWBO has more structured residential centers of its own as well. The FWBO has also been instrumental in setting up a network of "right livelihood" businesses in which many members work. The most successful of these is Windhorse Trading—a chain of retail stores with six warehouses, nineteen retail outlets, and an annual income of close to $15 million. The idea is that by living and working together FWBO members can reinforce one another's commitment to the Buddhist path and provide the most supportive overall living environment for spiritual practice. As one observer of the FWBO put it, "His [Sangharakshita's] goal is not so much to let Buddhism filter out into the forms of the wider community, but to create a new community for Buddhists."[14]

Finally, there are a growing number of Buddhist-oriented groups that focus on meeting social goals, including welfare services such as helping AIDS patients or Tibetan refugees, education (for example, the Naropa Institute), political activism in the peace or environmental movements, and building community among people from different Buddhist traditions. The common thread that runs through such groups is their effort not only to meet such pressing social needs but to use their collective efforts as part and parcel of their spiritual path.

There is a vigorous movement in both Asia and the West to create a more "engaged Buddhism." Although the term means different things to different people, in the most common usage it has come to include "a broad range of approaches, unified by the notion that Buddhist teachings and practices can be directly applied to participation in the social, political, economic and ecological affairs of the nonmonastic world."[15] The origins of the term are generally credited to the influential Vietnamese monk and social activist Thich Nhat Hanh:

When I was in Vietnam, so many of our villages were being bombed. Along with my monastic brothers and sisters, I had to decide what to do. Should we continue to practice in our monasteries, or would we leave the meditation halls in order to help the people who were suffering under the bombs? After careful reflection, we decided to do both—to go out and help people and to do so in mindfulness. We called it engaged Buddhism. Mindfulness must be engaged. Once there is seeing, there must be acting. . . . We must be aware of the real problems of the world. Then, with mindfulness, we will know what to do and what not to do to be of help.[16]

Despite the popular image of Buddhism as a religion that retreats from the world, the twentieth century has seen numerous examples of Buddhist political activism around the globe. The most important organization of socially engaged Buddhists in the West is the Buddhist Peace Fellowship. Founded in 1978 by a group of Buddhists that included Robert Aitken, the roshi of the Diamond Sangha in Hawaii, its mission statement says that its intention is to "bring a Buddhist perspective to the peace movement, and to bring the peace movement to the Buddhist community." Headquartered in Berkeley, California, the Buddhist Peace Fellowship has chapters in seventeen other American cities and affiliates in six different countries. It is run by a fifteen-member board of directors and an international advisory board that includes some of the world's most prominent Buddhists. In the last few years the fellowship has been active in numerous human rights issues, has given its financial support to several social service projects in Asia, including medical teams for displaced Burmese and support for children in Tibetan refugee camps, and has coordinated events to urge the control of nuclear weapons, landmines, and community violence. The Buddhist Peace Fellowship also organized BASE (Buddhist Alliance for Social Engagement), which provides six-month training programs for people working in social service or social action. BASE participants combine weekly meetings for meditation and study with fifteen to thirty hours a week working in hospices, homeless shelters, prisons, medical clinics, and activist organizations.

Although the BPF focuses most of its efforts in the political arena, it is far from the only Buddhist group engaged in social or political activism. The San Francisco Zen Center, for example, helps support a hospice for AIDS patients, and the Zen Community of New York under the leadership of Bernard Tetsugen Glassman has been extremely active in combating homelessness in Yonkers, New York. The community's Greyston Bakery has trained more than two hundred chronically homeless people and has provided some forty people with jobs. The Greyston Family Inn provides permanent housing and support services for homeless families. The activity that has generated the most publicity has been Glassman's "street retreats," in which the participants give up their credit cards and their respectable clothes and live with the homeless for ten days, mixing regular periods of meditation with a strong dose of life on the streets.

Whether it is AIDS, human rights in Asia, the peace movement, protecting the environment, or fighting homelessness, socially engaged Buddhism has definitely drawn its agenda from the left side of the political spectrum. Unlike the Christian or Jewish communities, there are few conservative voices to be heard among Western Buddhists.

Despite the dedication, commitment, and enthusiasm of many activists, many other members still feel more comfortable maintaining the traditional Western division between "church" and state. Over two-thirds of the members of Buddhist organizations I surveyed disagreed with the idea that their center should become more involved in political issues. Of course, political activism by individual Buddhists is an altogether different matter, and had I asked about that I suspect that most of the respondents would have given it their hearty agreement. On the other hand, most of my respondents did not express such reticence when it came to involving their group in charitable causes. If fact, 53 percent agreed that their group should become more involved in charitable activities.

The Common Ground

At first glance, it may appear that a place like the San Francisco Zen Center, with its three large centers, elaborate rituals, and formal discipline, has almost nothing in common with the casual little sitting groups that have sprung up in so many cities and towns. But despite the profusion of different styles, traditions, and approaches, the new Buddhism growing in the West has a surprisingly large core of common practices and beliefs.

First and foremost is the practice of meditation. Of those responding to my survey, 92.4 percent ranked meditation as the single most important activity their group carried on. The members of the Tibetan groups gave more importance to rituals and ceremonies than the others, but 86.5 percent of them still ranked meditation number one. More important, most members actually carry on a regular meditation practice. Only 10 of the 359 people who answered the question said they did so less than once a week. The typical respondent reported that he or she meditated almost every day for an average of a little over forty minutes at a sitting. Of course, as is the case with surveys of church attendance, it may well be that my respondents are exaggerating, and the fact that my survey was distributed at group meetings means that it was more likely to reach the dedicated members who attend such functions more frequently. Nonetheless, the reported level of involvement in meditation is so great that there is still little doubt about its importance in their daily lives.

Interestingly enough, there were no great differences between those practicing in different traditions. The most common meditation period reported by the members of Zen groups was forty minutes, and it was thirty minutes for the Vipassana and Tibetan groups and the one nonsectarian group surveyed. The members of the Tibetan groups, however, were most likely to go in for very long meditation periods of an hour and a half or longer. The respondents to my survey reported using a profusion of different meditation techniques, but over 50 percent said their practice involved either counting or following their breath. Those in Vipassana groups, on the other hand, were much more likely than the others to label their thoughts as a meditation technique. (For example, a meditator who had been caught up in a daydream would not struggle to cut off her thoughts but would label them as "thinking" or "daydreaming" and just allow them to whither away.) Koan study appears to be limited to Zen practitioners. About a quarter of the respondents in the Zen groups reported doing koan practice, while none of the others did. Members of Tibetan groups were the most likely to use visualization or formless meditation and were much more likely to use multiple (three or more) meditation techniques. In addition, 87 percent of the respondents at least occasionally supplemented their sitting practice with walking meditation, although only 11 percent said they do so on a regular basis.

Another key element of the new Buddhism is the meditation retreat. Almost 93 percent of my respondents had attended at least one retreat. The typical respondent had been involved in Buddhist organizations for about nine and a half years and had attended twelve retreats, thus averaging a little over one retreat a year. Most retreats lasted from one to ten days, although the length did vary a bit from tradition to tradition. The Zen retreats seldom exceed seven days, while ten days was common among Vipassana groups; 39 percent of the respondents from Tibetan groups reported attending a three-month retreat.

In addition to these common practices, the new Western Buddhism has a body of common knowledge and beliefs that teachers and students share in public talks and their person to person interactions. Whatever differences may exist in Asia, it is actually quite difficult to find any hard-and-fast doctrinal disagreements in the West. Vipassana teachers tend to rely more on the original teachings of the Buddha, while the Vajrayana teachers draw on a broader range of sources that include Indian Mahayana and Tantric texts but usually not the East Asian works that are so central to the Zen tradition. But in the West, these differences are primarily a matter of emphasis, and teachers and students often freely borrow from all traditions.

Space does not permit us to explore all the beliefs common to Western Buddhists, but several things do stand out. To start with, the members of groups from all traditions share a common goal: liberation from suffering and delusion. Stated in positive terms, all these groups believe not only that there is a state of perfect wisdom called enlightenment but that there is a path that can lead each of us to it. They agree, moreover, that to follow that path we must let go of our ego-centered hopes, fears, and attachments. Thus most Western Buddhists would accept the influential Vipassana teacher Joseph Goldstein's view that "liberation through non-clinging" is the key point upon which all Buddhists agree. In the words of the Buddha himself: "Nothing whatsoever is to be clung to as I or mine. Whoever has heard this teaching has heard all of the teachings. Whoever puts this into practice has put all of the Dharma into practice."[17] Closely related to this understanding are two other fundamental ideas. The first is often termed the principle of interdependent co-origination, or what Thich Nhat Hanh calls more simply "interbeing." Everything, in this view, is related to and caused by everything else. Nothing stands alone as a discrete individual entity, whether it is this whole planet or what we have been taught to see as our own personal selves. The second idea sounds a bit obvious, but its consequences are profound: everything changes. Nothing in this world or any other can safely be clung to as permanent, everlasting, or eternally dependable. It all changes.

Although they express it in many different ways, Buddhists from all traditions also recognize a responsibility to be kind to others and help them escape their suffering. Ethical behavior has been a fundamental element of the Buddhist path right from Sakyamuni's original teachings. Like their Asian counterparts, however, Western Buddhists approach this issue from two different perspectives. Some teachers urge their students to exert themselves to follow the Buddhist precepts of ethical behavior and lead moral lives. From this standpoint, ethical behavior is an important tool that aids in the struggle for liberation. Other teachers look at things the other way around, seeing ethical behavior as the natural product of a liberated mind. From this perspective, an intentional cultivation of moral behavior is rooted in the egoistic desire to be a better person and is ultimately a barrier to liberation despite whatever beneficial effects it may have.

My survey explored Western attitudes toward three beliefs common to Asian Buddhism: karma, rebirth, and the ability of the Buddhas or bodhisattvas to extend their help to those who ask for it. The strongest agreement was with the idea of karma. Ninety-three percent of the respondents agreed or strongly agreed with the statement, "What happens to us in this life is determined by the kind of karma we create." Even though it is not a traditional part of the Western view of death, 81 percent also agreed that "after death, we are reborn into another life." Finally, about 66 percent agreed that "if I call on them, the Buddhas and Bodhisattvas will help me with my problems." Although there were no significant differences among the different traditions on that last question, members of Vipassana groups tended to be the most skeptical about both karma and rebirth (although substantial majorities accepted both ideas).

Given these similarities in doctrine and practice, it is not surprising that all Buddhist paths seem to produce similar fruit. The two most widely admired Buddhists living today, Thich Nhat Hanh and the Dalai Lama, Tenzin Gyatso, come from very different Asian traditions that have had little contact with each other over the centuries. Yet both men exude a remarkably similar aura of humility, peace, and compassion. Of course, such a high degree of realization is extremely rare, but even the average members queried in my survey report that Buddhism has had a very significant influence on them. When directly asked, "How great an impact has Buddhism had on your daily life?" none of the 354 people who answered that question said it had no impact, while 25.6 percent said it had a significant impact and 70.5 percent said it had a very significant impact. There was, moreover, an overwhelming consensus that the influence was a very positive one. When asked to evaluate the statement, "My Buddhist practice has had a very positive influence on my life," over 99 percent of the respondents said that they agreed (29 percent) or strongly agreed (70.2 percent).

So what are the fruits of a long-term commitment to Buddhist practice? For one thing, meditation can produce many profound experiences including the blissful state of complete absorption, sometimes known as *samadhi*, in which the thought process calms and the ego is in abeyance. Practitioners may also have a sudden enlightenment experience, known as *satori* or *kensho* in the Zen tradition, in which the separation between the self and the universe completely dissolves and there is only an indescribable unity. A sense of profound peace, great ecstasy, and a virtually unlimited array of other profound experiences are also reported by meditators. Nonetheless, any experience, no matter how wonderful, is transitory and the ultimate fruit of the Buddhist path is liberating wisdom that breaks the bonds of ego attachment. It is not that the self-concept and the personality just disappear but that they are understood so completely that they are recognized as transitory and unimportant, and the vicious circle of self-centered fear and desire is finally broken. As the great thirteenth-century Zen master Eihei Dogen put it: "To study the Buddha is to study the self. To study the self is to forget the self. To forget the self is to be actualized by the myriad things (that is, enlightened)."[18] Finally, whether it is called compassion, loving-kindness, or simply an open heart, an abiding mark of realized Buddhist masters from all traditions is their passionate concern for the well-being of others.

At the same time, all Buddhist paths share some common pitfalls as well. The powerful meditation techniques they teach can produce profound experiences and provide penetrating insights, but when used unwisely they can also become a way to cover over and ignore deep-seated emotional problems or perplexing social difficulties. An experienced meditator can hide in a blissful state of samadhi instead of facing what needs to be faced. The Buddhist emphasis on letting go of one's attachments ("nonclinging") can inadvertently promote a passionless, distant attitude toward life in some people and even disrupt important personal commitments. As Stephen Butterfield writes:

> The very idea of detachment may be particularly annoying to a meditator's non-Buddhist lover or spouse. . . . We may feel less than thrilled at the news that our bodhisattva partner has decided to take on all sentient beings as family members, or that our anger, jealousy, and insecurity have become the objects of tonglen.[19]

Western critics of Buddhism sometimes even characterize the whole tradition as a kind of spiritual escapism that leads it followers to hide in the artificial tranquillity of the monastery. While it is debatable how well such generalizations apply to Asian Buddhism, they are certainly wide of the mark when it comes to the very worldly variant of Buddhism growing in the West. That does not, however, mean that no Western Buddhists use the meditative skills they develop to escape from harsh realities they would rather not face.

Another common problem is that "spiritual achievements" along the Buddhist path can be used to inflate the ego instead of to see through it—what Trungpa Rinpoche called "spiritual materialism." After undergoing deep meditative experiences or having some profound personal insights, it is easy for even the most sincere practitioners to fall into the trap of feeling they have achieved something special, perhaps seeing themselves as somehow superior to others who have not had such experiences. Such attitudes lead to a kind of spiritual snobbery which is a significant barrier to further spiritual growth. As Suzuki Roshi put it:

> When you make some special effort to achieve something, some excessive quality, some extra element is involved in it. You should get rid of excessive things. If your practice is good, without being aware of it you will become proud of your practice. . . . This kind of bad effort is called being "Dharma-ridden," or "practice-ridden." You are involved in some idea of practice or attainment, and you cannot get out of it.[20]

The Spectrum of Difference

Despite all they share, each tradition of Western Buddhism has its own special attractions and its own perils as well. For those seeking the exotic, Vajrayana Buddhism has few equals among the world's major religions. It uses the powers of the imagination in unique ways to challenge our taken-for-granted sense of reality, and it shows great skill in working with the messy reality of human emotions. Vajrayana also offers an encyclopedic understanding of the Buddhist tradition, as well as an unequaled repertoire of techniques and practices to use along the path. On the other hand, however, those strengths can become their own pitfalls. The exotic trappings of Vajrayana Buddhism can easily contribute to the kind of spiritual materialism Trungpa warned against, and its powerful visualization techniques, in which one imagines oneself to be an enlightened deity, are especially dangerous. As Robert A.F. Thurman put it: "If you haven't dis-lodged what is called 'the rigid self habit' then you can become a kind of megalomaniac. You can believe that you are God and have created a special mandala world of your own. The mind can get you into a fan-tasy world where you become attached to this magical and miraculous self."[21]

Of all the Buddhist traditions, Zen teachers seem least likely to impose some external form on their students' experience. One prominent Vipas-sana teacher I interviewed said that she left her early Zen practice be-cause the only meditation instruction her Japanese teacher would give her was to "die on your cushion." The genius of the paradoxical Zen koan is that it can stimulate intense inquiry into the true nature of things with-out providing some preordained answer. In the Zen style of shikantaza meditation, one attempts to see one's experience just as it is without im-posing any particular interpretation and structure. The detailed guidance and meditation instructions given by teachers in other traditions provide more help to the student, but they inevitably encourage students to see things the way their teachers do without necessarily experiencing the un-derlying reality on which that vision is based. Of course, such openness can also leave some students floundering without direction. Perhaps in compensation, the Zen tradition tends to place greater emphasis on ex-ternal discipline, formal rules, and determined effort. Although this structure provides the student with concrete direction, it can also en-courage a kind of rigidity and emotional repression. Passionate emotional outbursts tend to make many "Zen people" uncomfortable. And as in all paths, there is always the danger that the meditator will become attached to the results of their effort.

One of the greatest strengths of the Vipassana tradition is its ability to present the heart of Eastern wisdom without the Eastern cultural bag-gage so many teachers have brought to the West. Some Vipassana teach-ers, such as Jack Kornfield, have also done a masterful job of using the concepts and approaches of the Western psychological tradition to help students understand Buddha dharma. This approach can, however, en-courage some students to try to use Buddhist teachings as a kind of ther-apy to make themselves feel better, rather than as an aid in breaking through the whole web of illusion that confines them. This is less of a problem with the more traditional forms of Vipassana practice, but that approach has difficulties of its own. The emphasis on the effort to uproot

personal desires and defilements typical of traditional Theravadan practice runs the danger of encouraging the kind of dry emotional flatness
and detachment for which the ancient Theravadin arhats were so often
criticized.

It is a lot harder to generalize about all the divergent approaches found
among the nonsectarian groups. To the extent that these groups bring
their members into contact with many different approaches and practices, they are capable of providing a far broader foundation than the
groups affiliated with only a single tradition. Moreover, the open, non-
hierarchical organization found in many of the nonsectarian groups
greatly reduces the danger of the kind of abusive student–teacher relationships that have come to light in the other traditions. At the same time,
it encourages more independence and autonomy on the part of the members. Yet this approach poses the risk that students will be satisfied to
take a bit from here and a bit from there without ever going very deeply
into any of it. Norman Fischer, former abbot of the San Francisco Zen
Center, argues against this kind of "dharma shopping," because "you will
take what you like from each tradition and you will never have to deal
with the part you don't like—and that is the part you can learn the most
from."[22]

THE RELIGIOUS DIMENSION   In the past, some Western scholars wondered if Buddhism was really a religion at all because it was so uncon-
cerned with the idea of God. While this question stems in large part from
the ethnocentric perspective of those raised in the traditions of Western
theism, both a religious and a secular style of Buddhism do seem to be
developing side by side in the West. At one pole are the groups that have
all the traditional religious trappings—robed priests, elaborate rituals, sacred images of supermundane figures, devotional practices, and clear criteria for who is and is not a member. At the other pole are the informal
groups of people who simply come together to learn from a particular
teacher or to support one another in their spiritual quest with few or
none of the traditional forms of religious practice. The nonsectarian
groups are the most likely to fall on the secular end of this spectrum, and
the Zen and Tibetan groups on the religious side. There are, however,
teachers from all traditions who have moved away from the Asian style of
religious Buddhism to take a more secular approach. Prominent examples
include Ken McLeod from the Tibetan tradition, Joko Beck and Toni Packer

from the Zen tradition, and Jack Kornfield and the teachers at the Spirit Rock Vipassana Center.

Although those who practice in one style or the other often place great importance on the particular approach they have adopted, much of this difference can be seen as a matter of personal taste—the rituals and ceremonies simply appeal to some and not to others. Although I have no data to back my claim, much of this difference may stem from one's early experiences with religion—those who found wonder in the rituals of the church or synagogue they attended as a child would seem to be far more likely to be attracted to the religious style of Buddhism than those who fell asleep during those services or were raised in a completely secular home. A good case in point is Stephen Batchelor, a leading Buddhist philosopher and advocate of a very secular approach he termed "Buddhism without beliefs" in one recent book. Batchelor says that he originally came to Buddhism out of a sense of rebellion against what he disliked in his own culture, but as he has grown older he has returned more and more to his own cultural roots. But that did not involve

some rediscovery of Christianity. In fact, I was brought up outside an explicitly Christian culture. . . . What I reconnected with, therefore, is not what we would call the religious traditions of the West, but rather the humanistic, secular, agnostic culture, which I feel a very, very deep sympathy with. . . . So in recovering my roots, I'm also recovering, as it were, a nonreligious identity.[23]

There is no question that the religiously oriented Buddhist groups offer a rich and powerful symbolic dimension that is absent from the more secular approach. Common rituals can help create strong feelings of community and solidarity among the participants. When pursued in the correct way they can become a powerful mindfulness practice, bringing the participants' full attention to the present moment. On the other hand, the more religious approach presents some very real pitfalls as well. As we have seen in countless religious wars throughout the centuries, the powerful sense of solidarity that rituals and common beliefs help create can also lead to an in-group/out-group mentality that excludes all who do not share in that ritual community. Groups that emphasize religious organization and ritual also run a greater risk that the maintenance of their institutions and traditions will become an end in itself and the real goal of Buddhist practice—personal liberation—will be obscured.

Toni Packer has been particularly outspoken on this point, questioning the value of identifying with any religious tradition at all.

> Can we question why we need to be something—Buddhist, Christian, Muslim, Jew? What is that something? Is it a thought, an image, a concept about oneself? Having a concept about oneself is a divisive thing, isn't it? It fragments the mind. . . . as long as I come to you as a Buddhist and you're a Catholic there's already division. Oh we may stretch hands across the border and call each other sisters and brothers and yet we both hang on to our identity because we can't let go of it. These divisions are the things that are blowing us up. The nuclear bomb is only a by-product of that.[24]

TEACHERS, STUDENTS, AND THE STRUCTURE OF AUTHORITY   One of the most important ways Western Buddhist groups differ is in the relationship between students and teachers. In some groups, teachers are powerful dominating figures who seek to control every detail of community life and do not hesitate to order their students around. In others, teachers take a more egalitarian and less directive approach. Some groups are structured to place virtually all the power in the hands of a single teacher, others are run more like constitutional monarchies, and still others are truly democratic. Some groups have a single head teacher, others have a group of more or less equal teachers, still others have no teacher at all.

A careful examination of the vast diversity of student–teacher relationships in Western Buddhism reveals three typical patterns.[25] Although each pattern is commonly associated with a different Buddhist tradition, advocates of all these approaches are found within the different traditions. Most teachers, moreover, probably act out different patterns in different contexts and at different times in their careers. Students' relationships with their teachers also inevitably change as their practice matures. "Over the years our relationship with a teacher will change," writes Jack Kornfield. "In time our teacher may fulfill many roles. They can be mentor and priest, confessor and guide, spiritual midwife and critic, mirror and exemplar of a radiant presence."[26] Of course, they may also take on a different kind of role such as the carrier of fearful authority or the indifferent object of reverence who never has time for or interest in the admiring student.

First off, there are the teachers who serve as "spiritual friends" to their students. This term is a rough translation of the Pali word *kalyana-mitta,* and it refers to the deep bonds of friendship and mutual affection that develop between those who are struggling to follow the spiritual path and those helping them to find their way. In the West, this pattern of teaching eschews hierarchy and minimizes the inequality in what is in some respects an inherently unequal relationship. First names are often used instead of formal titles, teachers are not given elaborate forms of ritual respect, and student–teacher interactions are seen more as a mutual exchange than as a mere transmission of knowledge or wisdom from one person to another. This relationship is something like the one between a wise older brother and a younger sibling who turns to him for guidance and support. This style of student–teacher relationship is most typical in Vipassana and nonsectarian groups, but because of its obvious affinity with the Western ideals of egalitarianism and democracy, it is becoming more common in the other traditions as well—especially among the newer generations of teachers born in the West.

In the second pattern, the teacher is seen as a figure of "spiritual authority." There is far greater social distance between student and teacher, and there is a stronger feeling that spiritual wisdom is being transmitted from one to the other. Teachers who assume the role of spiritual authority are often given special titles such as roshi or lama, and they are shown various degrees of ritual deference, which can include everything from simply leaving the meditation hall before everyone else to being the object of prostrations and chants proclaiming their exalted status. In the context of an established Buddhist center, this spiritual authority also tends to come with a great deal of temporal authority over the center's operations and the daily lives of its students. In the West, this approach is most typical of Zen groups that have, often unknowingly, absorbed a Confucian model of the patriarchal extended family from their Asian teachers. As in Asia, subordinates are expected to give respect and obedience to their superiors, and the superiors are expected to show parental concern for the well-being of their subordinates. Despite the great prestige and power Asian teachers enjoy, it is not unlimited power. In Asia, both teacher and student are tightly constrained by traditional social conventions that tend to provide a significant measure of protection against the abuse of the teacher's power. Many of these traditional restraints did not, however, make the boat over to the West, and numerous Buddhist centers that have invested their teacher with such great authority are still struggling to develop some sort of Western equivalent.

Finally, there is a third pattern in which the teacher plays an even more exalted role, which might be termed a "guru." Such teachers are seen as a divine embodiment of true enlightenment and are actually worshiped by their followers. Not only does the guru-teacher receive the respect and secular power of the spiritual authority, but he or she is far freer of traditional social restraints. This pattern of student–teacher relations is, of course, most characteristic of the Tibetan tradition, since students often take a vow of allegiance to their guru and perform a variety of ritual devotions and visualizations centered on the guru. The cultural model of the "spiritual authority" in the West is something like a strict but benevolent patriarch of a traditional family; the guru, however, has a kind of divine status that has few parallels here. Perhaps the essence of this relationship is complete surrender to the guru. Trungpa Rinpoche writes that

> we might feel proud that we gave one of our fingers to our guru: "I cut off my ear as a gift to him," or "I cut my nose as an expression of devotion to him. I hope he will take it and regard it as a sign of how serious I am about the whole thing. And I hope he will value it because it means so much to me." To the crazy wisdom guru such sacrifice is insignificant. Vajrayana surrender is much more painful and powerful and intimate. It is a problem of total communication; if you hold anything back, your relationship will be false, incomplete, and both you and your guru will know it.[27]

It is no coincidence that the descriptions of such relationships and the devotion they involve often take on an erotic coloring. Not that they necessarily lead to sexual relations (although occasionally they do), but that there is supposed to be the same kind of intimacy and intense libidinal energy between student and teacher that there is between two lovers.

From one perspective, these three approaches merely reflect differences in style that appeal to different kinds of students. Some students seek a strong parental figure in their teacher, while others are uncomfortable with anyone who claims spiritual authority and want something more of a wise friend; still others seek someone to idolize and revere. Regardless of the motivations of the students, however, each style has its own pitfalls. The dominating teacher runs the risk of encouraging dependence and immaturity in the students and, of course, that leaves the students more vulnerable to abuse if the teacher is unwise or unscrupulous. On the other hand, a more nondirective style encourages more independence, but it may allow some students to avoid the difficult challenges they most need to face. While the role of teacher as spiritual authority seems to be in no danger of disappearing, one of the biggest questions confronting Western Buddhism is whether or not the Asian style of guru devotion can survive this hostile cultural environment. In the view of many Westerners, such relationships are an affront to individual dignity and a threat to society's primary values of personal autonomy and egalitarianism.

It is a mistake to attempt to understand these patterns of student–teacher relationships in isolation from the institutional context in which they occur. The smaller Buddhist groups tend to have a loose, informal structure, and their decision-making process is not so unlike the early Buddhist sangha, which acted only by group consensus. Since there are few rules, regulations, or requirements in these small groups, teachers have little in the way of formal constraints on their behavior. But since they also operate without much institutional support or charisma and have a relatively small number of students, they are subject to the influence of members who may "vote with their feet" and drop out of the group or simply fade into apathy.

Not surprisingly, the larger Buddhist groups have been gravitating toward the kind of governance structure established for religious groups in Western law. Like most churches and synagogues, large Buddhist groups tend to be legally incorporated entities that in theory are run by an official board of directors. But the relationship that develops between the board of directors and the head teacher (if there is one) is far more determined by the personality and behavior of the teacher than by the technicalities of the law or even the formal governance procedures of the center. Although in theory the power may rest with the board of directors, in actual practice the head teacher usually enjoys a position of unrivaled authority. After all, the fundamental assumption in these groups is that the head teacher possesses a level of wisdom and insight far beyond that of ordinary members, and those who come to doubt it would have little reason to stay in the group. In many groups, the head teacher actually appoints the board. But even where board members are selected by consensus of the existing board or are elected by the general membership, the head teacher is still a dominating figure who plays a major part in determining what role the board of directors will have in the organization. Some teachers who play the role of spiritual authority want control over all the day-to-day operations of the center and in such cases the board may act as nothing more than a legal rubber stamp. Other teachers, especially those more inclined to the role of spiritual friend to their students, are less interested in such matters and are more than happy to turn most administrative duties over to their board. In fact, many Western teachers brought up with the values of democracy and egalitarianism intentionally encourage the members to exercise active control of the center.

Whatever kind of routine relationship develops between the head teacher and the board of directors, things change radically in times of crisis. When charges of abuse and misconduct are brought against a teacher, the board's legal authority suddenly takes on new importance. Not only must it make the ultimate decisions about whether or not to ask the teacher to resign, it often plays a pivotal role in attempting to reconcile the demands of different factions of the sangha. Although it is a bit early to tell for sure, the added strength the board gains after such crises seems likely to last long after their resolution.

Another key to understanding the dynamics of power in Western Buddhism lies in what it means to be a teacher and how one achieves that position. It should be obvious from our discussion that being considered a Buddhist teacher involves a lot more than simply teaching Buddhism. A college professor, for example, who gave classes on Buddhism but did not maintain a Buddhist practice would not be considered a "teacher" by most Western Buddhists. In addition to teaching others about Buddhism, the teacher is expected to have a deep experience with Buddhist practice and to have gained a level of realization far beyond that of ordinary members. But exactly how much the teacher is expected to differ from the members and how great the social distance between them is expected to be varies considerably from group to group. In fact, many nonsectarian groups do not have anyone who plays the role of teacher, even though they may have long-term members who have key positions of leadership and play a considerable part in guiding their less experienced colleagues.

One of the great paradoxes of Buddhism is that the respect, prestige, and authority the teacher receives are a powerful encouragement to the very kind of ego attachments that Buddhist practice is expected to help the practitioner transcend. More than a few Western Buddhists have been deeply troubled when, for example, they have seen high-ranking Tibetan teachers being chauffeured around in a limousine, attended by a team of servants, or giving their dharma talks from a golden throne. Traditional cultural forms or ego delusion? The question is not an easy one for many Westerners to answer. In fact, some nonsectarian groups intentionally avoid naming anyone as "the teacher" to avoid all the potential for confusion it can create. Toni Packer, who was named as Kapleau Roshi's successor at the Rochester Zen Center, left and started her own center in large part because she felt that the role she was being forced to play as a teacher was a source of egocentric delusion for both her and her students. Although she now heads a large center and gives retreats in numerous places around the world, she still refuses to call herself a teacher.

In addition to the style favored by individual teachers, their authority and their social distance from students is also affected by their group's method of training and selecting teachers. If it is relatively easy to be recognized as a teacher, there are likely to be more of them with less social distance from their students. As the requirements for qualifying as a teacher increase, the number of teachers naturally declines while social distance tends to increase.

As we have seen, there are a bewildering number of traditions, lineages, schools, and approaches in contemporary Buddhism. Since there is no universally accepted central authority, virtually anyone can claim to be an enlightened teacher or some kind of Zen master. To win recognition from an established lineage is, however, quite another matter. A few groups, such as the Spirit Rock Meditation Center, have established official teacher training programs that the aspirant must complete before being recognized as a teacher. The Spirit Rock program is designed for laypeople, not monastics, but it is open only to advanced students who must be invited to participate. This program involves four years of regularly scheduled meetings, classes, and retreats, in which students are given advanced training in Buddhist doctrines and practice, as well as special instruction in how to teach Buddhism and deal with the problems they are likely to encounter in their relations with students. The intensive three-year Tibetan-style retreats first begun in the West by Kalu Rinpoche are not specifically designed to be teacher training programs, but their graduates are generally given the title of lama and are considered ready for teaching duties.

Most Western Buddhist groups do not, however, have a formal teacher training program. Rather, as students mature in their practice, their relationships to other students change over the years and they naturally begin to take on various kinds of new responsibilities. The larger centers may have a considerable group of these "senior students" who are frequently called on to provide beginning meditation instruction, answer questions from newcomers, and give occasional talks and presentations. In the smaller nonsectarian groups, the more advanced practitioners may take on the teacher role without much supervision or any official sanction. The established centers, however, generally require some kind of formal approval from the head teacher before a senior student can assume full status as a teacher. (One important difference between senior students and teachers is that while the former often teach beginners and the general public, they are not usually allowed to train advanced students or to sanction others to teach.) In some centers, the sanction to teach comes directly from the completion of a teacher training program, but more often it is simply awarded by the head teacher when he or she feels that the student is ready—a process that often involves twenty years or more of dedicated practice. Some traditions hold official "dharma transmission" ceremonies that bestow a ritual authorization to teach and publicly acknowledge the new teacher's status.

In addition to those given authority to teach through their years of practice and training, the Tibetan tradition recognizes two higher ranks: the *geshe* (or *khenpo*) and the *tulku*. The geshe is the holder of a monastic degree that generally takes fifteen to twenty years of rigorous academic study to earn. The highest status, *geshe lharampa* (a sort of Tibetan Ph.D.), requires another eight to nine years of work. Tibetan geshes have been very influential in the academic study of Buddhism here in the West, but it is the tulkus—those who have been officially recognized as the reincarnation of a deceased lama—who have been the major force in establishing the Tibetan style of religious practice. The discovery and authentication of the reincarnation of a respected lama is a complex process that often involves a prophecy that the lama makes before his death, various forms of divination, and a formal testing procedure to see if the candidate can identify various items owned by the previous lama. In some cases, it has even become a political battle, like the one currently being fought by China's communist government and the traditional Tibetan hierarchy over who is to be recognized as the next Panchen Lama.

Although a few Westerners have been granted the title of geshe or tulku, their numbers are small, and no matter how advanced their practice, ascent to such ranks is not a realistic possibility for most people born in the West. Of course, one could chose to move to India or Nepal to study at one of the monasteries that offer the rigorous course of training necessary to earn the title of geshe. But it is no easy matter for a Westerner to win admission to such schools, and that is only the beginning. They must then thoroughly master a foreign language (examinations tend to take the form of oral debates, and fluency in Tibetan is an absolute requirement) and leave their homeland for years on end—barriers that are not faced by ethnic Tibetans. Becoming a tulku is another matter altogether, for, at least in theory, there is nothing at all that one can do to win such recognition. A few non-Tibetans have recently been recognized as reincarnations of Tibetan lamas, but the vast majority of the tulkus teaching in the West are Tibetans. Moreover, Western children who are recognized as tulkus are less likely to receive the lifelong monastic training that makes the Tibetan tulku so unique among the world's religious leaders. These barriers to full participation have meant that the highest levels of leadership in most Western Vajrayana groups continue to be filled by ethnic Tibetans. This situation has created considerable frustration among some advanced Western students who would have received higher status and more authority if they had been practicing in one of the other Buddhist traditions.

There are, of course, many more distinctions of power beyond those among the head teacher, students, and board of directors. Like most organizations, the larger Buddhist centers exhibit a complex pattern of stratified relationships that can shift unpredictably from time to time. Sometimes the hierarchy is an informal one derived solely from the patterns of personal interaction that participants develop, but more often they are bolstered by official titles, positions, and ranks. More committed members are, as we have seen, often distinguished from their more casual counterparts by their participation in a precepts ceremony that symbolizes their dedication to the Buddhist path. Many centers also support a group of monks with special privileges and responsibilities who are set off from other members by such things as distinctive robes or shaved heads.

Some members of Zen groups are also recognized as priests and given special responsibilities and ceremonial duties. The definition of what it means to be a monk or a priest, however, varies considerably from one center to another. Traditionally, monks are renunciates who practice celibacy and live by a strict code of discipline. In the Japanese tradition, priests perform ceremonies and teach the public but are not required to follow the strict monastic code and its prohibition on family life. In the West, these terms have taken on a variety of meanings. Although most groups do not have priests, in those that do the title is generally conferred upon people who have shown leadership and a long-term commitment to their practice and have learned to perform the ceremonies and rituals the center carries on. Although many still believe that being a monk means being celibate, Western Buddhist centers have frequently found that the requirement for celibacy is simply too unpopular and have loosened the rule. For example, Seung Sahn created a new category of "bodhisattva monk" for members of his Zen groups who want to take on the role of monk without the celibacy. What sets a monk apart from other Buddhists if he or she is not celibate? Again the standard varies from group to group, but generally monks live in a retreat center or monastery and are expected to dedicate their lives to Buddhist practice. However defined, monks and priests clearly have higher status, greater power, and more responsibilities than other members.

Whether or not a center has formally recognized monks and priests, an important distinction inevitably arises between the full-time residents of the centers and those who merely commute to various functions or stay for short periods during retreat. The former group has the power and authority, whereas those in the latter group are relegated to a subordinate position. In discussing the distinction between the ordained monks and the lay practitioners at Zen retreats, C. Victor Sogen Hori writes that

> the ordained monks wear robes, sit at the top end of the *zendo,* share a room with only one or two others, and in general hold all the important offices and give the orders during *sesshin* [meditation retreat]. . . . The lay practitioners wear rather plain clothing compared to the robes of the monks, sit in lower positions in the *zendo*, sleep eight or ten to a cabin, and in general are passive participants in running the *sesshin*. . . . In effect, the distinction between ordained and lay divides the people at *sesshin* into two social classes with quite different membership, power, and status. This distinction between monks and laypersons looks something like the familiar distinctions between management and worker in an American business corporation.[28]

Indeed, Hori thinks this distinction is so important that he actually dubs this approach "managerial Zen." The development of this kind of class division among the membership may be influenced by the teacher and the approach of each individual group. Nonetheless, long-term residents in these centers seem to almost inevitably develop an "in-group" mentality that sets them off from the nonresidential members who come and go at whim, often inadvertently breaking the established rules or disrupting the informal arrangements that keep any large organization operating.

Five

❋

SEX, POWER, AND CONFLICT

It seems that the new Buddhist centers springing up in the West should have been truly enlightened organizations, free from the conflicts so common in other social institutions. That's certainly what most of their members believed. After all, weren't those centers led by enlightened teachers and staffed by people with a fervent commitment to the loftiest spiritual goals?

The crises that swept through one center after another in the 1980s were a profound shock to the Buddhist community, and the reverberations of those and more current scandals are still being felt. More than a few members described their experience as a kind of coming of age that shattered their idealistic image of their teachers and of the fruits they could expect from the Buddhist path. Most students stuck determinedly to their teacher's side, but others pushed for reforms, walked out to follow a more independent spiritual path, or gave up their quest altogether.

Not surprisingly, the explosions that rocked Western Buddhism were touched off by the same incendiary questions of sex and power that perplex the rest of Western society. What are the proper roles of the two genders? Are women exploited by a male-dominated hierarchy? When are sexual relations appropriate and when are they exploitative? How much do people have a right to know about their leaders' personal lives, and how much can those leaders justifiably keep private? How much power should those with special knowledge and abilities be given, and what should be done when they abuse it? To explore these difficult issues, we first turn to one of the darker pages in the history of Buddhism—its treatment of women.

Women on the Buddhist Path

In theory, Buddhism should never have had the problems of sexism and discrimination that plague the world's other major religions. For one thing, Buddhism doesn't have the doctrinal barriers to full equality that many of the Western religions do. Since there is no all-powerful deity, Buddhism has no problem with the male "god language" to which feminists have raised such strong objections. Although Buddhism has developed an elaborate set of rules for its celibate monks, its ethical principles for laypeople are much more general, and they never give specific religious sanction to gendered inequality. In fact, no specific family norms of any kind have been incorporated into Buddhist belief. While the traditional Christian marriage ceremony instructs a wife to obey her husband and Islam gives males an even wider range of power and authority in family matters, Buddhism is largely silent on these topics. And even if it weren't, the ethical norms of Buddhism are not God given, so they are much easier to change as patriarchal social traditions weaken in the postmodern era.

On a deeper level, since the primary objective of Buddhism is spiritual realization and that realization occurs among both women and men, gender discrimination makes little theological sense. All Buddhist schools agree that the state of enlightenment the seeker strives to realize is the same in everyone regardless of gender, age, or social background. Many of the great Mahayana sutras tell us that this ultimate reality is beyond the realm of all dualities, which of course includes that of female and male. Moreover, since the highest ethical imperative of Buddhism is to save all beings from suffering and the way to escape suffering is Buddhist practice, it seems absolutely incongruous that women would be denied equal access to the techniques and training necessary to that practice. Yet more often than not, that is exactly what Asian Buddhism did.

The question of gender equality was apparently an issue right from the earliest times, and one of the most often cited stories in the Buddhist canon deals with this issue. According to the story, only men were admitted into the monastic community that originally formed around the Buddha, but in a few years he was approached by a large group of women that included his aunt and stepmother who asked for ordination. The Buddha originally rejected their pleas, but the women refused to give up. After leaving in dejection, they cut their hair, donned monastic robes, and followed the wandering Buddha to his next stopping place, where they again pleaded to be admitted to the sangha. This time the Buddha's trusted attendant Ananda took up their cause, and the Buddha finally relented. But before he would let them in, the women had to accept eight special rules, in addition to the regular monastic regulations, that strictly subordinated them to male authority. This was a rather grudging acceptance, for in this story the Buddha says that the reign of true dharma would have lasted 1,000 years had only men been admitted to the monastic order; with the admission of women, however, it would last only five hundred years.

Why was the Buddha so reluctant to accept women as monastics? Or to put the question more accurately, since many scholars believe that this story actually originated several centuries after the Buddha's death and served to justify the accommodation that had already been worked out between institutionalized groups of monks and nuns, why were women relegated to second-class status as Buddhist practitioners? Clearly, the Buddha never doubted women's ability to achieve enlightenment and he explicitly recognized the accomplishments of many different female practitioners. Alan Sponberg writes that "the earliest Buddhists clearly held that one's sex, like one's caste or class, presents no barrier to attaining the Buddhist goal of the liberation from suffering."[1] The problem doesn't rest with Buddhist practice or belief but with the patriarchal nature of ancient Indian society. While the men of ancient India commonly gave up worldly ties to pursue spiritual realization, women did not. The whole idea of women renouncing male authority and abandoning their family obligations to follow the life of a spiritual seeker was deeply unsettling to a society that viewed women primarily as child bearers and servants to their men. The compromise sanctioned by this story—that women be admitted as monks but be subordinated to male authority— seems intended to allow an avenue for women's spiritual growth while minimizing the opposition of sexist society.

As time went on, the celibate monastic community that guided early

Buddhism became increasingly negative toward women. The literature from this period is full of depictions of women as wanton sexual temptresses and discussions of the vileness of women's bodies. Such portrayals, however, probably sprang more from the attempt to rein in monastic libidos than any inherent Buddhist misogyny. The monks were often lectured about the vileness of their own bodies as well and were urged (among other things) to use a decaying corpse as an object of meditation. A female birth was widely regarded as an unfortunate one in early Buddhism (as it still is in many Asian countries), but such beliefs seem to come more from a realistic assessment of the status of women in Asian societies than Buddhist ideology. More troubling was the idea that while a woman might become an arhat, she was incapable of becoming a Buddha until she was reborn as a man. Because of such attitudes, and the strong opposition to allowing women to escape their traditional duties by entering the monastic life, the order of Buddhist nuns eventually died out in all Theravadin countries. Some women lived monastic lives nevertheless, but they were not able to receive full ordination. To this day, the Theravadin tradition remains the most resistant to the ideal of full equality for women.

With the advent of Mahayana, Buddhism's position on the status of women became more complex. Some Mahayana texts contain the same misogynist rhetoric found in earlier works, but there are also a considerable number of texts proclaiming women's potential for great religious insight. The female adept became a common character in many sutras, and some magical bodhisattvas were able to change their gender, and even the gender of others, at will. As the Mahayana was transmitted to East Asia, this schizophrenia continued. The Zen sect, like its Chinese predecessor, Ch'an, maintained the spiritual equality of women in theory, although often not in practice. For example, one prominent twelfth-century Chinese master in the Lin Chi tradition left some very explicit commentary on the question of gender. To one female student he said: "This matter (that is, enlightenment), does not depend on being a man or a woman, a monk or nun or a layperson. If on hearing one word from a teacher one suddenly breaks off (the chain of deluded thought), that is complete realization." And in another commentary: "For mastering the truth, it does not matter whether one is male or female, noble or base. One moment of insight and one is shoulder to shoulder with the Buddha."[2]

Soto Zen took much the same view of gender. Eihei Dogen, the founder of Soto Zen in Japan, strongly proclaimed the full spiritual equality of women. Yet, as in China, his monastic followers never put those egalitarian dictums into full practice, and nuns always remained subordinate to monks. But unlike Theravadin Buddhism, such places as Korea, Japan, Taiwan, and Hong Kong still have active monastic communities for women.

Although the monastic opportunities for women in Tibet are far more restricted than in East Asia, Vajrayana Buddhism's doctrinal attitudes toward women are, according to feminist scholar Rita Gross, "very favorable—much more favorable than in any earlier form of Buddhism and among the most favorable attitudes found in any major religion in any period of its development."[3] Although female imagery is rare in Mahayana Buddhism and virtually absent in Theravada, it abounds in the Vajrayana tradition. Female tantric deities run the gamut from blissful serenity to bloodthirsty passion. Sky dancing *dakinis,* in the words of Miranda Shaw, "leap and fly, unfettered by clothing, encircled by billowing hair, their bodies curved in sinuous dance poses. Their eyes blaze with passion, ecstasy, and ferocious intensity."[4] The denigration of women is, moreover, considered one of the fourteen "root downfalls" of Vajrayana Buddhism. Indeed, it was the female partner who was most often the object of worship in tantric sexual rites.

Because the tantric movement had it origins outside the male dominated monastic world, it was far more open to women and to members of the lower castes as well. In fact, Miranda Shaw argues that despite the androcentric bias in most of the historical record, many of the founders of the tantric movement were actually women. But as this powerful new movement forced its way into the monasteries and universities, it was increasingly co-opted by the traditional male hierarchy. Although the theory and the imagery of tantric Buddhism continued to cast women in a very favorable light, they were nonetheless systematically excluded from positions of power and influence in the Buddhist hierarchy.

As Buddhism entered the West, then, its institutional structures, whether Theravadin, Tibetan, or Zen, were overwhelmingly male dominated, and in most cases they operated to exclude women from full participation in the highest manifestations of their religious life. Buddhist doctrine, on the other hand, was a complex mixture with an egalitarian core and an accretion of other beliefs that often reflected the patriarchal attitudes of traditional societies.

When Asian Buddhists first began teaching in the West, they were not only confronted with a radically different set of cultural assumptions, they found themselves in a radically different sociological position as well. In Asia, Buddhism was a more or less conservative, established religion and most of its members were simply born into the faith. But in the West, Buddhism had to attract new members, and its appeal was greatest among bohemians and left-leaning intellectuals and professionals—the same groups that were least likely to be receptive toward traditional Asian attitudes about the proper role of women in religious life. As a result, most teachers simply ignored the more sexist elements of the tradition and focused on the core beliefs that transcend gender distinctions.

As Western teachers take over from the Asians, the last vestiges of sexist doctrine are being laid to rest. The norms emerging in the new Buddhism are clearly those of complete gender equality in all aspects of religious life: no encouragement for women to stay home and raise the children, no male god language, and no restrictions on full female participation as priests or monks, or in other leadership positions. Even male Buddhist teachers (perhaps *especially* male teachers) often go to great lengths to include female imagery in their talks and to avoid sexist language. Part of the reason is certainly that the teachers share the same liberal background as most of their students. But in addition, though Western Buddhists generally show great deference toward their teachers, students seem more willing to challenge what they perceive as their male teachers' sexism than almost any other aspect of their performance.

All this does not mean, however, that no Western Buddhist groups still maintain sexist doctrines. The most blatant example is found in the Friends of the Western Buddhist Order. The order's founder, Urgyen Sangharakshita, has expressed the view in many of his writings that women are less spiritually capable than men. His head disciple, Subhuti, made this view quite explicit in his 1995 book, *Women, Men, and Angels,* in which he posits that there are five stages of evolution from Animal, which is the lowest, to Woman, Man, Artist, and finally to Angel, which is the highest. Although members of the FWBO are in no way required to accept the belief that women are somehow at a lower evolutionary level, the official sanction for such views at the highest levels of the organization obviously does not bode well for the equal treatment of its female members.

Moreover, the fact that the vast majority of groups are firmly commit-

ted to the full equality of women does not mean that women have actually achieved full equality in the new Buddhism. While there are a growing number of female teachers, some of whom are taking over top
administrative positions (with the exception of the Tibetan groups that
are usually guided by ethnic Tibetan men), women are still substantially
underrepresented in those positions of power. Overtly sexist doctrines
have been expunged, but many women complain of a more subtle male
bias in the way the teachings are presented and in the organization of
practice. Moreover, the shortage of female teachers as role models in
some groups creates feelings of alienation and exclusion among some
women.

Since the doctrinal barriers to full participation have largely been
eliminated in the West, why aren't there more women in top positions?
One obvious answer is that the men in positions of power, whether Asians
or Westerners, are still influenced by the sexist attitudes of their culture
to favor members of their own gender. Even if they believe in the full
equality of women, cultural differences between the world of men and
the world of women mean that male leaders are likely to relate more easily to members of their own gender. Another factor involves behavioral
differences between the genders. Feminists often argue that males tend
to be more hierarchically oriented than females, and whether the cause is
biology or socialization, it does appear that males often strive more aggressively for high institutional position.

Finally, another extremely important factor is the special demands
family life often places on women. The deep realization that is the essential foundation for dharma teachers usually demands decades of intense
practice. Among celibate monks, there is little difference for males and
females, but that style of practice is certainly not the norm for Western
Buddhists. While married men have sometimes been able to carry on intensive practice while their wives shouldered most of the child-rearing
and family responsibilities, that option has seldom been open to women.
And for the ever growing numbers of single mothers, that kind of all-
consuming dedication to practice is simply out of the question. It is not
surprising that my survey, which primarily reached dedicated long-term
members of Buddhist groups, found that while there was no statistically
significant difference between the percentage of females and males who
were married, the women were significantly less likely to have children.[5]

Despite such obstacles, or perhaps because of them, Buddhist women have been working to develop new channels of communication and struggling not only to understand their common problems but to foster a stronger sense of community. In 1979, a group of women practicing at the Diamond Sangha in Hawaii began publishing *Kahawai: A Journal of Women and Zen* to explore women's experience in Buddhism. Over the years, this journal has published special issues on such important topics as childbirth, homosexuality, abortion, and the sexual abuse of power. In 1981, Judith Simmer-Brown of the Naropa Institute helped organize the first conference on Women and Buddhism in Boulder, Colorado, and it was followed by several others. In their quiet way, these meetings were something truly revolutionary in the history of Buddhism. Never before had women practitioners and teachers from so many different Buddhist traditions come together to share their common experiences and concerns. The topics covered included everything from basic Buddhism to feminism and the sexual abuse some participants have experienced at the hands of their male teachers. All this interest has also stimulated numerous new books with such titles as *Daughters of the Buddha, Buddhist Women on the Edge, A Gathering of Spirit: Women Teaching in American Buddhism, Turning the Wheel: American Women Creating the New Buddhism,* and *Buddhism after Patriarchy.*

It is doubtful that the new Buddhism can achieve complete gender equality without fundamental changes in the wider society, but it has unquestionably made enormous progress from its Asian beginnings. *Inquiring Mind,* the journal published by the Spirit Rock Meditation Center, recently reported on forty-eight Vipassana teachers leading retreats around the country and of those exactly half were women.[6] My survey of Western Buddhists showed a general satisfaction with the status of women in Buddhist groups. When asked about the statement "I feel that discrimination against women is a serious problem in American Buddhism," over two-thirds of those answering disagreed or strongly disagreed. Their views were even more positive about their own Buddhist group. Eighty-five percent of the respondents agreed or strongly agreed with the statement that "I think women have an equal chance to attain a leadership position in this organization." Interestingly, there was no statistically significant difference between the male and female respondents on either question.

Although most members recognize the strides Buddhist centers have made toward gender equality, it is also generally agreed that they have not done a very good job of dealing with the special problems of families with children. Many Buddhist centers now offer some kind of "family day" with special programs set up to include children, and a few provide a limited schedule of child care to encourage parents to participate in ceremonies and group activities. But the larger question of how to help parents participate in rigorous meditation and retreat schedules has simply not been answered. One of the main virtues of the celibacy most Westerners reject is that it frees renunciates from family obligations and allows them to focus single-mindedly on their practice. It is no coincidence that the Buddha named his son Rahula, which translates to English as "the fetter."

Given the inevitable shortages of time and resources, most Western Buddhist centers have failed to come up with any viable institutional alternatives to allow the full participation of parents with heavy child-rearing responsibilities. One exception is Thich Nhat Hanh, who provides a separate retreat within a retreat for children whose parents are also in attendance. The children, who range from roughly age five to twelve, sleep with their parents and attend a special segment of his dharma talks directed to them. Otherwise they spend most of their time in organized activities away from their family. These retreats, however, take a very "soft" approach with a permissive schedule, and it is doubtful that children could be as easily integrated into more rigorous retreats with a demanding schedule.

Parents in most groups who want to carry on a regular schedule of intensive meditation retreats must make their own arrangements for child care or wait until their children are grown. Those unwilling to postpone their spiritual quest have to come up with numerous child care strategies. In some cases, one parent provides the child care to free the other to attend intensive practice sessions and in others the partners take turns swapping those duties. When a considerable number of families with children are associated with a particular practice center, they sometimes organize rotating child care arrangements so that one parent or family can cover for the children of several others.

In some cases these arrangements work surprisingly well, but oftentimes parents end up frustrated by their inability to keep up with the practice schedule, feeling guilty about neglecting their children, or both. Barbara Rhodes, one of Soen Su Nim's leading American students, told one interviewer that "I did a strict practice until I had my daughter. . . . It was wonderful, I mean I wish I was over there (the meditation hall) right now! . . . After she was born, I had to stay here with her. So it's been very hard. I still get very torn."[7] Jan Chozen Bays, a Zen priest and close student of Maezumi Roshi, expressed the feeling of many parents who also have intense outside commitments in these words: "One thing I feel now is that I wish I had spent more time with my children when they were growing up. In my very intense drive to go into Buddhism as deeply as I could . . . I really feel I missed something with my kids."[8]

From one perspective, there is a fundamental contradiction between the demands of traditional Buddhist practice and those of parenthood and family, but in a deeper view there is no conflict at all. If parents seek to bring the attitude of practice into their daily lives, a crying baby can be as much a reminder to come back to the here and now as the great bells of the temples. Teachers from all religious traditions recognize the enormous spiritual value of selflessly caring for others which is, of course, the essence of parenthood. As Carol Ochs puts it in her book, *Women and Spirituality:*

> The decentering of self achieved through asceticism can be accomplished as well through true devotion, which is first and foremost physical caring. In caring for their infants, mothers . . . [are] merely doing what must be done, their spiritual development proceeds without pride and without strain—it gracefully unfolds.[9]

Of course, it is far easier to expound the spiritual virtues of parenthood than to actually remain centered amid the swirling demands of family life. As Jane Baraz put it:

> Before I became a mother, I used to go on long retreats. I thought of my spiritual practice as primarily fueled by many weeks of silence, inspiring Dharma talks and being with others committed to the same path. . . . As a parent setting unpopular limits and making the effort to stay mindful in the midst of temper tantrums doesn't feel nearly as comfortable as sinking into a quiet rural setting filled with compassionate acts and inspiring words. However, family life has become my classroom for learning the basic attitudes of respect, kindness, and responsibility. . . . Parenting at times has been a demanding teacher, letting me know quite clearly when I am not paying attention.[10]

There's no doubt that parenthood offers a great opportunity for practice. Many great teachers have held meditation in action to be far superior to meditation in stillness, but it is also far more difficult, especially for those in the beginning stages of their practice. Many Western Buddhist centers are struggling to develop more effective strategies to provide child care during retreats, to include children in their social and religious activities, and to help parents integrate their child-rearing duties into their spiritual path. The San Francisco Zen Center's Green Gulch Farm, for example, offers a monthly young people's lecture and an occasional family day of mindfulness in their flower and vegetable garden. The Spirit Rock Meditation Center offers a day-long retreat on parenting as a spiritual practice and has women's retreats with special day care arrangements. The Shambhala Meditation Center in Boulder, Colorado, offers two sittings a week with shared child care, and it has been experimenting with a family nyinthun—a three-hour meditation session in which children are expected to play quietly near their meditating parents. In Halifax, Nova Scotia, Shambhala operates a middle school for children from age six to eleven that begins and ends each day with five minutes of sitting meditation. Despite such efforts, however, much more needs to be done before parents, especially those with young children, have equal access to the resources most Buddhist centers offer.

Men's Buddhism and Women's Buddhism?

For the first time in its long history, the Western expansion of Buddhism brought large numbers of men and women together to practice side by side in an egalitarian atmosphere. The inevitable consequence was that many traditional Buddhist forms had to change. Feminists who have written about Western Buddhism, such as Rita Gross, Sandy Boucher, and Lenore Friedman, feel that a distinctive style of women's practice is developing here that is quite different from the traditional masculine style. In general, these writers argue that female teachers are more oriented toward practice in daily life and place less emphasis on intensive retreats and the aggressive "samurai" approach to achieving enlightenment. Women students and teachers, in their view, place more importance on feelings and emotion in their practice and are less comfortable in hierarchical organizational structures.

Although there is undoubtedly some truth in such observations, we also run the risk of serious distortion if we posit some dichotomy between men's and women's practice based on our stereotypes of gender differences. If we look at the most influential women teachers in the West, such as Sharon Salzberg in the Vipassana tradition, Pema Chodron in the Tibetan tradition, and Joko Beck and Toni Packer in Zen, we find extremely divergent styles of practice. Some women teachers such as Joko Beck pursue what could easily be called a "samurai" approach with an emphasis on long sittings and vigorous practice, while others do not. Sharon Salzberg is in the most traditional, conservative wing of Western Vipassana, while Toni Packer has made such sweeping changes that she no longer even calls herself a Buddhist. Pema Chodron, a celibate nun, has always remained intensely loyal to her sexually adventurous teacher, Chogyam Trungpa.

The survey data collected for this book are far from unanimous on this point, but they clearly show far more similarities than differences between female and male Buddhists. Less than a third of the seventy-four variables examined in the survey showed a statistically significant difference between the genders, and some of those concerned such tangential issues as average age and length of membership in the group being studied. None of the questions that asked the respondents to evaluate their teachers or their organizations showed significant gender differences. For example, women and men were equally likely to say that Buddhism had a very positive influence on their life, and equally small numbers thought that meditation periods in their group were too long and difficult.

A survey is a clumsy way to evaluate the subtleties of meditation practice, but it is the only relatively objective measure we have, and it shows men and women to be remarkably similar on most of the key variables measured. In contradiction to the stereotypes expressed by some Asian teachers that women practitioners are more lazy or less motivated than men, there were in fact no statistically significant gender differences between average length or frequency of meditation. Nor, contrary to other assertions, was there any difference in the number of meditation retreats attended by women and men or their average duration. Men and women generally employed the same types of meditation techniques as well. Of the seven groups surveyed, only one showed any significant difference in the techniques used by women and men. And even then, it is hard to attribute much importance to the fact that in that one group men tended to do more formless "just sitting" meditation while women were somewhat more likely to alternate among several different styles of meditation. It is more difficult to measure overall progress along the Buddhist path, but the Tibetan groups that have clearly institutionalized stages through which their members pass show no indication of sharp gender differences. The survey showed no significant difference between the percentage of men and women who had finished the preliminary *ngondro* practices or those who had received special empowerments (*abhishekas*).

The only important difference involving meditation practice came from the Rochester Zen Center. Because this group has traditionally emphasized the importance of experiencing *kensho* (a mind-opening enlightenment experience), I asked its members if they had ever had such an experience and if its authenticity was confirmed by their teacher. I found that the men were significantly more likely than the women to say they had had a kensho experience (27 percent of the women compared to 55 percent of the men). Some might take this as evidence of greater determination or a more "samurai" goal orientation among male practitioners, but there are other plausible explanations as well. One possibility is that the "male ego" simply makes men more likely to interpret common meditation experiences as a kensho. That seems unlikely, however, since there was no significant difference in the percentage of men and women who reported that their kensho has been confirmed by their teacher, and by all accounts it is extremely difficult to deceive a Zen master on such matters. There is, however, another possibility. Although the difference was not statistically significant (isolating out the responses from the Rochester Center greatly reduced the sample size, thus making a finding of statistical significance considerably more difficult), the average male respondent reported being a member of the Rochester Center about three years longer than the average woman, which could account for some of this difference.

If their meditation practice and attitudes toward Buddhism are generally so similar, what are the important differences between men and women? The survey showed that, as in many other religious organizations, the majority of all the active members were women—about 57 percent. There was, however, a statistically significant difference in the gender ratio of the respondents from the different groups that were surveyed.[11] The two Vipassana groups and the one nonaffiliated group (whose practice and organization has more similarities to Vipassana than to the Zen or Tibetan groups) in the sample had the highest percentage of female members. Since the Vipassana groups are the least hierarchical and tend to draw more heavily upon the Western psychological tradition, this finding is very much in line with the expectations discussed above. The Rochester Zen Center was one of two groups in which male respondents outnumbered female (56/44 percent). Again, this finding is consistent with our expectations, since its style of practice is the most demanding and tightly organized of any of the groups studied. What was surprising, however, is that the Dzogchen Foundation had the highest percentage of male respondents (60 percent) and yet doesn't appear to have the characteristics we would associate with a "masculine" style of practice. The sample size for the Dzogchen Foundation was, however, unusually small. This finding appears to be a statistical anomaly, since Lama Surya Das, who heads the foundation, estimates that around 60 percent of his students are actually women.

Questions about basic Buddhist beliefs and doctrines brought out some modest gender differences. Large percentages of both women and men agreed that "what happens to us in this life is determined by the kind of karma we create" and that "after death we are reborn into another life." A much thinner majority agreed that "if I call on them, the Buddhas and bodhisattvas will help me with my problems." There were, however, clearly more skeptics among the men than the women on all three questions.

Another area in which women and men in the sample differed was in the reasons they gave for becoming involved with Buddhism. There were no significant differences in the percentages of males and females who said they were attracted to Buddhism by a desire for spiritual growth, but females were more likely to be attracted by people they had met who were involved in Buddhism (64 percent of the women and 51 percent of the men)[12] and they were also more likely to say they became involved in Buddhism to help them deal with some personal problem (75 percent of the women compared to 60 percent of the men).[13] Much larger gender differences were found concerning the influence of psychedelic drugs. Not only were men significantly more likely to have used a psychedelic drug, but the men who had used such drugs were also more likely to say that it helped stimulate their interest in Buddhism. Altogether 45 percent of the male respondents but only 22 percent of the females said that psychedelics encouraged their involvement in Buddhism.

Finally, there were some interesting demographic differences between male and female respondents. There wasn't much difference in average age, but there was a significant difference in their distribution. While the average age is right around forty-six for both sexes, males aged thirty-nine to forty-nine slightly outnumbered their female counterparts, while there were significantly more females in the younger and older age groups. The reason for this difference is not entirely clear, but it may be related to the use of psychedelic drugs and the counterculture that surrounded it. The only cohort in which the men outnumbered the women was among the baby boomers born directly after World War II—the generation that saw the growth of the hippie counterculture and the explosion in the use of psychedelic drugs. Government surveys of self-reported drug use showed a sharp decline in the use of psychedelic drugs during the mid 1980s and early 1990s, and younger men who came of age during this period also seem to be less interested in Buddhism. As we have seen, the use of psychedelic drugs was never as important a route into Buddhist practice among women, and their numbers do not drop off as rapidly among cohorts in which the use of those drugs is more rare.

These significant gender differences may tempt the reader to conclude that the survey data actually show a very marked distinction between the male and female respondents, but such an interpretation would be based on a misunderstanding of the meaning of *statistical* significance. Unlike everyday speech, in the realm of statistics "significance" means only that the odds are low that the differences a survey found between two groups were actually caused by a random error in the samples collected. In this case, it means that the odds are good that there actually was a difference between the women and men we questioned. But that doesn't tell us how *big* the difference was, and in fact most of the differences were not that large. There was, for example, a statistically significant difference between the percentages of men and women who agreed that "what happens to us in this life is determined by the karma we create," but the *strength* of that relationship was not very great. About 94 percent of the women and 90 percent of the men agreed with this statement; thus the vast majority of men and women hold the same opinion about this question.

Since there were no statistically significant differences on the majority of the variables we examined and in most cases where there was a difference its magnitude was relatively small, the overall picture that emerges is one of remarkable similarity between the genders. We should not, however, carry this conclusion too far. Surveys have their limits, and they are likely to be insensitive to more subtle difference in orientation. Because women and men pursue similar spiritual practices, express similar opinions about their effectiveness, and evaluate their Buddhist groups in similar ways does not mean there are no important differences in their needs and outlooks. Indeed, the differences the survey did reveal are very much what we would expect given the sharp gender distinctions drawn by our society. The men were more skeptical about basic Buddhist doctrines and were more likely to have experimented with illicit drugs, while the women were more likely to be attracted to Buddhism by personal relationships and the need to deal with individual problems.

Given the gender polarity of our society, it is not surprising that many of the larger centers now have special retreats for women that not only focus on the common problems they face in their practice but also encourage a sense of solidarity and community among female practitioners. Specialized retreats are now also being offered for other groups, such as gays and lesbians, Vietnam veterans, and those in the helping professions. Ultimately, enlightenment means seeing through dualistic thinking and identifications, including those based on gender, sexual orientation, or past experience. But that does not mean that we must all take the same path to reach that end.

Lust and Enlightenment

In one way or another, the issue of gender always seems to get entangled with the conundrum of human sexuality. Buddhism's attitudes toward sex, like its attitudes toward gender, are complex and contradictory. Indeed, few of the world's other major religions seem to have as wide a range of views on sexual passion. Depending upon the teacher one follows, lust is seen as everything from a vile defilement to the most direct path to complete enlightenment.

It is never possible to be sure if the statements attributed to the Buddha in the Pali Canon and other early scriptures are really his, since they were not set down in writing until centuries after his death. On the matter of sex, however, there is little doubt about his attitude. The Four Noble Truths—the bedrock of the Buddha's teaching—hold that suffering is caused by desire and that the way to end suffering is to end desire. Not surprisingly, sexual passion was high on the list of the desires to be uprooted. In one of the Buddha's earliest discourses, the Fire Sermon, he is held to have said that "all is burning . . . burning with the fire of passion, hate, and delusion. When the blaze of passion fades, one is liberated."[14] When his followers asked him about sexuality, the Buddha often told them that "there is no delight in passion; real delight is to be free of passion." This rejection of sexuality is reflected in the early Buddhist ideal of the arhat, who was seen as a kind of sexless saint who had completely transcended all physical need.

For most seekers, however, sexual passion was not something that simply fell away of its own as they gained spiritual maturity. It had to be fought. Spiritual seekers were told to abstain from all sexual contacts no matter how powerful the passion urging them on—an injunction that has bedeviled Buddhist monks and nuns from that time until this. In one of his most famous statements on the subject, the Buddha is said to have told a monk who was seduced by the wife he had left behind when he joined the sangha: "Oh misguided man, it is better for you to put your penis into the mouth of a hideous poisonous snake than into the body of a woman."

How were healthy young men and women supposed to maintain their celibacy? The first line of defense the Buddha recommended was to avoid the opposite sex. The Buddha warned his monks: "The one thing that enslaves a man above all else is a woman. Her form, her voice, her scent, her attractiveness, and her touch all beguile a man's heart. Stay away from them at all costs."[15] When a monk asked the Buddha how members of the order should act toward women, he replied, "Do not look at them."

"But what if we must look at them?" the monk asked.

The Buddha replied: "Don't speak to them."

"But what if we must speak to them?" he persisted.

"Keep wide awake," was the Buddha's final response.[16]

When monks were forced into contact with the opposite sex, the Buddha recommended that they look at every female as their mother, sister, or daughter, which, according to the Buddhist belief in rebirth, they probably had been in one lifetime or another. Finally, for his followers of a sensual temperament, the Buddha often recommended meditation upon a rotting corpse or the loathsomeness of the human body—a technique the Buddha himself apparently used. According to the legend, when the beautiful daughters of the demon Mara tried to seduce him away from his quest for enlightenment, the Buddha responded: "Beautiful you many seem, but from the crown of your heads to the soles of your feet you are nothing more than bags of skin filled with blood, pus, and filth."[17] The Buddha often sent his followers to the charnel grounds to meditate on the dead bodies they found there. The idea of merely going to look at a rotting corpse, much less meditating on it, seems rather strange to contemporary Westerners, but the practice was highly recommended not only to conquer sexual desire but as a firsthand lesson in the impermanence of life.

The Buddhist order didn't rely solely on the monks' own efforts to win their sexual struggle, however. There were also strict external restraints. The rules for the monastic order, known as the *Vinaya*, contain a detailed list of forbidden sexual behaviors and punishments for each. If a monk's penis, for example, entered any orifice of a human being (male or female) or animal, even if the penetration was only the depth of a sesame seed, it was grounds for expulsion. Masturbation was also forbidden, and nuns were specifically warned against the use of any kind of dildo. Responding to various cases of sexual impropriety, the Buddha first made it an offense to have any bodily contact with the opposite sex and then extended the rule to any improper contact with members of the same sex or with animals. Eventually, monks were prohibited from even being alone with the opposite sex or sleeping under the same roof with them.

With the development of Mahayana, new views of sexual passion were laid alongside the old. Most Mahayana monks still lived under the traditional *Vinaya* rules, and many Mahayana writers continued to express the same virulent antipathy toward sex. At the same time, however, some of the great Mahayana sutras began to challenge the spiritual superiority of the celibate monk. The heroes in these great Buddhist works began to include laypeople, women, and even youths and children. In one of the most popular of all Buddhist sutras, a family man named Vimalakirti confounds the monks with his great understanding, and a magical little girl transforms the great arhat, Sariputra, into a woman to show how unimportant gender is to the quest for enlightenment. The sutra even talks of women who intentionally became courtesans in order to lead their customers to the true dharma.

In China, the development of Ch'an/Zen took the Mahayana in a new direction. But, like many of their other attitudes, the classic Zen masters' approach to sex is a puzzling one to most contemporary Westerners. To judge by their written records, at least, they simply ignored the whole issue. With a few minor exceptions, the great koan collections said nothing about sex, and the same is true of most other Zen writings as well. Dogen Zenji's classic *Shobogenzo,* for example, provides a detailed discussion of Zen doctrine and practice, including everything from cooking to proper toilet procedure, but says virtually nothing about sex.

Although Zen masters did not dwell on the issue, down through the centuries the expectation was that Zen monks and priests should be celibate. In nineteenth-century Japan, however, the Meiji regime that was struggling to industrialize Japan and promote its state-supported version of the ancient Shinto religion, rescinded the rule of celibacy for Buddhist monks, apparently on the theory that family obligations would make them more susceptible to imperial influence. These changes obviously proved popular among the Japanese clergy, since the vast majority are now married men. Marriage also spread among the Buddhist clergy in Korea during the period of Japanese colonialism, but it touched off a bitter conflict with traditionalists who saw it as a form of cultural imperialism from their Japanese masters.

Even where celibacy was the expected norm, however, it was often ignored. The famous "Monk Dance" of Korea, for example, depicts a Buddhist monk as a sly sexual aggressor. Although it probably owes as much to the mudslinging of other religious groups as the monks themselves, Buddhist monastics do have a reputation of licentiousness throughout East Asia. There were also many famous Zen rebels who openly rejected sexual asceticism as a path to enlightenment and frequented taverns and brothels. One of the most famous of these was the Zen priest Ikkyu, who was reputed to have been the bastard son of the Japanese emperor:

> Follow the rule of celibacy blindly and you are not more than an ass.
> Break it and you are only human.
> The spirit of Zen is manifest in ways as countless as the sand of the Ganges.
> Every newborn is a fruit of the conjugal bond.
> For how many eons have the secret blossoms been budding and fading?[18]

Although this camp of Zen Buddhists included many unique and idiosyncratic individuals, in general they held sex to be no different from any other human activity; one should not be obsessed with either avoiding or pursuing it. As the head of one major Japanese monastery put it:

So many Buddhists believe that it is necessary to seclude oneself in the mountains in order to really practice Zen. That is a great error. One should be able to do Zen even in a brothel. Those who are agitated by sex should place the blame squarely on themselves and not accuse others of causing temptation. I have known plenty of courtesans who understood Zen better than most trainee monks.[19]

So in addition to Buddhism's original rejection of sexuality, the Mahayana added a second perspective: sexuality was simply one more part of life that did not necessarily inhibit or promote the quest for enlightenment. The third turning of the wheel of dharma that produced the Vajrayana schools now prominent in Tibet also produced a third view of sexuality. For the tantric revolutionaries who founded this school, sexual passion was neither a barrier to realization nor just one more part of life; it was a powerful tool that when properly used could propel seekers directly to enlightenment (or cause them immeasurable harm if misused). In fact, some tantric texts held that enlightenment *required* practice with a sexual consort and that the Buddha's enlightenment was actually due to the sexual bliss he had experienced with his wife. According to one tantra:

> The aspirant should strive for spiritual attainments
> With the mantra and consort
> Found on the secret path.
> The secret path without a consort
> Will not grant perfection to beings.
> Thus, attain enlightenment
> By applying oneself most diligently
> To the activities of erotic play.[20]

Real tantric sex, however, bears little resemblance to everyday lovemaking. Most contemporary books that claim to present the "secrets of tantric sex" are not really much different than traditional sex manuals, for they show little concern with the true objective of the tantras—what Miranda Shaw calls "passionate enlightenment." Tantric sex is a religious ritual and an intense practice of joint meditation. Practitioners visualize themselves and their consorts as deities who directly embody the principles of enlightenment. They worship each other and arouse their sexual passion by gazing at each other, by laughing together, by holding hands and touching, and eventually by sexual union. Through physical union, they combine their energies to reach the highest states of enlightened awareness and to realize what is called the merging of "emptiness and bliss." The theory of tantric yoga holds that the body is traversed by 72,000 channels through which flow subtle energies known as winds. The shared rituals, the intense concentration, and finally the union of the consorts intensifies this energy to excruciating levels until it shatters the egoistic obstructions to the free circulation of the winds, which are then drawn into the central channel (roughly following the spine), where they produce a profound state of enlightenment.

Even in Tibetan Buddhism, however, this kind of sexual yoga is still a relatively rare practice, considered suitable for only the most advanced practitioners. Less advanced monks are usually instructed to pursue this practice by merely visualizing a consort, and the tradition of celibacy is still a strong influence on Tibetan practice. The current Dalai Lama, for example, recently told a conference of Western Buddhist teachers that only those whose practice was so advanced that they had no sexual desire whatsoever and whose equanimity was so great that they would just as willingly drink a glass of urine as a glass of wine are qualified for sexual yoga with a consort. In response, the American scholar of Vajrayana Buddhism, Robert Thurman is reported to have quipped: "So what your Holiness is suggesting is some kind of a *taste* test." When asked to name any lamas he thought were at this level, the Dalai Lama admitted that he could not. Most members of the Tibetan hierarchy do not, however, take such a conservative posture. Since sexual yoga—along with most other high tantric practices—is expected to be kept secret, it is difficult to judge how widespread it actually is. For example, at the time of his death, Kalu Rinpoche, one of the most admired lamas of the twentieth century, was believed to be a celibate monk. But a book since published by his tantric consort has shown otherwise.

The Buddhist teachers who traveled to the West thus brought with them a wide range of attitudes toward sexuality and its place on the spiritual path. The first impulse of many teachers was simply to transplant the celibate monasticism that is central to most Asian Buddhism, but the West hasn't proven to be fertile ground for this approach. Strict Asian standards of modesty and decorum have traditionally kept a tight lid on the public expressions of sexuality, but the celibate who ventured out into

Western society was inevitably bombarded with every imaginable kind of sexual stimulation, from couples necking in the park to girls in skintight dresses and huge billboards of muscular young men showing off the latest underwear. In fact, the timing of Buddhism's arrival in the West could hardly have been worse for its tradition of celibacy. When Buddhism was taking root in the 1960s and 1970s, the sexual revolution was at its height and the whole movement of the culture was toward greater freedom, not greater restraint. The idea that sexual passion was a defilement to be up-rooted just didn't ring a responsive note with Westerners in the late twentieth century.

Many Buddhist groups nonetheless manage to maintain a small group of monastic celibates. But their numbers have remained low, and perhaps more importantly, their lifestyle never seems to elicit the kind of awe and respect it does in Asia. Temporary vows of celibacy during a period of re-treat or especially intense practice are another matter, however. It is rela-tively easy to convince Westerners that celibacy during such times is an effective way to reduce distractions and focus their efforts. Getting them to carry that practice over into everyday life has proven a much more daunting task.

This has led to a concern among some traditionalists that Westerners' distaste for celibacy makes their quest for enlightenment far more diffi-cult, if not completely impossible. Anyone who has tried to pursue an in-tensive Buddhist practice while raising a family knows firsthand the great difficulties involved. And many people, from athletes to Freudian psycho-analysts, believe that sexual energy that is not released can be channeled and redirected to provide the power necessary for other pursuits. On such grounds, many doubt that someone leading an active sex life can ad-vance spiritually as far or as fast as the celibate monks who devote all their energies to the quest for enlightenment. Tantric sexual practice, which intentionally arouses sexual energy and then turns it to spiritual purposes, would seem to offer a powerful alternative to celibacy, but this kind of high tantra remains extremely rare in the West, and for that matter in the East as well. Even among the respondents from the Tibetan-oriented groups in my survey, 86 percent said they had never practiced tantric sex, and the practice is undoubtedly far more rare among those pursuing other styles of Buddhist practice.

Although no major Buddhist groups in the West have promoted tantric sexual practices on a large scale, some groups certainly developed a wide-open sexual style during the 1960s and 1970s. One of the best-known examples was the sangha headed by Trungpa Rinpoche:

> In the early years of the sangha, there was a lot of groping for alternatives to monogamy. . . . Multiple sex partners, drinking, and wild parties characterized the tone of the Vajrayana community, which emanated from the leadership. If a husband or wife had an affair, the spouse was more or less expected to regard the triangle as a practice opportunity: a chance to be spacious and accommodating, and to work with the "neurosis" of jealousy by doing tonglen. Demands for sexual exclusiveness were not respected. It was understood when you went to Seminary that you would probably have an affair with at least one other Seminarian, whether either of you were married or not.[21]

In the decades since then, things have settled down considerably, even at the most liberal centers. The growing fear of AIDS, the conservative trend in Western culture, and the aging of the baby boomers seem to have promoted something of a counterrevolution against the forces of sexual liberation. Moreover, the series of crises and scandals involving the sexual behavior of several teachers provoked many members to undertake a searching reevaluation of their attitudes and behavior.

One of the most important outcomes of this process was a new emphasis on the five lay precepts that have traditionally served as Buddhist guideposts for proper behavior (no killing, stealing, sexual misconduct, lying, or intoxication). Growing numbers of Buddhist teachers are giving prominent attention to the importance of the precepts in both their public talks and in more informal settings as well. Many Buddhist groups now hold precept ceremonies in which members publicly affirm their commitment to attempt to live up to those principles.

But this interest in the traditional precepts has not been without its own problems. On the one hand, while the rules for monks were spelled out in minute detail, the lay precepts are rather general and vague. While that posed little problem in Asian cultures with a high degree of consensus about ethical issues, advising a contemporary Westerner to avoid "sexual misconduct" is likely to be far less helpful, since so many people disagree about what that means. On the other hand, when Buddhist teachers attempt to be more specific, as Thich Nhat Hanh has done, many people simply refuse to accept their interpretation; the result is to alienate those who follow divergent standards. Even during ceremonies in which members "take the precepts," some of the initiates pointedly decline to stand and accept one or more of the specific standards. A related problem lies in interpretation. The traditional understanding is that the precepts are something like signposts pointing in the right direction, not rigid commandments that mark the violator as a sinner. Yet with the pervasive influence of the Judeo-Christian tradition in Western culture, the precepts are inevitably transformed into just such commandments in the minds of many members—thus adding to the burden of guilt and the sense of inadequacy so many Asian teachers have commented about in their Western students.

It would, however, be a mistake to overemphasize the extent of the changes that have occurred in the last decade. Right from the start the extremes of celibacy and indulgence were always the exceptions, not the rule, in the West. It was the Japanese Zen teachers who were the most influential force in the early days of American Buddhism and, following the practice of their homeland, they were usually married men with families. With this kind of model, most Western Buddhists came to take a relatively neutral view of sex—as neither a great asset nor a great obstruction on the path of enlightenment—and to follow the conventional sexual ethics of their subculture. Thus, unlike the Judeo-Christian religions, Western Buddhist groups have not usually advocated a particular set of sexual standards such as premarital chastity or the condemnation of homosexuality. The one exception is provided by Thich Nhat Hanh's groups, whose interpretation of the precepts holds that sex should be restricted to those with a "committed relationship."

Gays, Lesbians, and the Buddha

Given the ringing condemnation voiced by so many conservative Christians, it is hardly surprising that Buddhism has had a particularly strong appeal among gays and lesbians searching for a spiritual path. There is not much in the way of quantitative data, however. My survey, for example, did not inquire about sexual orientation, but many Buddhist centers have earned a reputation for a friendly environment in the homosexual community.

One important reason for this is that the liberal, highly educated people who are attracted to Buddhism are among those who are least likely to harbor the antigay bigotry so common in our society. As Michael Hyman writes in an article on his experiences as a partner in a gay Buddhist couple:

Zen Centers tend to be populated by liberals who are mostly but not always free of deep sexual prejudice. . . . While there may be a wide spectrum of response to the arrival of a gay person on the scene, Buddhism does not orchestrate it. For gay Buddhist couples, beyond Vajradhatu and San Francisco, my experience has been one of normal welcome or ho-hum. We are still rather unusual entities, looked at quizzically by some, encouraged by others, openly rejected by very few, and certainly not in the name of Buddhism.[22]

The Buddhist scholar Jose Ignacio Cabezon came to similar conclusions about the tolerance of most Buddhist centers:

To my knowledge no North American Buddhist institution has ever marginalized its lay homosexual constituency, nor have any ever impeded the full participation of lay homosexual men and women by, for example, requiring their abstinence. To my knowledge, no gay Westerner has ever been denied Buddhist ordination because of his or her sexual orientation.[23]

Cabezon goes on to make the obvious point that many individual Buddhists nonetheless harbor antigay sentiments. For example, when the Buddhist review *Tricycle* published an interview with Jeffrey Hopkins on gay tantric sex, it turned out to be one of the most controversial pieces it had ever run, and the editors received more than fifty antigay letters from its presumably Buddhist readers. On the other hand, while it is certainly not part of their official doctrine, at least one Buddhist group, the Friends of the Western Buddhist Order, has been charged with actively promoting homosexuality among its male members.

What role has traditional Buddhist doctrine played in fostering an atmosphere of tolerance and respect? Although Asian cultures do not conceptionalize the division between "gay and straight" in quite the same way we do in the West, Buddhist doctrines imply to many that the division between heterosexual and homosexual, like the distinction between male and female, is merely one more dualism that needs to be transcended. If there is no abiding self, what importance can the intellectual structures we build our identities around really have? Buddhist doctrine has never, of course, existed in a cultural vacuum and, as in the case of gender, Buddhist institutions have often absorbed the prejudices of their social environment. From the earliest time, the code of monastic conduct prohibited all kinds of sexual behavior but drew little distinction between heterosexual and homosexual activities. For example, any monk who engaged in sexual intercourse was to be expelled from the order regardless of the gender of his or her partner. Although early Buddhism doesn't appear to have placed any special stigma on homosexual relations as such, it did pick up the popular prejudice against the *pandaka*—a group stigmatized not so much for their homosexuality as for their "lacking in maleness" and effeminacy, and for assuming the passive "feminine" role in intercourse. Although there are cases where pandaka in the order are treated tolerantly, the Buddha is also reported as saying that admitting pandakas into the order was not conducive to increasing the number of believers, and their ordination was banned.

As Buddhism spread throughout the rest of Asia, its attitudes toward homosexuality remained pretty much the same. The interpretation of the third precept forbidding laypeople from engaging in "sexual misconduct" was generally determined by the vagaries of local culture. All ordained monks, however, were forbidden from engaging in any kind of sexual relations, whether heterosexual or homosexual. Given their strict gender segregation, reports indicating that homosexual activities were nonetheless common in many monasteries are not surprising. In Japan, the Esoteric (*Shingon*) School of Buddhism even became associated with the medieval samurai idealization of sexual love between men and boys. But in general, the Asian Buddhist attitude toward homosexuality has ranged from neutrality to mild aversion.

The current Dalai Lama, who heads the sexually conservative Gelupa sect of Tibetan Buddhism, is certainly the world's most prominent Buddhist leader today, and he seems to have expressed both viewpoints, which has caused considerable confusion among gay Buddhists in the West. In a special meeting with gay and lesbian leaders in San Francisco on June 11, 1997, the Dalai Lama forcefully rejected all forms of discrimination. "Discrimination is very sad. . . . It is wrong for society to reject people on the basis of their sexual orientation. Your movement to gain full human rights is reasonable and logical . . . and there is no harm in mutually agreeable sexual acts."[24]

At the same time, however, the Dalai Lama went on to reiterate the doctrine traditionally accepted by the Gelupas, which derives from the first-century Indian scholar Ashvaghosha. It asserts that for Buddhists sexual misconduct is determined by "inappropriate partner, organ, time, and place" regardless of one's sexual orientation. While this may sound neutral toward sexual orientation, the forbidden organs include the mouth, anus, and "using one's hand," and the inappropriate partners include men for men and women for women. The Dalai Lama went on to say that no one could be excluded from the Buddhist sangha for breaking this precept and that sexual expression, whether homosexual or heterosexual, was preferable to harming oneself or another from pent-up sexual frustration. His remarks have nonetheless raised concern among liberal Western Buddhists, perhaps in part because he is often mistakenly seen as a kind of Buddhist pope. But as he pointed out in those meetings, the Dalai Lama has no special power to issue edicts or change Buddhist doctrine. Such reforms can only come from discussion and consensus building among the sangha. Moreover, other Tibetan leaders, such as Dudjom Rinpoche, the head of the Nyingma lineage until his death in 1987, apparently did not see homosexuality in terms of sexual misconduct at all.

In the Western world—with its large gay community stalked by the AIDS epidemic and struggling for social acceptance—something more than passive tolerance seems to be required. It is not surprising that the San Francisco Zen Center was one of the first Buddhist organizations in the West to actively reach out to the gay community. In 1980, several gay men who had been practicing with the SFZC ran an advertisement in a local gay newspaper and created the Gay Buddhist Club, which was eventually renamed Maitri—the Buddhist word for friendliness. One of the early members was Issan Dorsey, a former drag queen, junkie, and hooker who had become a Zen priest. At the time, Dorsey was the director of SFZC's city center, and he put its resources at the disposal of the group. "At first we'd just sit around and smoke cigarettes and complain about how hard it was to practice and be gay. Gradually, we began to meditate for a while before our discussions, and pretty soon there was a Buddha and incense and flowers."[25] A few members of the group began to sit zazen regularly in the basement of their house at 57 Hartford Street near the heart of San Francisco's famous Castro gay district. After some serious ups and downs, the house evolved into the Hartford Street Zen Center with Dorsey as its abbot. Located at the virtual epicenter of the AIDS epidemic, Dorsey tenaciously struggled to create the Maitri Hospice for dying AIDS patients, where he himself succumbed to the disease in 1990.

Some Buddhist centers now have special retreats for their gay members. The Spirit Rock Center, for example, hosts a yearly retreat for gay men, one for lesbian women, and a third for both. Nondenominational groups such as the Bay Area's Gay Buddhist Fellowship and the smaller lesbian group, Dharma Sisters, provide support and encouragement to gay and lesbian practitioners.

Some Western Buddhists have expressed concern about the fragmentation of the sangha that may result from the formation of such "identity-oriented" groups. From the liberal perspective so dominant in Western Buddhism, people are people. Whether straight or gay, rich or poor, male or female, they need to learn to get along together. But many gays and lesbians argue that they have special needs that only they can meet for each other. For example, Kobai Scott Whitney writes:

> If gay people organize to practice Buddhism together, it is not because we desire separation from mainstream Buddhism, but rather because we need the opportunity to share with, and encourage, one another. . . . Any group which has been oppressed by a dominant culture feels powerless. The first step out of powerlessness is to organize the individuals who have experienced the oppression. They can then begin to heal themselves, first by sharing their experiences with each other, and later, by feeling the power they *do* have as a group.[26]

Buddhism in Crisis

The 1980s were a time of crisis in Western Buddhism, as one center after another exploded in acrimonious disputes about the conduct of their teachers. Although the troubles that rocked so many Buddhist centers have frequently been described as sex scandals, power was often as close to the heart of those conflicts as sex. Some revelation about a teacher's sexual behavior usually provided the spark that set off these explosions, but it was the huge inequality in power between teachers and students that gave those sexual contacts such an enormous potential for abuse. Moreover, the misuse of power was seldom limited to sexual matters. Allegations of hypocrisy and deception were as much at issue as the teacher's sex life, and other concerns, such as money and alcohol, were often thrown into the mixture as well.

The upheaval that resulted in the ouster of Richard Baker as the abbot of the San Francisco Zen Center was the first crisis of the 1980s, and it provides a good illustration of how power, money, and sex combined to create problems in the American sangha. Suzuki Roshi, the founder of the San Francisco Zen Center, was a warm straightforward man, but his successor, although charming and well-spoken, was more aloof and cool. A natural leader, Baker attracted a diverse group of creative and powerful people around him from Gary Snyder, the Beat poet, to Jerry Brown, who was then the governor of California. Under Baker's stewardship, the Zen Center grew at a frenetic pace. In fifteen years, it went from an annual budget of $6,000 to $4 million. It acquired property worth somewhere around $20 million and built up a network of affiliated businesses staffed by Zen Center students, which included a hip vegetarian restaurant, a bakery, and a grocery store. Although no one ever accused Baker of amassing a personal fortune at Zen Center's expense, he did live a life of comfort and elegance that stood in stark contrast to the austerity expected of his students. His salary was modest, but Baker traveled extensively, entertained visiting dignitaries in high style, and was even provided a luxurious BMW for commuting and chauffeuring around important visitors. As time went on, Baker became less and less available to help students with their spiritual practice, and resentment mounted over what was perceived as his extravagance. The spark that set off the growing discontent was an affair Baker had with the wife of an influential member of the sangha. As the news of his indiscretion spread, the community split into pro- and anti-Baker factions, and reports began to surface about other affairs Baker had had. The key issue seemed not so much to be that these relationships were abusive but that he concealed them from the sangha. And perhaps more importantly they did not fit the lifestyle the community expected from a spiritual master. After months of conflict, the Zen center's board of directors forced Baker to resign.

This crisis was something of a coming of age for the San Francisco Zen Center. Membership plummeted as many of the students who sided with

Baker walked out. Others became so disillusioned that they left Buddhism altogether. There was a pervasive feeling of confusion and loss—much like a family that had just gone through a divorce. Zen center members turned to professional "facilitators" to help them through the crisis. They learned that, like a dysfunctional family, they had become experts at denial and concealment, and they needed to make the Zen center more open and more democratic. Numerous Zen center businesses were spun off and basic changes in organizational structure were made. The board of directors was shifted from an appointed body to one democratically elected by the members of the Zen center. In the biggest break with tradition yet, the abbot is now appointed to a four-year term with a fixed limit on the number of reappointments.

Three years later this new organizational structure was tested by a different kind of leadership crisis when Reb Anderson, who was then abbot, was held up at knifepoint while jogging near SFZC's downtown center. Instead of responding with Buddhist equanimity, Anderson returned to the center, retrieved a gun he had taken from a suicide victim years before, and roared off in hot pursuit. He spotted a man he believed to be his attacker outside a nearby housing project and chased him inside, while shocked neighbors called the police. "Zen Master Gets in Trouble for Pulling Dead Man's Gun" was the way the headline in the *San Francisco Chronicle* read, and the Zen center was once again in the midst of a crisis. Anderson offered to resign, but the board only requested he take a six-month leave of absence and brought in Mel Weitzman—the respected abbot of the Berkeley Zen Center and long-term student of Suzuki Roshi—to share administrative and religious responsibilities as "co-abbot." The multiple abbot arrangement worked out so well that the center continued it after both Anderson and Weitzman reached their term limits. The San Francisco Zen Center once again seems to be flourishing.

After the explosion in San Francisco, similar crises swept through one center after another. Four hundred miles to the south, the Zen Center of Los Angeles was soon embroiled in turmoil over the conduct of its Roshi, Taizan Maezumi. Unlike Baker, Maezumi Roshi was not an American dharma heir, but an Asian who had founded the center and led it since its inception. Once again, the scandal concerned allegations of sexual affairs between the Roshi and his students. This time, however, the mix was not sex and money but sex and alcohol, for once the sexual allegations became public many of the Roshi's students also began to voice concern about their teacher's drinking. Although Maezumi Roshi continued to lead the center until his death in 1995, he did openly admit his alcoholism and agreed to enter a treatment program. Numerous students left during the upheaval, and it even looked for a time that financial problems might force the Zen Center of Los Angeles to close its doors. Like the San Francisco Zen Center, the Los Angeles center brought in outside counselors to help them handle their crisis and instituted structural reforms to help deal with future problems. The community survived and seems to have learned from its experience. In the late 1990s, when Maezumi Roshi's successor was alleged to have made unwanted sexual advances toward a student after a sesshin (the intensive seven-day meditation retreat practiced at most Zen centers), he was quickly removed from office.

One by one allegations surfaced about other Asian teachers, including a supposedly celibate Vipassana teacher who was leading a retreat at the Insight Meditation Center in Barre and several other Japanese Zen masters. One of the most important teachers to be affected was Soen Sa Nim, the Korean Zen master who admitted to having long-term affairs with two of his senior students while claiming to be a celibate monk. Many of his students felt betrayed when they found out the truth, and his network of American centers was plunged into the same kind of crisis that occurred in the San Francisco and Los Angeles Zen Centers. The Kwan Um School did not undertake the kind of structural reforms pursued by the other two Zen centers, and Soen Sa Nim is still very much its undisputed spiritual and administrative leader. As the crisis abated, these centers turned their efforts toward finding new members in the outside community. Today, total membership in the Kwan Um School is once again on the rise, but most of the new members are now nonresidents. Some centers have even shut down their residential programs.

Perhaps not surprisingly, the biggest crisis in all of Western Buddhism struck in Chogyam Trungpa's sangha. Trungpa's behavior would certainly have scandalized most other sanghas. He was driven around in a chauffeured Mercedes and had numerous servants. Although he was a married man with children, he had sexual encounters with many of his students. He was also a heavy drinker. He would sometimes deliver his lectures with a glass of sake in his hand and even have to be helped from the stage at the end. Alcoholism is widely credited with causing his death at age forty-seven. Yet Trungpa was never hypocritical about his behavior. In fact, he explicitly taught the "crazy wisdom" of using even the most out-rageous behavior as part of the spiritual path. As one long-term student put it, "His method of practicing Vajrayana was to drink the poison—to take on the actions of *samsara* (the unenlightened world of desire and attachment) and bring them under the power of enlightened mind."[27] Trungpa always warned his students against rushing into the tantras, and he pointed out on many occasions that "drinking the poisons" was a highly dangerous endeavor.

Probably as a result of this openness, no scandals like the ones at other centers ever erupted during Trungpa's life. Students either accepted Trungpa's lifestyle and that of his senior students or went elsewhere. Trungpa's successor, Osel Tendzin, was not as fortunate, however. Tendzin took over leadership of the Vajradhatu community in April 1987 and continued the hard drinking and wide-open sexuality of his teacher. Less than two years later, a scandal exploded that literally tore the community apart. In December 1988, the Vajradhatu administration told their mem-bers that the Regent, as Tendzin was called, had known he was infected with the AIDS virus for nearly three years and that except for some months of celibacy he had neither protected his sexual partners nor told them the truth. It eventually came out that the Vajradhatu board of directors itself had known of the problem for more than two years and done nothing about it. The Regent had apparently passed on the virus to a young man in his twenties who in turn infected his girlfriend. When Rick Fields, a historian of Western Buddhism and long-time Vajradhatu student, asked Tendzin what had happened, he answered: "I was fooling myself. . . . Thinking I had some extraordinary means of protection I went ahead with my business as if something would take care of it for me."[28]

This announcement split the Vajradhatu community right down the middle. Although many members demanded Tendzin's resignation, he re-fused to step down, saying that "to withdraw would violate the oath I took with my guru, and it would also violate my heart." The board of directors consulted Tibetan elders in Nepal and India, who suggested a traditional Tibetan solution: the Regent should go into retreat. Tendzin and a num-ber of his students did go into retreat in Ojai, California, but he refused the board's request to give up teaching and continued to act as both spir-itual and administrative head of Vajradhatu. A bitter power struggle raged on for months and the community seemed on the verge of disintegration. Finally both sides sent delegations back to Asia, and senior lamas recommended that Tendzin go into a strict retreat for a year. Tendzin complied, keeping his nominal authority but giving up his teaching and administrative roles. He died while still in retreat on August 26, 1991. The next day, Trungpa's eldest son, Osel Mukpo, was appointed the new spiritual leader of Vajradhatu.

The latest scandal in Western Buddhism was touched off by a 1997 article in the *Guardian* newspaper that was followed by an anonymous seventy-page document, *The FWBO Files,* posted on the Internet. The most serious allegations centered around activities in the FWBO's Croydon Centre in the late 1980s, where it was claimed that some FWBO members were coerced into homosexual activities and that one man killed himself as a result. The center's head was accused of pressuring other men at the center into having sex, using a corrupted version of Buddhist doctrine. (All FWBO centers are sex segregated and Croydon admitted only men.) The idea was that spiritual friendships are essential to spiritual development and that they could be inhibited by the fear of homosexuality among men. So the only way to overcome that fear was to actually engage in homosexual activities. In defense of the FWBO, one of the original twelve members ordained by Sangharakshita in 1968 told one reporter that

> what happened in Croydon was an aspect of certain attitudes around in the FWBO, but taken to an extreme. In Padmaloka, you had a lot of people who were gay. It did get a bit out of hand and it got disbanded in 1989. But I've never heard of anything unethical going on there. It was just a rather tangled sexual mess.[29]

So far almost all of the scandals have centered around male teachers. We don't know if women will fall victim to the same problems as they move into top positions of power, but we do know that at least one has. A quarter Dutch, a quarter Jewish, and half Italian, Alyce Zeoli was born in Brooklyn. With little or no contact with organized Buddhism, she developed into a powerful teacher and was eventually recognized as a tulku by Penor Rinpoche. She took the name Jetsunma Ahkon Lhamo and built up a large following. Like some of her male counterparts, she also took on a series of younger "consorts," most of whom were her students. She lives a luxurious lifestyle and some charged that over half her center's budget went to her salary and clothing expenses. One of her students even had her arrested for assaulting her in a fit of anger.

THE SEXUAL CONUNDRUM   Although Western Buddhism was shocked to discover that its disciplined pursuit of spiritual enlightenment did not exempt it from the same kind of problems experienced by the government, corporations, schools, and churches, there is at least some solace in the fact that it was not alone in its struggle to deal with the primordial sexual impulse in an ambivalent and rapidly changing society. Amid the confusion and reevaluation, two questions arose again and again: "Why would an enlightened spiritual master have sex with a student?" and "When is that a problem?"

Although idealistic Western students often believe that a Zen master or lama has transcended all physical needs and acts only for the good of all, that degree of realization is extremely rare. Even Buddhist teachers with considerable enlightened self-awareness have the same impulses as the rest of us, and their behavior can often be attributed to the same causes. The head of a flourishing Buddhist organization, like a popular entertainer or the CEO of a successful corporation, is constantly surrounded by an admiring group of followers. Thus on one level, teachers have sex with their students because the students are attractive and available. Indeed, many students are the ones who instigate the sexual contact. Moreover, the demands on the head teachers in large Buddhist organizations are enormous, and they often have little time to cultivate friendships on the outside. If a teacher is going to start a new relationship or have a casual affair, his or her students are often the only available candidates.

The role of the teacher is a very isolating one in another way as well. Although admired and respected, the teacher can never be "one of the guys." He or she is always set off, different, special. Not only do teachers have tremendous power over the lives of students (a circumstance that hardly promotes friendship and easy camaraderie), but they are expected to be a living example of the fruits of the Buddha's teaching. Given such heavy expectations, a sexual affair with an admiring student can be one of the few ways to break through those feelings of isolation and establish deeper human contact. That same isolation can also lead teachers to harbor an unrealistic view of their actions and their potential impact on their students and the wider community. For example, Soen Sa Nim denied any personal motivation in carrying on affairs with those two senior students, claiming that he was only trying to strengthen them and their role in the community. Osel Tendzin presented a far more extreme example of self-deception. He apparently believed that his spiritual powers were so great that they would actually prevent him from transmitting AIDS to his sexual partners.

All these pressures are, moreover, likely to be intensified for the Asian teachers, who must cope with an alien culture they often don't fully understand. The sexes mix openly here, and women are far freer in their style of dress and in their sexual behavior. To judge by external signs, one might well believe that Westerners have a free, uninhibited attitude toward sex and not realize the deep cultural neurosis that often lies beneath the surface. As one of Trungpa's most insightful students, Judith Simmer-Brown noted, students are often very interested in sex with their teacher but feel betrayed if it actually happens. Many Asian teachers probably did not understand the psychological consequences a sexual encounter might have for a student who appears so sexually liberated.

From the student's standpoint, it isn't hard to see why the teacher is an attractive object. For one thing, the teacher is often so idealized that he or she might well seem like an almost perfect sexual and emotional partner. For another, teachers are enormously powerful figures in the Buddhist community in general and especially in their own group. Not only is that kind of power extremely attractive to many people, but the teacher has the ability to give a favored student all manner of rewards. The most important of these is often just time and attention, for within these communities there is often intense competition to win the teacher's favor. A student is likely to gain in status and authority within the group from a "special" relationship to the teacher. Finally, the student–teacher relationship is uniquely deep and intimate. As Judith Simmer-Brown put it: "The relationship with one's teacher is profound, groundless, and naked, whether or not it is a sexual relationship; it can be insulting, intimidating, gratifying, but it is always intimate."[30] It is easy to see how the kind of deep communication that occurs in these relationships can lead to physical intimacy as well.

On the other hand, of course, there are strong taboos and social restraints on this kind of relationship, and it is difficult to judge how frequently sexual contacts between Buddhist teachers and students have actually occurred. The number of scandals that broke in the 1980s and the numerous rumors that circulate through the Buddhist community tend to indicate that they have been quite common indeed, and the one piece of qualitative data we have supports that conclusion. In 1985 the influential Vipassana teacher Jack Kornfield published the results of his informal survey of fifty-four spiritual teachers, which included Buddhists, Hindus, and Jains. Of those, fifteen said they were celibate, but thirty-four of the remaining thirty-nine teachers said that they had had a sexual relationship with one of more of their students.[31] Although this survey was not based on a random sample, the fact that such a high percentage of teachers admitted having sex with their students is certainly an important finding. It does, however, seem possible that the structural reforms and the growing public attention this issue has received in the last decade may have changed things since the 1980s.

Given the fact that sexual relationships between students and teachers appear to be relatively common, the question of when and if they are really a problem has become one of the hottest issues in Western Buddhism. On one side are those who argue that they are not a problem at all. As we have seen, Buddhist groups draw their membership from the most liberal segments of Western society, which generally accept sexuality as a normal part of a healthy life, and Buddhism itself has never considered sex sinful in the way Western religions often do. After all, those in this camp argue, this is sex between two consenting adults. By what right does someone outside the relationship step in and judge it, especially when one of the participants is a Buddhist master whose realization may make many aspects of his or her behavior incomprehensible to others? Defenders of these relationships also point to successful marriages between some teachers and their students and argue that a complete prohibition on this kind of behavior would tend to make the social isolation of Buddhist teachers even greater than it already is. At the other extreme are those such as psychologist Peter Rutter who argue that a sexual relationship in which there is a great imbalance in power between the two partners—whether it is between a boss and a secretary, a therapist and a patient, or a spiritual teacher and a student—is always unethical and damaging to the weaker party.

As usual, the truth seems to lie somewhere between the two extremes. In addition to surveying spiritual teachers, Jack Kornfield also spoke to many students who had been sexually involved with their teachers. He found that about half reported that their relationship had undermined their practice, their relationship with their teacher, or their feelings of self-worth, and about half said it had not. Certainly, the enormous imbalance in power between the revered teacher and the aspiring student creates enormous potential for abuse, but it does not have to occur.

One obvious kind of problem occurs when unscrupulous teachers use their positions to pressure a student into an unwanted relationship. More subtly, the teacher may encourage or at least ignore false and unrealistic expectations about the benefits a sexual relationship might bring. Miranda Shaw reports that while she was researching her book on women in Tantric Buddhism, several Tibetan lamas approached her with offers of a "tantric sexual relationship" when in fact they actually knew little or nothing about those practices. A former student at the San Francisco Zen Center told one writer that "until he [her teacher] began to relate sexually to me, he had been the most important man I'd ever met, a wonderful teacher. . . . I very much hoped that by breaking through to the forbidden area I would somehow, magically break through to all that was held frozen and paralyzed within me." But as "soon as we became sexually involved, any possibility of real spiritual intimacy with him ended. . . . It felt like incest to me—it was very physically unrewarding, and after every time, I would feel just destroyed.[32] In addition to having such unrealistic expectations, many of the seekers attracted to Buddhism are, as Lama Surya Das points out, very psychologically vulnerable.

In fact, vulnerability and openness are in some sense essential to the practice relationship between Buddhist teachers and students, which is even closer than that between a priest and parishioner. The nearest analogy in traditional Western culture is probably that of the therapist and client. Psychologists have long recognized the phenomena of transference and countertransference in which the patient develops a powerful attraction based on an idealized image of the therapist, and the therapist develops a corresponding attraction to the open, needy patient. Having sexual relations with patients has, of course, long been considered grounds for disciplinary action and may result in the revocation of a therapist's license. Although psychiatric patients are likely to be uniquely vulnerable, the same crises that drive some people into therapy drive others to seek out spiritual mentors, and the same dangers exist.

In seeking to understand the impact of these relationships, we need to keep in mind the fact that they usually occur in the context of a tightly knit community that has grown up around a particular teacher. Students who are sexually involved with the teacher may well see their special access and responsibilities as a source of added status in the group. On the other hand, however, if they are expected to hide the relationship, the secrecy and deception may place them under intense psychological stress. And if the secrets do come to light it can have explosive effects on the community itself. Since the teacher is seen as a living exemplar of the goals of Buddhist practice, his misbehavior may weaken some students' faith in the whole Buddhist path.

Despite all these problems, the fact is that many teachers and students have carried on nonexploitative and mutually fulfilling relationships. Jan Chozen Bays, a pediatrician who now heads a Zen group of her own, gave the following description of her long-term affair with Maezumi Roshi of the Zen Center of Los Angeles:

> To me the sexual aspect of it was very minor, and Roshi would say the same thing too, if you talked to him. It really was almost *fusing* with another person. It's very difficult to explain. Most people see the relationship as a traditional "affair" and it certainly has aspects of that—you know everybody wants to be loved and part of your expression of that love is physical—but that was really a minor part of it. I was becoming so close to this person that I really was fused with him in a way that my identity was submerged. That's part of Dharma transmission, to become one with your teacher so that you can see through their eyes. . . . There is a real danger of trying to make a relationship more than it is. You know, to say this was a sacred relationship or a mysterious relationship or a mystic relationship—somehow to justify a relationship on that basis. I don't mean to do that. But it was a very profound, very special relationship. And it taught me a lot about love.[33]

POWER AND COMMUNITY   Although allegations about a teacher's sexual behavior often provided the spark that touched off the explosions in these Buddhist communities, other powerful conflicts were already simmering beneath the surface. Indeed, the split in the Rochester Zen Center that occurred when Toni Packer left involved the same dynamics as the incidents discussed above, but in that case there were no sexual issues at all. The Buddhist centers that sprang up in the West were, after all, a kind of radical sociological experiment unlike anything seen in Asia, so it isn't surprising that this period of creative growth was marked by upheavals and conflict.

Some of the thorniest issues involve power and authority. Most Western centers were started by charismatic Asian teachers who brought their Asian ideas about deference to authority with them. The teacher set up the center, did the teaching, explained the tradition, made the decisions, and controlled the money. His word (this generation of teachers was virtually all male), as the expression goes, was law. The ideal of democratic governance so deeply rooted in Western culture simply had no relevance. Even centers that have Western leaders and elected boards of directors recognize that no matter how they are organized, when push comes to shove, the teacher's authority must be respected or he or she should be replaced by someone else they do respect.

When these centers were first formed, students unquestioningly followed the teachers, who were struggling to bring Buddha dharma to the West. For most nonresident members, the question of the teacher's power never became much of an issue, although sexual misconduct or alcohol abuse were more likely to arouse their concern. For the residents of these centers, things were quite different, however. The community became their home, their family, their primary group, and often their employer as well. The teacher's authority inevitably extended well beyond spiritual matters into their routine everyday lives. As the pressures of communal living and their relative poverty mounted up, some students felt frustrated and trapped. Although her sentiments are certainly more extreme than most, one student of Soen Sa Nim gave voice to those frustrations in an interview with Sandy Boucher:

> The people who are in charge, none of *them* has really questioned Soen Sa Nim. If you live in these communities for years, it's not just how you feel about your teacher, it's your home, it's all your friends, it's where you're raising your kids—do you have enough independence in your own life to move, give up your job, your community? It's like you give up everything! . . . It's fascistic. And Soen Sa Nim is a dictator. . . . there is an inherent lack of democracy, where power comes from the top down, where decisions are often made in secret without a genuine process of consultation with the group as a whole.[34]

These residential communities have often been compared to a dysfunctional family. Most of the students have a strong psychological investment in an idealized image of the teacher as an enlightened master; after all, that makes them rather special too. When problems crop up, the usual response from the community and especially from its senior students is denial and cover-up, and that in turn often aggravates the problem. As Jan Chozen Bays said of Maezumi Roshi's drinking: "We in subtle ways encouraged his alcoholism. We thought it was enlightened behavior that when he would drink, elements of Roshi would come out that we had never seen before. He would become piercingly honest. People would deliberately go—everybody did this—and see what he would say and do when he was drunk, and how he could skewer you against the wall."[35] Most of the explosions in Western Buddhist centers not only involved an allegation of misconduct by the teacher but an ongoing cover-up by his or her closest followers that ultimately left those outside the inner circle feeling manipulated and abused.

Regardless of the teacher's behavior, however, the long-term residents of these centers often face mounting difficulties as the years add up. Most residents live very modest lifestyles—small rooms (sometimes shared with other people), lack of privacy, long hours, and low pay. So it was bound to create jealousy and resentment when a teacher like Baker Roshi or Trungpa Rinpoche lived a luxurious life that included personal servants and chauffeured limousines. But an even more fundamental problem was that long-term residents often found themselves at a kind of social dead end. When they first move in, many of them undoubtedly harbor secret fantasies of someday becoming a great teacher themselves. But only a few turn out to be gifted teachers, and for the rest there is simply no clear career path available. In Asia things are completely different. In Japan, for example, after a few years of training in a monastery, a monk usually moves out to head up a village temple. But in the West there are no local temples, and even many very advanced students seem to have no place to go when their years of training are complete. So although a crisis involving their teacher's conduct precipitated the exodus of many residents from these centers, there were many underlying causes as well.

THE RESPONSE   Institutionalized Buddhism is a new phenomenon in the West, and these crises marked an important turning point in its development. Perhaps their most significant result has been the growth of a new sense of honesty and realism in the Buddhist community. It seems likely that the charismatic spiritual teacher will always be a central feature of Western Buddhism, but there is a growing recognition that, as Jack Kornfield has often pointed out, it is possible to be highly developed in some aspects of one's spiritual life and still be neurotic or immature in others. Complete realization is rare indeed, and the actions of even the greatest teachers must be questioned when they appear wrong. Of course, it takes great courage to stand up and challenge a powerful and revered teacher, but those raised in the individualistic culture of Western democracy seem to be uniquely suited to the task.

The highly decentralized nature of Buddhist institutions in the West makes it more difficult to sanction powerful teachers who abuse their position, but it also promotes a cornucopia of competing options and directions for informed students to pursue. Before these scandals broke, teachers' failings tended to be guarded like family secrets. While denial and cover-up is still the first response of many communities, it is becoming harder and harder to carry off successfully.

As a result of these crises, some of the larger Buddhist centers have carried out significant structural reforms. As we have seen, the board of directors in such places as the San Francisco and Rochester Zen Centers are now elected by the members instead of appointed by the teacher. Another crucial change is that most of the larger centers now have a number of respected teachers, which serves as a natural counterbalance to the abuse of power by any single individual. It is obviously easier to remove an unpopular teacher when there are other qualified people to take his or her place. Some centers now have a "teachers committee" that makes decisions which would formerly have been made by a single charismatic individual. While all the teachers at a center can be expected to have a natural desire to protect their organization from unfavorable publicity, it is hardly in their interest to cover up the misdeeds of one of their colleagues, especially since they are in a sense competitors for the allegiance and respect of the same students.

Many of the larger centers have also created official codes of ethics and formal procedures for handling complaints. In most cases, these codes are modern interpretations of the traditional Buddhist precepts, which proscribe such things as killing, stealing, false speech, and sexual misconduct. The codes used by both the San Francisco Zen Center and the Insight Meditation teachers (which includes the two main Vipassana centers in North America at Spirit Rock, California, and Barre, Massachusetts) expressly forbid all sexual relations between teachers and students. If a student and teacher wish to become physically involved, they are required to terminate their student–teacher relationship and wait a specified period of time (three months for the Insight Meditation teachers and six months at SFZC). In addition, married Insight Meditation teachers are instructed to refrain from any "adulterous relationship" whatsoever. Although the selection procedures vary, many centers have also established ethics committees to hear complaints and resolve disputes.

Another kind of response to these problems has developed out of the growing contacts among Western Buddhists from different organizations, lineages, and traditions. A symposium dealing with these issues entitled Sex, Power, and Buddha Nature was held in 1990, and in March 1993 the Western Buddhist Teachers Network, an association of Western teachers, held a ten-day conference with the Dalai Lama in Dharmsala, India, at which the issue of sexual misbehavior by Buddhist teachers was given considerable attention. The conference was organized by the prominent American lama Surya Das and was attended by such influential teachers as Jack Kornfield and Bodhin Kjolhede. Another of the attendees, Buddhist philosopher Stephen Batchelor, prepared an open letter to the Buddhist community that was signed by all the Western teachers. It laid down a code of conduct for teachers in the West and stated among other things that students should not hesitate to publicize any unethical behavior of which there is irrefutable evidence and that no person can stand above the norms of ethical conduct. Although the Dalai Lama originally expressed his support for the letter, it ultimately failed to win his official imprimatur. Later that year, the Spirit Rock Center hosted the Network's teacher conference on the art of teaching, which unexpectedly became a forum for expressing the pain and grief that many of the participants had experienced as a result of their sexual relations with their teachers.

As a result of the increasingly open examination of this problem, informal networks of teachers and senior students formed to deal with complaints and problems that individual centers have failed to resolve. The Buddhist Peace Fellowship, a broadly based organization advocating the principles of engaged Buddhism, became a kind of informal clearinghouse for such allegations after it was listed as a resource for the victims of sexual harassment in an influential book, Sex in the Forbidden Zone, by Peter Rutter. Alan Senauke, the Zen priest who is the current director of the fellowship, estimates that they now receive five to ten complaints of various sorts a year.

Although the Buddhist Peace Fellowship generally tries to work behind the scenes to create a cooperative resolution of individual problems, there is public evidence of the growing strength of this new movement to oppose student/teacher sexual relations. In November of 1994, a woman identified only as Janice Doe brought a $10 million suit for sexual harassment against a prominent Tibetan teacher, Sogyal Rinpoche, the author of the bestselling book *The Tibetan Book of Living and Dying*. She was encouraged to bring the case by a number of Western Buddhist teachers who saw it, as her lawyer put it, as a way "to prevent future abuse." Sogyal Rinpoche's supporters, on the other hand, saw the case as an effort by jealous Western teachers to discredit an Asian teacher who outshines them. As Robert Thurman, the eminent scholar of Tibetan Buddhism, put it: "There is a group of Western Buddhist teachers who feel they should now be honored and respected themselves as teachers, and who represent a very puritanical tendency. I think they're envious of Asian teachers who maybe misbehave a little bit around the edges, but who are more respected than they are. I'm not saying there is a conspiracy. But there are certainly people who have been abetting this attack."[36] Whether these actions are a conspiracy or a defense of the Dharma is, of course, very much in the eye of the beholder, as are one's conclusions about the appropriateness of the civil courts as a forum for settling this kind of dispute. Although the charges against Sogyal Rinpoche generated a great deal of controversy in the Buddhist community, they were ultimately resolved quietly in an out-of-court settlement for an undisclosed sum of money.

Summing Up

Much of this story of sex and power in Western Buddhism can be read as part of the adaptation of Asian Buddhism to the West. Buddhism entered the West during a time of growing spiritual thirst, but Western society lacked the cultural matrix necessary to evaluate the claims and the behavior of the teachers working to quench that thirst. As Mariana Caplan put it, "because Western culture offers very little spiritual education to the majority of its inhabitants, people interested in spirituality lack knowledge regarding how to discriminate between what is genuine and what is not. There is plenty of religion. . . . but by and large, the West is a desert in terms of educating its own about spirituality."[37] In Asia, everyone knows how Buddhist teachers are supposed to behave, and someone who violates those expectations is likely to be viewed with a skeptical eye. Many of the problems that have surfaced in the West can be traced to the lack of the cultural background necessary to provide Buddhist centers and their students and teachers a framework to guide and evaluate their endeavors. But the spread of Buddhism and other forms of spirituality new to the West are inevitably laying the foundation for a cultural matrix that may eventually turn these kind of difficulties into self-limiting problems.

The most important transformation Buddhism has undergone, and the one that seems most likely to be a permanent fixture in the West, has been the growing power of women and the trend toward full gender equality. Although it may be too optimistic to say there is complete equality in any Western institution, the differences between the roles of women in Eastern and Western Buddhism are remarkable, and all the indications are that the socially structured gender inequalities remaining in Western Buddhism will continue to erode.

The issue of the power and authority of the teacher is more complex. Seen from one direction, it appears that many of the groups that are now headed by Western teachers have moved a considerable distance toward the egalitarian ideals of this culture. Few teachers currently wield the kind of virtually unlimited power enjoyed by the first generation of Asian missionaries, who were literally irreplaceable. Yet there are limits to how far this trend is likely to go. The relationship between Buddhist teachers and their students is in some sense inherently unequal. The whole enterprise is based on the assumption that the teachers have greater wisdom and greater realization and that they can use them to help their students on their spiritual path. Centers that have decided to elect their board of directors and make other democratic reforms will certainly find it easier to replace an incompetent or unethical teacher, but when the teacher is respected and admired, as is usually the case, he or she will continue to wield enormous power within the organization. Nonetheless, as the members of Buddhist groups and Westerners in general grow more sophisticated about what to expect from spiritual teachers, a stronger set of controls should naturally develop.

Since Buddhism never developed a strong set of norms about sexual behavior among the laity, its adaptation to Western sexual mores was not a difficult process. In fact, it seems that Western Buddhism has to a large degree merely followed the cultural trends of its new home. In the 1960s and 1970s, many groups practiced the wide-open sexual style common in the liberal quarters from which they drew most of their members. The 1980s and 1990s saw a conservative counter-reaction to the "sexual revolution," and attitudes in all sectors of society, including organized Buddhism, tended to become more conservative. Although cultural liberals never returned to the traditional condemnation of premarital sex, they did fervently endorse the movement to define and eliminate sexual harassment, which in turn had sweeping consequences for student–teacher relationships in many Buddhist groups. If popular mores swing back in a more liberal direction, we might expect to see similar changes among Western Buddhist groups.

Six

✳

WHY BUDDHISM?

Like our politics, we get our religion along with our mother's milk. Any new religious movement must confront established faiths backed by habit, tradition, and vast organizational resources. That is especially true of Western Buddhism, since it is such a radical departure from the mainstream of Western religious tradition. Few Westerners think of fundamentalists, evangelicals, orthodox Jews, mainstream Catholics, liberal Protestants, Mormons, and even Muslims as sharing much in common, but compare those faiths to Buddhism and their similarities quickly become apparent. They all stem from common roots, they all accept the validity of some of the same religious texts, and most importantly, they are all built on a belief in a single all-powerful God who created the world and determines the fate of all humankind. Buddhism shares none of this: no common ancestors, no common texts, and no creator God. Moreover, few of the systematic techniques of spiritual practice that are so essential to the new Buddhism are anywhere to be found in the mainstream Western religions. A Protestant or Jew who became a Catholic would learn different doctrines, symbols, and rituals, but in becoming a Buddhist would be exposed to a radically different set of assumptions about the most basic nature of the world and would begin a completely new kind of spiritual practice. Such sweeping changes obviously do not come easily, and yet as we saw in the first chapter, Buddhism is one of the fastest growing religions in the West. So then, why Buddhism?

The Circles of Involvement

It would seem that the first thing we should do in this kind of study is to set up some criteria for who is or is not a Buddhist. As it turns out, however, that is not a very simple or even necessarily a very useful thing to do. We might say that someone is a Buddhist if they join a Buddhist group, but the boundaries of such groups are not usually very clearly defined. Most groups have some category of people known as members, but that usually involves nothing more than a willingness to make a specified financial contribution. Moreover, many people who have a very active Buddhist practice are not involved in any particular Buddhist group. Another approach would hold that someone becomes a Buddhist by performing certain rituals such as the *jukai* ceremony, but many groups do not have such rites. Even among those that do, many long-term members have never participated in them. Alternatively, a Buddhist might be defined as someone who carries on certain practices such as regular meditation, but that of course would include many people who do not consider themselves Buddhists at all. Perhaps we could isolate certain core beliefs and define those who accept them as Buddhists, but it isn't at all clear what those beliefs would be: The law of karma? Reincarnation? Impermanence? Interdependent coorigination? The role of attachment in causing suffering? Selflessness? The truth of the Buddha's teachings? And what would we do with someone who believes in some but not all of the beliefs we defined as essential to Buddhism? What about a Hindu who shares those beliefs? In the final analysis, the most viable approach is probably the one suggested by Thomas Tweed: someone is a Buddhist if they define themselves as one. That approach certainly works well enough for most religions, but it too has some special difficulties when applied to the new Buddhism growing in the West. One of the central focuses of Buddhist practice is to see through the illusion of the separate self with all its fears, desires, and identifications. So in a very real sense, identification of oneself as a Buddhist is exactly what the practice does *not* recommend. As Jack Kornfield puts it:

It is important to realize that to identify oneself as a meditator or a spiritual person or even a Buddhist can be another way we get caught or lose one's true balance. . . . The purpose of meditation is not to create a new spiritual identity, nor to become the most meditative person on the block, who tells other people how they should live. The practice is to let go.[1]

There is, moreover, good evidence that many people who are deeply involved in Buddhism would not define themselves as Buddhists. Editor Helen Tworkov estimates that about half of the 60,000 readers of *Tricycle: The Buddhist Review* don't considered themselves to be Buddhist. Although the respondents to my questionnaire had been involved in Buddhist organizations for an average of about nine and a half years, nearly a third still did not identify themselves as Buddhists.

Thus, it seems best to approach the issue from a different direction. If we set aside the issue of identity, the question then becomes, who is involved in Buddhism and to what degree? One useful way to conceptualize this variable is as a series of concentric "circles of involvement." On the outer edge are those with only a casual interest in Buddhism, and at the core are the most dedicated practitioners.

Countless people have been indirectly influenced by Buddhist ideas that have filtered out into our popular culture, and they stand on the outer fringe of our concentric circles. The Zen tradition, for example, has helped foster a wide understanding of the spiritual benefits that complete absorption in a particular task can bring. Numerous people who know little or nothing about most aspects of Buddhism have come to approach such everyday activities as playing the piano or going for a run from a truly Buddhist perspective. The Buddhist ideal of equanimity and emotional balance is also gaining growing acceptance among many Westerners, as is the value Buddhism places on living in the present moment and not in our memories of the past or our projections about the future.

Another broad source of Buddhist influence comes from the example set by prominent Buddhists such as the Dalai Lama. Many people who have no interest in Buddhism have been profoundly impressed by his lack of dogmatism and the compassion he has shown in the face of China's brutal repression of his people.

The next circle includes the so-called bookstore Buddhists who have been influenced by popular books on Buddhist beliefs and practices but have never gotten involved in any organized Buddhist group. In recent times, this group has been joined by the "cybersangha"—frequent visitors to Buddhist Web sites and chat groups—as well as the "audiovisual Buddhists" who get their Buddhism on tape or video cassette. Although there is little demographic information about this group, the sales figure for Buddhist books indicates that it is a sizable one. Starting over one hundred years ago, Edwin Arnold's poetic account of the life of the Buddha, *The Light of Asia,* has gone through eighty American editions and has sold somewhere between 500,000 and a million copies since it was first published in 1879. Only a handful of other Buddhist books have sold as many copies as that, but as the titles have proliferated the total volume of Buddhist books sold has grown exponentially. Thomas Tweed reports that *Books in Print* lists 197 titles that begin with the world "Zen," including such esoteric subjects as *Zen and the Art of Kicking Butts: The Ultimate Guide for Quitting Smoking Forever, The Zen of Programming,* and *Zen and the Art of Changing Diapers.* In my own local bookstore, I counted 272 different books on various aspects of Buddhism and Buddhist practice; more specialized shops may easily have twice that many. The Bodhi Tree Bookstore in West Hollywood, for example, carries about 1,900 Buddhist titles.

Many of those who are active in Buddhist groups and have a strong relationship to a particular teacher dismiss these bookstore Buddhists as dilettantes and dabblers experimenting with a trendy New Age infatuation. The truth, however, is much more complex. In this age of mass literacy and instant communication, average people have a far wider range of texts available to them than even the most privileged monks of past generations. Information and advice that in past times could only have been gained directly from an experienced teacher are now easily available in books and on tape.

The earliest books on Buddhism in the West were often full of inaccuracies and strange distortions, but by the 1950s the works of people like Alan Watts and D. T. Suzuki presented the public with a sophisticated picture of Zen and its subversive view of the nature of human life. As time went on, the books not only came to reflect the full diversity of the Buddhist tradition, but began to devote far more attention to actual Buddhist practice. In 1965, Philip Kapleau Roshi published *The Three Pillars of Zen,* which contained specific instruction on Zen meditation, and since then most of the best-selling books have been the ones that offer direct practical advice on how to practice. Thich Nhat Hanh's *The Miracle of Mindfulness* has sold about 125,000 copies since its publication in 1975, and his *Being*

Peace has sold twice that many since it came out in 1988. But the most popular of all Buddhist books in the West is Suzuki Roshi's *Zen Mind, Beginner's Mind.* First published in 1970, it is now in its thirty-seventh edition and still selling 30,000 copies a year. *Publisher's Weekly* estimates that there are almost a million copies of Suzuki Roshi's book in print. Despite the continuing popularity of books by such well-known Asian Buddhists as Thich Nhat Hanh and the Dalai Lama, in the last few years books by Western teachers have taken over the market and stimulated an unprecedented growth in sales. Lama Surya Das's *Awakening the Buddha Within,* for example, sold more than 100,000 copies in its first year and a half of publication, and the number of titles by other Western teachers has grown at an astounding pace. Peter Turner, executive editor of Shambhala Publications, one of the largest publishers of Buddhist books, comments that "these authors are establishing a middle path that brings together traditional meditation practices with their everyday lives with spouses, children, political beliefs. This approach to Buddhism isn't that common in Asia, but it is essential to what is happening to Buddhism in this country."[2]

There is no question that the support of fellow practitioners and the direct personal contact with qualified teachers offered by most Buddhist groups provide a unique opportunity for growth. But the solitary practitioner can certainly practice as frequently and with as much dedication as anyone else, listen to tapes of the same lectures students hear during meditation retreats, and read answers that have been given to the same kinds of questions he or she is likely to ask. Indeed, Richard Hayes, who runs the Buddha-L on-line discussion group, reports that the question "do you need a teacher?" elicits more debate among the participants than any other issue.

In the next circle are those who have actually gone on to get involved in a Buddhist group. Within this circle, there are, of course, widely different levels of participation. On the outer ring are those who occasionally visit a Buddhist group or center when it holds an event of particular interest or when they feel some special personal need. In larger cities that have many active Buddhist groups, there are a wide variety of lectures, workshops, meditation retreats, and other activities available to the public. Most centers also offer a regular schedule of meditation and public talks to anyone who is interested. Many of these occasional participants take part in activities at several different centers without forming a bond with any particular group. In smaller communities, there is often only a single meditation group, which is less likely to have its own facilities or a resident teacher. Nonetheless, most of these groups have regularly scheduled meetings for meditation, group discussion, and listening to tapes or lectures, as well as periodic visits from one or more of the many teachers riding the "dharma circuit." Many Western communities still do not have any organized Buddhist groups, and those interested in seeking contacts with the Buddhist community must often commute long distances to attend a lecture or meditation retreat.

Although it is safe to assume that these occasional participants are generally less dedicated practitioners than those who are more regularly involved with Buddhist centers, commitment to practice and involvement in Buddhist organizations are not the same thing. Some people maintain a very disciplined meditation practice and regularly participate in intensive retreats but seldom attend other Buddhist activities, while others become deeply involved in the affairs of a particular Buddhist group but are far more lax about their practice.

As people become more involved in organized Buddhism, they tend to form a commitment to a particular group, which usually comes to perform important social as well as spiritual functions in their lives. The sangha has traditionally been considered one of the three jewels of Buddhism, along with the Buddha and the dharma, but until recently the emphasis in Western Buddhism has been on meditation and personal cultivation rather than building community. In the last few years, however, there has been a growing recognition of the importance of the community of practitioners. Although the overwhelming majority of the respondents to my questionnaire ranked meditation as the most important activity carried on by their Buddhist group, social activities with other members was ranked second, well ahead of rituals and ceremonies. On the average, they reported visiting a Buddhist center fifty-four times a year, or a little more than once a week. Many Buddhist leaders would agree with Thich Nhat Hanh when he says that "without a Sangha body, sooner or later you will abandon the practice."[3] In fact, the influential Nhat Hanh goes so far as to say that Maitreya, the legendary Buddha to come, will not take the form of a single individual but of the entire sangha.

The next circle of involvement is made up of the small group of people who go beyond regular participation to make their Buddhist practice the central focus of their daily lives. Many of the larger Buddhist centers have residential facilities, and some of these people actually live in a center, either working for the organization itself or commuting to an outside job. Others hold official positions in their organization and carry on the administrative functions necessary for the survival of any organized group. Then there are the groups of long-term "senior students" who form around prominent teachers, many of whom are headed for careers as teachers themselves. Finally, in the innermost core of the Buddhist world are the teachers who have been authorized in some fashion or other to guide others along the Buddhist path. Most Buddhist organizations also recognize an even more elite group of "senior teachers" or a single head teacher who has been authorized not only to teach the public but to train a new generation of teachers as well.

Another critical dimension in someone's involvement in Buddhism is intensity of practice. As pointed out above, those with a strong social involvement in Buddhism tend to have the deepest practice, but that is not always the case. Some of the greatest Buddhist teachers spent most of their formative years in isolated retreats with few contacts with any other people, Buddhist or otherwise. Here in the West, there are undoubtedly many highly accomplished practitioners who have had little or no involvement with the Buddhist community.

It is also important to remember that two people who are involved in the same Buddhist activities may have taken a very different course to get there. The most common pattern among those who become deeply involved appears to be a steady progression from the fringes into the inner circles. About 60 percent of my respondents reported that their involvement in Buddhism was increasing, a third said it was staying the same, and only 7 percent said it was decreasing. Such a progression may occur relatively rapidly but more often develops over a period of years. Most never reach the inner core, however, but stay in one of the outer circles for an indefinite period of time. Then there are the "experimenters" who try out Buddhism for a while and then quit, and another group that might be called the "crisis Buddhists." They turn to Buddhism to find help with some pressing personal problem but then drift away as things settle down, perhaps to return later when new difficulties arise.

The Western Sangha

What kind of people are attracted to the new Buddhism? There is virtually no reliable information about bookstore Buddhists, but it does seem safe to assume that they are literate and reasonably well educated. Those who actually get involved in a Buddhist group are easier to study. Although my survey reached only a small sample of groups, so far as I know it is the only broadly based attempt to measure the demographics of the new Buddhism, and it provides a lot of useful data. In addition, the leaders of these groups generally have a fairly clear idea about the composition of their own group, and there is also a kind of conventional wisdom in the Western Buddhist community about the kinds of people it attracts.

It is generally agreed that although both sexes are always represented, Western Buddhism, like so many other religions, attracts more women than men. About 58 percent of those who responded to my questionnaire were female and 42 percent male. There were, however, some significant differences between the groups surveyed, and the Rochester Zen Center, which is known for its demanding "samurai" style of practice, actually had a majority of males.

There is no doubt that the membership of the new Western Buddhism is overwhelmingly white—only about one in ten of my respondents identified themselves as Asian, Black, or Hispanic—a matter that has been of considerable concern to Buddhist leaders. When asked about their family's religious background, 8.6 percent said it was nonreligious, 16.5 percent Jewish, 25.6 percent Roman Catholic, 42.2 percent Protestant, and 1.9 percent Buddhist. A comparison of these findings with the demographics of the entire U.S. population confirms the often made observation that Jews—who make up only 3 percent of the total population of the United States but more than five times that percentage of my respondents—are more likely to be attracted to Buddhism than other Americans. My survey did not, however, support the common belief that people with a Catholic background are also more likely to become involved in Buddhism. The percentage of Buddhists from a Catholic family was virtually identical with the overall percentage of Catholics in the American population. Those with Protestant backgrounds, on the other hand, appear less likely to get involved. Whereas they made up 42 percent of my respondents, they constitute 56 percent of the total American population.

My data clearly indicate that American Buddhism appeals most strongly to the middle and upper-middle classes—another fact that is generally recognized in the Buddhist community. About a third of the respondents reported their family income to be between $30,000 and

$60,000, while another 19 percent fell in the $60,000 to $90,000 range. About 20 percent of the respondents had incomes over $90,000 and about 30 percent fell on the other end of the spectrum, making less than $30,000. Although these income figures were somewhat higher than the national average at the time the survey was conducted, the educational level of American Buddhists was right off the charts. Of the 353 people who responded to the question on educational achievement, only a single person reported having failed to finish high school, and less than one in twenty said that their education stopped with high school graduation. Eleven percent said that they had some college, 32 percent were college graduates, and surprisingly, more than half of the respondents (51 percent) had advanced degrees. Thus it may be that the participants in new Buddhism represent the most highly educated religious group in the West today.

Just as these Buddhists are far more educated than the average American, they are far more liberal as well. Almost 60 percent of the respondents said they were Democrats, while only 2.6 reported a Republican affiliation. Surprisingly, the Republicans were outnumbered by members of the tiny Green Party by more than three to one (the Greens were 9.9 percent of the total sample). A self-ranking on a left-to-right political scale also produced a distribution heavily skewed to the left. On a one to ten scale with one being the furthest right and ten the furthest left, the average respondent ranked him- or herself as an eight.

These new Buddhist groups clearly attract people of all ages. My youngest respondent was nineteen and the oldest seventy-eight. But most of the respondents were in their middle years, roughly from their late thirties to their early fifties, with a mean average age of forty-six. This finding confirms the conventional wisdom in the Buddhist community that American Buddhism has its greatest appeal to the baby boom generation. The question of whether there is something unique in the experience of the baby boomers that makes Buddhist practice especially attractive or if they were simply the first generation of Westerners with the opportunity to get involved cannot be answered until we see if later generations become more involved in Buddhism as they age. Although my survey could not measure the changes in the age composition, reports from numerous different participants indicate that a significant shift has occurred since the "Zen boom" of the 1970s, when the membership was considerably younger than it is today.

Although the overall tone of Western Buddhism has certainly become more mainstream over the years, it is generally agreed that it continues to have a particularly strong appeal to bohemians, intellectuals, and artists. My survey found, for example, that Western Buddhists are much more likely than the general public to have experimented with illicit drugs. When asked "have you ever used psychedelic drugs (excluding marijuana)?" 62.5 percent answered yes—a far higher proportion than in the general population. The number of "celebrity Buddhists" has also grown rapidly in recent years, which is hardly a surprise, since actors, writers, and musicians are often most comfortable in the kind of cosmopolitan, left-leaning environment found in most Buddhist groups.

Geographically, Buddhist groups are scattered throughout North America and Europe, but they are most likely to be found in the most cosmopolitan urban areas. In the United States, that means urban metropolises on the East and West Coasts, and in Canada it is Toronto and the province of Ontario. The guide to the meditation-oriented Buddhist centers of North America edited by Don Morreale found that 22 percent of the American centers were in California and 38 percent of the Canadian centers were in Ontario. In Great Britain, the heavest concentration of Buddhist centers, like the heaviest concentration of the population, is in and around London.

Why Buddhism?

It seems that the first place we ought to turn to understand why people get involved in Buddhism is to the sociology of religion. But few of the current theories about why people join new religions fit Western Buddhism very well. The sociology of religion has its roots in a nineteenth-century rationalism that saw religion in general and Christianity in particular as a kind of superstitious holdover from the past. It nonetheless seems to have taken on so many assumptions about the nature of religion from the Judeo-Christian tradition that it must undergo a very significant reorientation before it can provide a convincing account of the Western (or Eastern) Buddhist experience. The sociology of religion has dropped most of its earlier hostility toward Christianity and assumed a more neutral view, but those Eurocentric assumptions are another matter. Many Western scholars simply don't know how to handle a religion whose assumptions and perspectives differ so greatly from the traditions in which they grew up.

The sociology of religion's most common tactic for dealing with Asian Buddhism is simply to ignore it, or even to deny that Buddhism is a religion—no mean feat given the fact that virtually no one outside the academy would call Buddhism anything else. Another common strategy is to recast Asian Buddhism into a theistic religion in the Judeo-Christian mold. For example, Rodney Stark and William Sims Bainbridge, two prominent scholars of contemporary religion, argue that all religions must have a God or gods (or some close equivalents) that intervene in human life. The notion that Buddhism does not mistakes

> the "religious" views of a small group of philosophers and court intellectuals for popular Buddhism. . . . In societies such as ours and that of classical India, there exist schools of thought, promulgated by professional scholars and intellectuals, that recast traditional religious ideas as philosophical systems having no reference to supernatural deities. Far from representing the dominant religious thinking of their societies, these philosophical systems are the extreme in secularization. Perhaps some members of the intellectual elite favor them, but they may have little impact on social behavior.[4]

While it is true that supernatural deities play an important role in some forms of Buddhism, in others, such as the extremely widespread and influential Theravadan tradition and the new Western Buddhism we are studying here, they do not. Moreover, no one familiar with the historical record of the Buddha's teachings would claim that the unconcern with supernatural deities required some kind of reinterpretation of religious tradition. The Buddha didn't deny the gods so many Indians believed in, but he didn't say much else about them either. About the only way that Stark and Bainbridge and the others who take their approach can handle Buddhism is to split it in two and dismiss its nontheistic tradition as secular philosophy. The fact is, however, that one cannot find those two sharply divergent Buddhisms out in the real world. There simply isn't much difference in the sociological, psychological, and spiritual role that Buddhism plays in the lives of people who believe that supernatural Buddhas and bodhisattvas can intervene in their lives and those who do not.

What about Western Buddhism? If it is considered at all, it is usually

classified under the heading of "new religions" among such often stigmatized company as the Peoples Temple (the cult that ended with the mass
suicide at Jonestown), the Unification Church (the Moonies), and the
Hare Krishna movement. Aside from the obvious irony of referring to a
tradition five centuries older than Christianity as a new religion, this clas-
sification just doesn't work very well from a sociological standpoint.
While these so-called new religions have very diverse ideological and
spiritual roots, what most of them share in common is a close-knit and
more or less exclusive social community, and a fervent commitment to
converting new members. Western Buddhism, on the other hand, has
neither characteristic. New Buddhist groups often pay even less attention
to attracting new members than do the more staid Christian denominations, much less the evangelical sects. In Zen, it was traditional that most
people who wanted to join a monastery were almost automatically refused.
The aspiring monk would then have to prove his determination by sitting
outside the gates of the monastery for days or even weeks until they
finally let him in. While it is not that difficult to join today's new Buddhist
groups, the general attitude is that people should come to Buddhist practice only when they are ready. The Buddhist path to spiritual awakening
requires a deep personal commitment that cannot come from persuasion
or peer pressure. There is, moreover, a strong feeling among many members of these groups that the kind of evangelism practiced by fundamentalist Christians is not only counterproductive but borders on forced
indoctrination that violates individual religious liberty. (The Soka Gakkai
is the one exception to this generalization, but they are not, as noted in
the introduction, included in this study as part of the new Buddhism.)

It is not surprising that most sociological theories of conversion don't
fit very neatly either. The whole concept of conversion seems a bit suspect
here, since it implies that the "convert" must switch from one religious
perspective or worldview to another. While this may indeed happen, it is
by no means necessary to be involved in a Buddhist group. Although most
Western religions would certainly not agree, Buddhists see no contradiction in being *both* a Buddhist *and* a Christian, Jew, or Muslim. In fact, about
12 percent of my respondents identified themselves as Christians and
more than 10 percent said they believed in Judaism.

Beyond the problems with terminology, there is a more fundamental
difficulty—most sociological theories of conversion view it as a process
of assimilation into an all-consuming social group with a distinctive

worldview that the convert comes to adopt. This orientation comes through clearly in Thomas F. O'Dea's classic little book on the sociology of religion:

> Social change, and especially social disorganization, results in a loss of cultural consensus and group solidarity, and sets men upon a "quest for community"—that is, looking for new values to which they might adhere and new groups to which they might belong. This implies that conversion—the acceptance of new religions—is itself closely related to needs and aspirations which are highly affected by the social circumstance of the people involved.[5]

While there is no doubt about O'Dea's second point, at least as far as Western Buddhism is concerned, the assumption that the quest for community is the primary motivation for religious reorientation is very much open to question.

The same assumptions are reflected in the influential theory of conversion developed by John Lofland and Rodney Stark from their work on the Unification Church. They hold that the process of conversion has four identifiable stages. It begins when potential converts are "picked up" and given their first exposure to the group. Next they are "hooked," that is, they are stimulated to develop an interest in the religious group. Then they are "encapsulated," or totally immersed in the ideology and emotional economy of the group, and, finally, they commit to the group and become full-fledged participants. Because Western Buddhist groups seldom engage in the kind of proselytization that this model assumes, it obviously has limited applicability to the case at hand. Although more recent theorizing, including some by Lofland himself, tends to assign the converts a more active role in their own conversion, the sense of community and social support offered by the new group is still usually seen to be of critical importance.

Nevertheless, a careful reading of the evidence does not indicate that the desire for a supportive social group and a greater sense of community is a particularly strong motivation for most Westerners who become involved in Buddhism. Although many groups of Western Buddhists are starting to place more emphasis on community building, the primary focus has always been on spiritual practice, not social relationships. Moreover, many Buddhist practitioners stay in the outer circles and never get very deeply involved in any Buddhist group. My survey also provides some interesting data on this point. I asked my respondents, who were located through their attendance at Buddhist groups, to state their level of agreement or disagreement with three relevant statements: "I became interested in Buddhism because of a desire for spiritual fulfillment"; "I became interested in Buddhism in order to help me deal with my personal problems"; and "I became interested in Buddhism because I was attracted by the people I met who were involved with it." Well over half the respondents strongly agreed with the first statement and 22 percent with the second, but less than 12 percent strongly agreed with the third. Of course, it is possible that the respondents were being less than honest because they felt that the first two responses were more appropriate reasons for getting involved in a religious movement. But their answers to another question clearly show that few of them were part of a tightly knit "encapsulating" community. When I asked my respondents "how many of your friends are involved in Buddhism?" 9.4 percent answered none, 31.3 percent said only a few, and 13.4 percent said one out of four. Thus the majority said that considerably less than half of their friends were involved in Buddhism. In contrast, only 23.1 percent said that more than half their friends were involved. More evidence against the idea that the "quest for community" is a primary motivation for involvement in Buddhism comes from a comparison of the average length of time the respondents had been involved in a Buddhist group (9.5 years) with the length of time they had been meditating (13.2 years). It is obvious that they would not have continued meditating for almost four years before joining a group if their primary motivation had been the need for social support and reinforcement.

In another variation on this theme, Stark and Bainbridge argue in their influential work *The Future of Religion* that interpersonal bonds between "cult" members and potential new recruits are the primary path into the cult. (Despite its negative connotation, Stark and Bainbridge use the term "cult" to describe any religion that offers something new or deviant from the perspective of society's dominant religious orientation, and that includes Western Buddhism. Asian Buddhism would be classified as a church in many places, since it is the dominant faith into which most people are born.) While this sounds plausible enough, and there is evidence that this generalization is actually true for many new religious groups, the data once again show that the conventional sociological generalizations don't seem to apply to Western Buddhism. When I asked my respondents, "How did you first become involved in Buddhism?" only 25 percent said it was because of their friends, while 47 percent said it was from books, lectures, or classes.

It would certainly be going way too far to say that the desire for a supportive social group has played no role in the spread of Buddhism in this anomic society. But such social motivations are clearly of less importance in Buddhism than they are in most other religious movements. What, then, are the primary reasons for the spread of Buddhism in the West? To answer that question, we must start with a description of the path that leads most people into Buddhism. Only then can we turn our attention to the complex and difficult task of explaining that behavior. The approach taken here is based on the commonsense notion that social actions require a motivation and an opportunity before they can occur. In the pages that follow, we will examine how social psychological and structural changes in postmodern society have combined to promote the spread of Buddhist in the West.

GETTING INVOLVED   Unfortunately, there isn't much available in the way of longitudinal data, but by combining the data from the cross-section survey and the depth interviews I conducted, it is possible to piece together a pretty good picture of the typical path that most Westerners follow into Buddhism. It is important to bear in mind, however, that the description that follows is only a generalization; many people's paths follow a very different trajectory. As touched on above, my survey found that most Westerners' first exposure to Buddhism was in their reading— about 40 percent of the respondents said it was from reading books— while 25 percent said it was from contacts with friends and another 9 percent said it was from both books and friends. No matter how they first learn about Buddhism, most people go through an initial period of exploration in which they read about Buddhism in a variety of books and magazines, talk with friends and associates about it, and perhaps attend lectures or other activities.

The next step is a big one: actually starting a meditation practice. Fifty or a hundred years ago, even Westerners who considered themselves Buddhist seldom got to this stage, but today an active meditation practice is considered an essential component of the Buddhist path—at least among the new Buddhist groups we are studying here. The earliest books on Buddhism available in the West were mainly about philosophy and not practice, but as Buddhism sank deeper roots into Western culture, numerous books, pamphlets, and audio tapes were produced that provided detailed instructions on how to meditate as well as advice regarding the problems beginners are likely to encounter. In addition, almost all Buddhist groups provide meditation instruction, and many Buddhist teachers travel extensively and give lectures describing the techniques of meditation to the general public. Of course, Buddhists are not the only ones interested in meditation, and some people who eventually get involved in Buddhist groups actually start their meditation practice in another tradition, such as Hindu-based transcendental meditation, before they switch over.

So far as I know, there is no information about the number of people who stay at this stage, meditating on their own in isolation from most other practitioners. Many teachers claim that those who lack community support will eventually abandon their practice, but there isn't any real empirical support for such claims. Most Buddhist teachers are surrounded by a throng of students clamoring for their attention, and they are unlikely to have much knowledge of such isolated practitioners. Many anecdotal reports, however, suggest that their number is sizable.

The third step is to get involved with a Buddhist group. My survey indicates that most respondents began meditating in their early thirties and that their first involvement with a Buddhist group came about four years later. The initial contacts with Buddhist groups are often rather occasional and tentative. Involvement tends to increase slowly over time as the participants learn the expectations of their group, assimilate its attitudes and values, and develop friendships and an identification with other members. Although most of my respondents had been active in Buddhist groups for a considerable period of time, as I indicated above, almost 60 percent reported that their involvement was increasing.

My survey also explored two activities that are widely believed to provide an entryway into Buddhism: practicing a martial art and using psychedelic drugs. Many of the martial arts traditions have their roots in Buddhist practice, and they encourage a mindfulness in action that bears a strong affinity to Buddhist teachings. So it is natural to wonder if the practice of a martial art stimulates some people's interest in Buddhism. About a third of my respondents reported that they had practiced a martial art. Of those, however, 65 percent said that their involvement in the martial arts did not help attract them to Buddhism, and another 12 percent said that it was actually Buddhism that started their interest in the martial arts. Thus the martial arts were an important pathway into Buddhism for about 8 percent of the entire sample, or about one respondent in twelve.

Another common belief in the Buddhist community is that the use of psychedelic drugs plays an important part in leading many practitioners into Buddhism. Numerous Buddhist teachers have admitted using psychedelic drugs, and Jack Kornfield goes so far as to claim that: "the majority of Western Buddhist teachers used psychedelics at the start of their spiritual practice."[6] Clearly, the members of Western Buddhist groups are far more likely than the overall population to have used psychedelic drugs. As we have seen, over 62 percent of my respondents had taken psychedelics, while government surveys indicated that to be true for only about 8 percent of the overall population. Psychologist Charles Tart took a survey at an Oakland, California, retreat given by the Rigpa Fellowship (a popular Tibetan group headed by Sogyal Rinpoche) and he found an even higher percentage (77 percent) of people who had used psychedelics. Indeed, it appears that those who practice in the Tibetan tradition are particularly likely to have used these drugs. Eighty percent of the members of the two Tibetan groups in my sample said they had used psychedelics—a significantly higher figure than for the Zen or Vipassana groups[7] and very close to Tart's figure. As one of Tart's subjects put it, "Tibetan Buddhism or Hinduism, with its flashy trappings and enormous numbers of deities and practices, was more like my psychedelic experiences than anything else I came across."[8]

Of course, the fact that someone used a psychedelic drug doesn't mean that it encouraged their Buddhist practice. It may simply be that those who are dissatisfied with contemporary society are more likely to experiment with both illicit drugs and unconventional religions. When queried on this point, however, fifty percent of my subjects who had used them said that such drugs had encouraged their involvement in Buddhism while fifty percent said it had not. Thus, almost one in three of the people I sampled felt that the use of psychedelic drugs had helped attract them to Buddhism, and in Tart's narrower sample it was about one in five.

There is an often heated debate in Buddhist circles about whether psychedelic experiences are "real" mystical experiences or some kind of drug-induced counterfeit. Without entering into that fruitless argument, it can certainly be said that the psychedelic experience does stimulate an interest in meditation among some users. Stark and Bainbridge see a kind of indirect influence from psychedelic use: "Some cults recruit heavily from the sons and daughters of the middle class who are dropping out of conventional society, and in many cases drugs may have contributed to dropping out."[9] Thus drug use promotes dropping out and dropping out promotes unconventional religious involvement. But once again, such broad generalizations do not seem to fit very well with what we know about Western Buddhism. We have already seen that average participants start in their thirties and are therefore not young dropouts, and the accounts of those who report that psychedelic drug use encouraged their involvement virtually never mention the kind of process Stark and Bainbridge propose. Rather, they talk about the effects of the drugs themselves. Some report that they got into meditation in an attempt to experience the same kind of high they got from psychedelics without the side effects of the drugs or that they were seeking a more intense, more real, experience than they were able to achieve through their drug use. Others say that their psychedelic experiences were a profound blow to their conventional view of reality. They may have watched seemingly solid objects dissolve into translucent patterns of energy or had the even more unsettling experience of seeing all the hidden games they play and all the self-delusion upon which their psychic economy depends. The result of such shattering experiences may be some kind of psychological breakdown, but they may also touch off a sincere search for something to help make sense of what happened. It is generally believed, however, that when people become committed to Buddhist practice their use of psychedelics takes on secondary importance and usually stops altogether. My survey did not ask about current drug use, but Tart found that despite a great deal of past experience with drugs few of his respondents reported being current users.

OPPORTUNITY   There is little doubt that one of the main reasons for the growing popularity of Buddhism in the West is that there are simply more opportunities for people to encounter Buddhist ideas and participate in Buddhist groups. But before we explore the reasons for the dramatic growth of such opportunities, we need to refine the concept of opportunity a bit. Most people think of an opportunity simply as the possibility to follow some course of action. For our purposes at least we must draw a distinction between a theoretical possibility and a real opportunity. Suppose, for example, that a Buddhist group built a retreat facility in a remote rural area with a strong fundamentalist orientation. Further suppose that the neighbors came to define it as a satanic cult and ostracized anyone who had friendly contact with it. In this case, while it would certainly be possible for someone in the surrounding community to stop in and learn about Buddhism, there would still be little realistic opportunity for most of the local people to become involved in this organization. A real opportunity is not just a possible course of action; it must also be *psychologically available* to the potential participant. Thus opportunity entails both a particular set of objective conditions and a symbolic understanding of those conditions that makes them appear attractive to a particular individual.

One of the most fundamental reasons, then, for the spread of Buddhism in the West is that modern technologies of transportation and communication have brought more and more Westerners into contact with it. Ideas, beliefs, and people themselves move around the world at a faster pace than ever before in human history. Just a century ago, only a tiny number of Westerners had any contact with Buddhism at all. Today, not only do tourists routinely visit all parts of the globe, but the growing interdependence of the world economy has created a kind of massive cultural exchange program among the workers and executives involved in multinational commerce. The tides of migration have also been an important force in this cultural diffusion. As we saw in chapter 3, the Japanese American community played a particularly important role in the introduction of Zen Buddhism to North America, and Sri Lankans and Burmese migrants played the same role in bringing Theravada Buddhism to Great Britain. Currently, refugees from the Chinese repression in Tibet are helping spread Vajrayana Buddhism around the world. But even those who never leave their hometown or have any direct contact with Asian Buddhists are still exposed to the media, which can bring a story or cultural event from anywhere around the world into their living room.

Another critical factor has been universal literacy and the rising level of education. Most Westerners receive their first exposure to Buddhism through books, so obviously the more literate the population, the more likely they are to encounter Buddhist thought. The unprecedented affluence of the postwar period has probably played a role as well. By allowing a greater degree of freedom from pressing financial obligations, it created the time for many more people to read, explore new ways of thinking, and attend lectures and meditation retreats.

The secularism and the spirit of open inquiry nurtured by higher education played a role in another critical development: the weakening of the cultural hegemony of the dominant Christian religions. At one time, the Anglo-Protestants of North America were not only able to define other Christian groups as un-American, they could simply dismiss non-European traditions as foreign superstitions (if they paid any attention to them in the first place). But as religion itself came under increasing challenge from rational secularism, the claims of any one group to represent the one undeniable truth became more and more suspect.

An even more important force in the breakdown of Anglo-Protestant hegemony was probably the successive waves of migration that transformed all the Western nations into multiethnic societies. Once the establishment was forced to grant some measure of grudging recognition to Catholics and Jews, greater acceptance inevitably came to those farther out on the fringes, including secularists, atheists, and the followers of Eastern faiths. Of course, the Judeo-Christian tradition is still a dominating force in the West, but it is far more difficult for a multicultural society in the throes of postmodern information overload to define all the world's other religious traditions out of its psychological horizons.

The sweeping social transformation of our social world that is sometimes termed modernization did, however, much more than just weaken the dominance of Anglo-Protestantism. It ate away at the religious worldview that provided the very foundations of traditional culture. Steve Bruce may be putting it a bit too strongly when he writes that this process of modernization was "in time, to see the widespread, taken-for-granted, and unexamined Christianity of the pre-Reformation period replaced by an equally widespread, taken-for-granted, and unexamined indifference to religion."[10] But despite the objections of a few sociologists, there seems little doubt that a kind of secular revolution has occurred that has displaced the religious worldview from its position of cultural hegemony. Even if we go to church on Sunday, a synagogue on Saturday, or a mosque on Friday (and most of us don't),[11] the rest of the week we live in a secular world far removed from the kinds of religious concerns that used to dominate social life. Most of the time it is hard-headed ends-means rationality, not religious faith, that guides our daily lives. Culturally, the relentless materialism of consumer capitalism has displaced Christianity from its hegemonic role in shaping Western attitudes, values, and beliefs. Some even say that the whole religious scene has been transformed into a "religious marketplace" where different denominations compete for followers, just as manufacturers compete to sell their soap or hairspray.

It might appear that the seemingly irresistible tide of rational secularism would be just as bad for Buddhism as the more established Western faiths, but that has not been the case for at least two important reasons. First, the general weakening of religious life has left a void in the lives of many people. In times of crisis, they often lack the framework necessary to make sense out of their suffering, and many see no path to fulfill their deepest spiritual longings—if indeed they are aware of them at all. Nature abhors a vacuum and such spiritual discontent has always been a boon to new religious movements. Second, although it is possible to make too much out of it, it does seem that the tenets of Buddhism, especially as practiced by the new Buddhist movement in the West, are more compatible with a secular scientific worldview that those of the more established Western religions. For one thing, the emphasis in these new groups is, as in early Buddhism, not on accepting any Buddhist doctrines or beliefs on faith but in testing out Buddhist practice and seeing firsthand if it really is what they claim. Some prominent Buddhists, such as Robert Thurman, actually characterize Buddhism as a "science of the mind" based on the same kind of systematic investigation of the inner world that the physical sciences have carried out in the outer world. Another key area in which Buddhism seems to have a greater affinity with the scientific perspective is in its view of cause and effect (karma). From its very beginnings, the Buddhist tradition, like modern science, has seen the events of the world as the result of the impersonal operation of cause and effect. Karma operates with the same kind of inevitability as the laws of modern science, and there is no intervening God who can step in and change the rules of the game.

On another level, most of the unique demographic characteristics of Western Buddhism noted earlier can be attributed to differences in opportunities and in the way Buddhist practice and belief resonates with different social strata. Thus one important reason Western Buddhism has its strongest following among the more privileged and more highly educated is that they are simply the ones most likely to have heard about it. But Buddhism is also an intellectual religion with a long scholarly tradition. The Buddha was as much a philosopher as a prophet, and many

Westerners are attracted by the view of human existence he presented. But ideas that intrigue those accustomed to grappling with abstract thought may seem boring and incomprehensible to the less educated. Moreover, the disciplined self-control demanded in so much Buddhist practice is very much in harmony with the ideals of the middle and upper classes. The polite decorum expected in most Buddhist centers would be second nature to those accustomed to attending a Presbyterian church or a synagogue in an upper-middle-class suburb, but wholly alien to those who sing boisterous gospel songs or speak in tongues in the storefront churches of the inner city. Furthermore, the relative lack of dogmatism and the willingness of many Buddhist leaders to submit their beliefs to the tests of reason and experience has particular appeal among intellectuals who are accustomed to the habit of critical thinking. Of course, Buddhism also has a long tradition of devotionalism that speaks to the needs of the less privileged strata of Asian societies, but that tradition has made far fewer inroads in the West, where Christian devotionalism is already firmly established.

Another important factor is the flavor of the foreign and exotic many Westerners find in Buddhism. Although some people are clearly put off by it, others feel a strong attraction to what they see as the different and unusual. That has proven to be especially true among artists, writers, intellectuals, and members of the counterculture who see themselves to be a bit out of the social mainstream. Those with a more countercultural orientation also tend to have weaker bonds to traditional religions and are therefore less likely to define involvement in Buddhism in some negative way.

The strong attraction Buddhism has for Western Jews can be attributed to three important factors. First, Jews are overrepresented among Buddhists because they are overrepresented in the segments of society to which Buddhism appeals most strongly: the highly educated upper middle class, intellectuals, artists, and bohemians. Second, since Jews traditionally played the part of outsiders in a culture dominated by Christian orthodoxy, they have been more willing to embrace ideas that mainstream society sees as deviant or foreign. Finally, although it is far from clearly established, it may be, as Stark and Bainbridge argue, that Jews are more interested in new religious movements because "Judaism has been more greatly eroded than Christianity by the process of secularization."[12]

The reasons for the underrepresentation of Protestants are not so immediately apparent, since they don't seem to have any obvious social or religious differences from Catholics in matters that would affect their attraction to Buddhism. My survey did not distinguish among different Protestant denominations, but I suspect that Buddhism appeals at least as strongly to those from the more liberal Protestant denominations as it does to Catholics; but there are far fewer Buddhists among those from fundamentalist backgrounds. One possible reason for this difference may be found in the research showing that many who "convert" to fundamentalist faiths actually come from a fundamentalist religious background themselves. When they face a psychological or spiritual crisis, instead of exploring new religious traditions, the fervent evangelism of their original faith may draw them back into the fold. Moreover, if those with a more secular background are more likely to become involved in new religious movements, as Stark and Bainbridge and others assert, it follows that fundamentalist Protestants will be the least likely to take that step, since they are clearly the least secular of all the major religious groups in the West.

BUDDHISM AND POSTMODERN SOCIETY   Surveys aren't necessarily a very good tool for finding out what motivates people. It is a relatively straightforward matter to describe our behavior, but the plain fact is that we often don't really know why we do what we do. The explanations we construct are usually ex post facto affairs that have more to do with justifying our behavior than understanding it. Nonetheless, there is something useful to be gained from asking people about their motivations as long as we maintain a healthy skepticism about what their responses really mean. As mentioned above, I asked my respondents to evaluate three statements about why they became involved in Buddhism: a desire for spiritual fulfillment, a desire to deal with their personal problems, and social reasons. Although a majority agreed with all three statements, there is little doubt that Western Buddhists see spiritual fulfillment as their primary motivation. Not only did 93.4 percent of those who answered agree or strongly agree with that statement, but it received more than double the percentage of "strongly agree" responses (53.5 percent) than either of the two other options. The desire to deal with personal problems came in second place—21.8 percent said they "strongly agreed" with that statement and another 46.9 percent "agreed" for a total of 68.7 percent. Finally, only 11.7 percent "strongly agreed" that they became interested in

Buddhism because they were attracted to the people who were involved in it, but another 46.6 percent "agreed" for a total of 58.4 percent. These findings were also confirmed by the depth interviews I conducted. When asked "Why did you get involved in Buddhism?" most people mentioned some kind of spiritual need or a particular problem they were facing, but they seldom mentioned a desire to get involved with a social group. If social support were someone's *primary* motivation, Christian evangelical groups would probably be more attractive for most people, since those groups tend to have an inclusive, extroverted style and put a great deal of effort into group activities. Even when carried on with other people, meditation is a solitary kind of pursuit.

My guess is that the survey respondents were more inclined to agree with the statement about spiritual fulfillment than the other two because it seems a higher, more noble motivation. But the distinction between the statements they were offered may not really be all that clear. After all, the lack of spiritual fulfillment or a supportive social group is in some sense a personal problem. So however it is conceptionalized, I think it is fair to say that people are drawn to Buddhism because they believe it can help them resolve some kind of nagging spiritual dissatisfaction—a feeling that somehow things aren't quite right.

The same thing could, of course, be said about almost any other religion. It may be that the spread of Buddhism in the West has simply resulted from the fact that people now have more contact with it. But I think that Buddhism's growing appeal has deeper roots that are to be found in its unique resonance with the social psychological dynamics of life in "postmodern" society. To understand why that is so, we need to step back and look at the big picture, especially the profound changes in human consciousness that have accompanied the evolution of society from simple bands of foragers to the bewildering complexity of contemporary life.

Although many traits have been dubbed the "essential" quality that sets us off from the other animals, self-consciousness is certainly one of the most likely candidates. It has often been noted that we are the only animal that knows it is going to die, and it might also be added that we are probably the only animal that knows it is alive. The birth of self-consciousness—that stunning realization by some lost ancestor that he or she existed as a kind of individual entity—must be considered one of the most pivotal events in all human evolution. Yet we know virtually nothing about when, where, or how it occurred with any certainty. What little we do know about the early evolution of consciousness comes from flimsy speculation based on a few surviving artifacts and some ancient myths and legends.

What does seem certain is that at some point in the past homo sapiens or our prehuman ancestors had no more self-consciousness than other animals and that the birth of self-consciousness involved a profound alteration in our psychological and social structures. Students of mythology such as the Jungian psychologist Erich Neumann, tend to put the origins of mature self-consciousness at a fairly late date. They argue that the mother goddess that was apparently the focus of the earliest human religions was a symbol of the engulfing power of nature, which in legend after legend destroys the symbols of autonomous human action. In this analysis, the figure of the conquering hero who appears in later myths to slay the dragons and other symbols of nature is the symbolic representation of the ego—victorious in its struggle to separate itself from the unconscious natural realm. As Neumann put it, "this means . . . not only that man's ego consciousness has achieved independence, but that his total personality has detached itself from the natural context of the surrounding world and the unconscious."[13] Regardless of what date we ascribe to this momentous development, it must have been a terrifying realization. Whatever heroic powers it might possess, humankind was now standing alone before the world, naked and mortal.

All this is not to imply that modern self-consciousness evolved in one great leap. In fact, many thinkers such as Ken Wilber believe there was an intermediate stage which consisted of a kind of group self-consciousness under which the individual was subsumed. It is risky to generalize from twentieth-century studies of tribal societies, since traditional peoples were often subject to social pressure from the modern world long before anthropologists reached them. Not to mention the fact the mere presence of anthropological researchers is likely to be an important source of change in and of itself. Nonetheless, fieldworkers have often commented on how much more important the group appears to be in such cultures than in the industrialized nations. For example, writing about a tribal people in the Philippines, Michelle Rosaldo asserts that "it seems misleading to identify individuality with the Ilongot sense of self . . . because the very terms they use in their account of how and why they act place emphasis not on the individual who remains outside a social whole but rather on the ways in which all adults are simultaneously automonous and equal members of the group."[14] Face-to-face interaction and group decision making was the normal way of life for tribal peoples, and as Joachin Wach pointed out in his classic study of the sociology of religion, there was a complete identity of natural social groups, such as the tribe, and religious groups. Religious life centered around collective rituals and ceremonies marking among other things changes in the group and its individual members, and it would seem to make sense to argue that identity was far more of a collective phenomenon than it is today.

Whatever truth there may be in the theories about the early evolution of self-consciousness, we know that profound changes in the structure of self-identity were still going on even in the relatively short period of time for which we have good recorded evidence. Although the members of all the traditional agricultural societies we know about certainly had a developed sense of self, it was quite different from the postmodern self that has now emerged in the industrial nations. I am not referring here to the strain of radical individualism that is so influential in the United States, but to the sweeping change that has occurred in the social context of the self. In traditional societies, self-identity was ascribed by convention, social institutions, and public consensus. Not only did everyone know everyone else in the traditional villages where most people lived, but there was a strong consensus about "who" each person was. Each individual had a predetermined status in the social hierarchy, a defining set of family relations, and a publicly known personal history. Identity was in this sense an externally constraining reality that the individual had little choice but to assume. This is not to say that it was an unchanging constant of personal life. Personal identity was certainly more stable than it is today, but it did change with the predictable stages of the life cycle and the sudden vicissitudes of daily life. In most cases, however, individuals had little control over the trajectory of their identity, and the underlying inertia of traditional society gave self-identity a kind of stability seldom seen in the postmodern world.

It was in this social context that Buddhism developed and refined its critique of self. In traditional Buddhist societies, however, the quest for enlightenment was an either/or kind of thing. One either adhered to one's traditional identity or, because of personal bent or social circumstance, took the radical step of "leaving home" and becoming a monastic or solitary yogi. It may be that the relative rigidity of traditional self-identity actually facilitated realization of "no self" when the seeker finally saw through it all. In any case, conventional self-identity was much less likely to come into question and the pursuit of such a realization was usually confined to a relatively small group of strivers.

The industrial revolution, which culminated in what is now commonly called postmodern society, shattered the old social consensus about self-identity and thereby radically transformed it. Perhaps the defining characteristic of this process has been the fragmentation of society into an ever growing number of divergent groups and the refraction of culture into a rainbow of different perspectives and viewpoints. The tightly knit community in which everyone had their place has been replaced with the anonymous institutions of mass society. In the place of the old social consensus, there now stands a cacophony of competing viewpoints. Freed from traditional constraints and expectations and forced to chart an uncertain course in a sea of ever changing social currents, postmodern humanity is bombarded with contradictory definitions, images, and demands. Since the social world no longer presents individuals with a consistent set of expectations about who they are and what they should be, self-identity undergoes a fundamental transformation. In the postmodern world identity is no longer a given; we must actively work to construct our own sense of who we are, which is then continuously revised in terms of the responses we elicit from others and our evaluations of our own performance. The noted sociologist Anthony Giddens has dubbed this process the "reflexive project of the self":

> In the post-traditional order of modernity, and against the backdrop of new forms of mediated experience, self-identity becomes a reflexively organized endeavor. The reflexive project of the self, which consists in the sustaining of coherent, yet continuously revised, biographical narratives, takes place in the context of multiple choice as filtered through abstract systems.[15]

Whatever we call this process, the maintenance of self-identity is a precarious enterprise in the postmodern era. The pervasive psychological uncertainty of our times has led us to ravenous hunger for identity. We passionately resuscitate the long forgotten ethnicities of our ancestors. We submerge ourselves in narrow "lifestyle enclaves" in which everyone at least appears to think, act, and feel the same. We adopt the latest fashions to show the world what trendsetters we are, or we cling determinedly to a traditional style we feel defines us as a levelheaded sort beyond the sway of trivial fads. Advertisers seek to sell us a self-image along with our cosmetics, clothing, or sport utility vehicle, and many are lured into the hopeless endeavor of trying to create a stable sense of who they are out of the products they consume. In matters of religion, the baby boomers have been dubbed a "generation of seekers," but in fact we have actually become a society of seekers straining to discover a religious identity that can anchor our precarious sense of who we are.

Much of the new Buddhism's appeal in the postmodern era can be attributed to the unique multilevel response it offers to this crisis of self. On one level, Buddhism, like other religions, offers support for an unstable identity and reinforcements to build our self-esteem. Buddhist seekers may easily come to identify themselves as wiser, more spiritual, and even more hip than their less enlightened brethren. The Buddhist sangha can provide its own sense of belonging and identity, and those who follow its moral teachings may enhance their self-esteem by seeing themselves as kinder or more ethical than others. Those who have had some success with Buddhism's meditative regime may also build a new identity around the spiritual insights they have experienced. "New Age" catalogs bristle with products from T-shirts to jewelry that proclaim one's Buddhist identity.

On another level, Buddhism, like the psychotherapies that have shown such an explosive growth in popularity in the postmodern era, can offer considerable help with the reflexive regulation of the self. Most Buddhist teachers in the West spend a good deal of their time dealing with such psychological issues as anger management, fear, guilt, and strategies for coping with the instability of life. As Jack Kornfield, a trained psychotherapist and leading Vipassana teacher, puts it:

> Almost everyone who undertakes a true spiritual path will discover that a profound personal healing is a necessary part of his or her spiritual process. When this need is acknowledged, spiritual practice can be directed to bring such healing to body, heart, and mind. . . . True maturation on the spiritual path requires that we discover the depth of our wounds: our grief from the past, unfulfilled longing, the sorrow that we have stored up during the courses of our lives. As Achaan Chah put it: "If you haven't cried deeply a number of times, your meditation hasn't really begun."[16]

Meditation certainly has its limits as a psychotherapeutic tool. If it is used incorrectly, the powers of concentration that it helps develop can become a way to ignore personal conflicts rather than resolve them. But it can also be a powerful tool for healing by helping bring hidden psychological conflicts and deeply rooted fears into the open. Mark Epstein, a psychoanalyst with long experience in Buddhism, writes that

> Far from being a mystical retreat from the complexities of mental and emotional experience, the Buddhist approach requires that *all* of the psyche be subject to meditative awareness. It is here that the overlap with what has come to be called psychotherapy is most obvious. Meditation is not world denying; the slowing down that it requires is in service of closer examination of the day to day mind. This examination is by definition psychological.[17]

A Buddhist teacher is far more likely to advise students to accept and carefully observe their conflicts and unpleasant emotions than to provide the kinds of techniques psychotherapists sometimes offer to try to get rid of them. But there is no doubt many students are led to Buddhist practice in an attempt to deal with their pressing personal problems and that they often experience the same kind of psychological benefits they would from psychotherapy.

At its deepest level, however, Buddhism goes far beyond psychotherapy. Its most profound teachings do not offer a new identity or a new set of techniques for managing our problems but deconstruct the whole project of the self—to bring us to see the pointlessness of our desperate efforts to construct, maintain, and protect our self-identity that consume so much of our lives. Even the deepest realization of "no-self" does not, of course, wipe out one's personality or socially constructed identity. Our concept of self is essential for life in contemporary society, for it tells us what we can expect from others and what they can expect of us. Although self-identity remains, the attachment to it—what Buddhists call self-clinging—and the suffering it causes do not. Self-identity is recognized as simply one more pattern of thought that arises and passes away as conditions dictate. There is no need to defend, protect, or improve it, since it has no real independent existence. While few Buddhist practitioners may reach that level of complete realization, even a small glimpse of this truth can have a profoundly liberating experience that not only strikes to the core of the crisis of self so common in postmodern society but provides a glimpse of true freedom and authenticity.

It would seem that the more difficult society makes it to establish a strong sense of self and the more precarious the effort to maintain it, the more attractive the teachings of no-self are likely to appear. So it is not surprising that in traditional societies with a strongly rooted sense of social place and identity, the Buddhist teachings offered to most people center on such things as the virtues of generosity and kindness and the importance of leading an ethical life, while the teachings of no-self have been directed to only a dedicated few. But in the new Buddhism emerging in postmodern society, the teachings on the suffering caused by self-clinging and the ways to be free of it have moved from the periphery to center stage. Buddhist teachers from all traditions have been wrestling with the difficult task of making such an esoteric doctrine accessible to a broad audience and showing students the direct results of self-clinging in their daily lives.

When teachers in the West are asked about the most essential point of Buddhism, for example, they often talk about "freedom" or "letting go." At first hearing that may not appear to have much to do with non-self, but when you explore such statements more deeply it becomes clear that what they are talking about is freedom from self-clinging. What is to be let go of is the attachment to self-centered thoughts. For example, the influential Vipassana teacher Joseph Goldstein writes that

> awareness of impermanence leads naturally to a deepening insight into selflessness or nonidentification. As we watch the different thoughts, feelings, and sensations coming and going, we notice that they seem to have a life of their own, that the whole process is occurring according to its own laws. Recognizing this, we simply stop identifying with what is coming up. When we don't identify, we stop clinging. In that vast and open mind of not clinging we again see impermanence and selflessness with greater clarity. We enter the great stream of dharma and it carries us along.[18]

In his enormously popular book, *The Myth of Freedom,* Trungpa Rinpoche gave the problem of attachment to self his own unique twist, calling it a great "cosmic joke."

> In order to cut through the ambition of ego we must understand how we set up me and my territory, how we use our projections as credentials to

prove our existence. The source of the effort to confirm our solidity is an uncertainty as to whether or not we exist. . . . The attempt to confirm our solidity is very painful. Constantly we find ourselves suddenly slipping off the edge of a floor. . . . then we must attempt to save ourselves from death by immediately building an extension to the floor in order to make it appear endless again. . . . [But] there was never any danger of falling or need for support. In fact, our occupation of extending the floor to secure our ground is a big joke, the biggest joke of all, a cosmic joke.[19]

Robert Thurman, a leading advocate of Tibetan Buddhism in the West, makes a very similar point when he writes that "every day, we wake up in the morning and are hit by the biggest intuitive lie known to human consciousness. That lie goes like this: 'It's me, it's me, I'm it, I'm the center of the universe. I come first. I hold it all together.' The bottom line is 'me.' It is not just that we are selfish; it is deeper. We perceive the self as the one sure thing, the only thing, that we can count on."[20]

In the Zen tradition, teachers sometimes take a more indirect approach—trying to lead students to their own discovery of the paradox of self. Sueng Sahn, the most influential Korean teacher in the West in the last thirty years, often assigns his Western students the koan "who are you?" or "what are you?" to grapple with in their daily meditation. But Western Zen, like the other traditions active here, does not hesitate to state the problem directly either. One of the vows recited daily at the Zen Center of San Diego goes right to the heart of the matter:

> Caught in a self-centered dream:
> only suffering
> Holding to self-centered thoughts:
> exactly the dream
> Each moment, life as it is:
> the only teacher
> Being just this moment:
> compassion's way.[21]

Seven

＊

THE NEW BUDDHISM TAKES SHAPE

When Buddhism first spread beyond its ancestral home in India, it took centuries to adapt to each new country and each new culture. Many of the leaders of Western Buddhism see the same kind of slow evolutionary development occurring here. It is often said that we will not know what shape Western Buddhism will take for generations to come. But, whether we like it or not, the frenetic pace of postmodern society has rewritten the equations of change. The story of Western Buddhism is told in decades, not centuries, but Buddhism has already made some of the most radical changes in its history. It would certainly be wrong to say that Buddhism has entered its final form in the West. What living religion has a final form? The goal for this last chapter, then, is to chart the trajectory of change along which this new Buddhism is moving, not to divine its ultimate destination.

The New Buddhism and the Old

It seems fair to say that the new, Western Buddhism is no longer in its infancy, but neither has it reached mature adulthood. Fresh, innovative, and diverse, it still shows a good deal of adolescent awkwardness as well. But like most adolescents, it is easy to see the seeds from which its character is growing and its differences from the parents that gave it birth. Buddhism as refracted through the prism of late Western modernity certainly bears a family resemblance to all its Asian ancestors, but the most striking likeness is to the original "Buddhism" Siddartha Gautama first taught in India over two millennia ago.

One obvious similarity is that Shakyamuni's followers weren't born into the faith but had to make their own decision to join. Thus we can assume that most of them must have felt the same kind of spiritual hunger that draws Westerners into Buddhism today. Siddartha himself never placed much emphasis on rites, rituals, and ceremonies, and neither do many of the new Buddhist groups we have examined in these pages. Even the most formal Western groups almost always have fewer such practices than the Asian traditions that gave them birth. Another striking similarity between the oldest and the newest forms of Buddhism is their egalitarianism. Despite the stories about the Buddha's hesitation to let women join the monastic sangha, in the context of its times original Buddhism was radically egalitarian. The Buddha did in fact admit women into the sangha and he was quite clear about their potential for full enlightenment. Moreover, he defied the rigid caste barriers of his society and admitted people from all social groups and strata. While there has never been any question about class restrictions in Western Buddhism, it has made enormous strides in allowing the full participation of women as both members and teachers. Although the point is somewhat controversial, many would argue that Western Buddhism has not only allowed the full participation of women but is itself being "feminized," that is, it is moving away from a more goal-oriented and hierarchical "masculine" approach to a softer approach that focuses more on the needs of individual members. It is also far more open to gays, lesbians, and other stigmatized groups than most traditional Western religions.

Most importantly, like most of the new Buddhists, Shakyamuni Buddha focused unwaveringly on the struggle for liberation. In both the newest and the oldest Buddhism, the highest goal is not faith and belief, proper behavior, or ritual devotion, but the direct experience of enlightenment. Both attach great importance to the practice of meditation and both feel that liberation must spring from each individual's own life and practice, not the intercession of the supernormal beings who have assumed such great importance in some forms of Asian Buddhism.

Despite these similarities, this new Western Buddhism is not some sort of fundamentalist movement seeking to return to the "true Buddhism" of the past. Eons of social evolution have left their impact in countless ways. For one thing, the new Buddhism has been able to draw on the philosophies, doctrines, and techniques developed during more than 2,000 years of Buddhist history. From the exquisite dance of contradiction in the great Mahayana sutras to the mysteries of the Zen koan, the new Buddhism has had tremendous wealth from which to draw. It has, moreover, been informed by continuous interaction with other faiths, both Eastern and Western, as well as the insights of the modern sciences and psychotherapies. All in all, the new Buddhism has a breadth of perspective unmatched in Buddhist history.

An even more striking difference is the turn the Buddhist path has made away from monastic withdrawal and into everyday life. The Buddha repeatedly urged his followers to leave behind their involvement with family, sex, and the material world, and devote themselves single-mindedly to the pursuit of liberation. Monastic renunciates were the heart and soul of the Buddhist movement in ancient India and for that matter in most of the rest of Asia. In the new Buddhism, the battleground in the struggle for liberation has shifted away from the monastery. Although Western Buddhists may withdraw from worldly activities for a few weeks for intensive retreats, and a few may even live in a practice center for a period of years, enlightenment is seen as something that must ultimately be realized right in the heart of the suffering and joy of daily life.

While this new Western Buddhism might not have surprised Shakyamuni Buddha, it is something of a puzzle to Asians who grew up in long established Buddhist denominations. To some, Western Buddhism just seems too different to really be Buddhism. Other Asians take considerable pride in the acceptance that their faith is gaining in the West, and a few even see it as a source of revitalization for Buddhism in general. There is little doubt that the onslaught of modern consumer culture has taken its toll on religious vitality in many Buddhist countries just as it has in the West. Buddhists in places like China, Vietnam, and Tibet have also had to face fierce political repression. As Asia continues its relentless drive for economic development, Western Buddhism may well provide a model for a new style of Buddhism that better meets the demands of the postmodern culture taking root there.

So far our focus has been on the new Buddhism itself, but in this final chapter we need to step back a bit and place it in the context of the Western scene of which it is now a part. Despite everything that has been said about the effects of secularization and multiculturalism on the Western faiths, Christianity is still the dominant religious force in the Western world. But year by year, the religious scene is becoming more fragmented, and Christianity's ideological hegemony more precarious. Over the centuries, Christianity itself has fragmented into hundreds of different denominations and traditions, while an almost bewildering range of new religious options and approaches have sprung up. Although the process has gone farther in some Western countries than in others, they have all been moving toward a real religious pluralism. Most of the Christian churches and Judaic denominations are recognized as legitimate mainstream faiths, while the rights of the nonreligious to their convictions are also coming to be a recognized part of this pluralistic mix. Nonetheless, some groups—often classified as cults, fanatics, or just weird—are still beyond the bounds of accepted religious practice. While some of the New Age faiths and practices are objects of laugher and derision, other groups are feared as dangerous, and still others, for example the militant atheists, are stigmatized for their refusal to accept the legitimacy of the dominant religious tradition.

At the present time, Western Buddhism seems to stand somewhere between those two poles. On the one hand, it is still seen as too foreign and exotic to be accepted as a mainstream religion, and its rejection of or at least indifference to the Western concept of a personal God marks it as a subversive influence for many of the faithful. But on the other hand, Buddhism's ancient tradition, strong emphasis on ethical behavior, and status as a major world religion make it far more difficult to marginalize than many of the new religious movements. Another real asset has been the Dalai Lama, whom many Westerners regard as a kind of Buddhist pope and symbol of the faith. His personal charisma as well as his position as a world political figure and steadfast proponent of global peace and understanding make him a very hard person not to admire. Hinduism, Taoism, and Sufism, the traditions that show the strongest similarities to Buddhism in the West, have no single person who can symbolize their faith and aspirations in quite the same way.

On a more individual level, most members of new Buddhist groups clearly fall at the more active end of the religious spectrum rather than among the apathetic and indifferent. Most Westerners (and for that matter most people in the rest of the world) just follow along in the religion into which they were born, with varying degrees of faith and enthusiasm, or slowly drift away from their religious moorings if they had any to begin with. The mere fact that almost all the participants in the new Buddhism are converts requires a much higher degree of commitment. Like converts to other traditions, these are people who are looking for something. People seeking answers to the existential problems that confront their lives. People for whom the religious quest has a pressing personal importance.

The motivations for religious conversions are as diverse as the people who make them. In general, however, it seems fair to say that those who join Buddhist groups tend to have a different religious orientation from those who join, say, the Mormon Church or a fundamentalist Christian group. Converts to those faiths are more likely to be seeking a supportive social group that reinforces their values and a faith that provides a sense of meaning and purpose in their lives. The Buddhists, on the other hand, have what might be termed a more "mystical" orientation. The reader may have noticed that up until now, I have used the term "mysticism" sparingly. The word implies a quest for some kind of a mysterious otherworldly experience, and at its heart Western Buddhism is nothing if not practical and down-to-earth. Yet it clearly falls much farther toward the mystical end of the religious spectrum than do the conventional Western religions. That is to say, it looks inward toward the direct personal experience of the ultimate rather than outward to the world of the established social order. Indeed, it is hard to describe the encounter with vast emptiness that is so central to Buddhist realization as anything but a mystical state.

Many outsiders see the new Western Buddhism as part of the diverse collection of traditions and approaches often dubbed the "New Age," thus putting it in the company of everything from spirit channeling to astrology and some of the more cultlike psychotherapies. This New Age approach to spirituality is so broad and encompassing that its fundamental assumptions are hard to define very clearly. Indeed, one of its most central characteristics is the unwillingness to judge one set of beliefs as true and another as false. As a result, many New Agers have accepted beliefs and practices that are so divergent that they appear contradictory.

In one sense, Buddhism is indeed an important component of the New Age movement, since it is one of the many major ingredients in that eclectic mix. At the same time, however, Buddhism and the other traditional faiths such as Christianity and Hinduism, which are also part of the New Age stew, have much more clearly defined boundaries, beliefs, and practices.

Few of the Buddhist leaders I interviewed would consider themselves part of the New Age movement. Not only are its basic tenets too vaguely defined to satisfy most Buddhist teachers, but the popular image of New Age spirituality carries a connotation of self-indulgence and superficiality that stands in stark contrast to the disciplined practice and strict behavioral standards demanded at most Buddhist centers. Yet it is hard to deny that there are important underlying similarities. If nothing else, they both draw adherents from a very similar and indeed overlapping group of Westerners who are seeking to fulfill their spiritual needs outside the mainstream of orthodox religion. There is, moreover, a mystical stream in the New Age movement that sometimes bears great similarity to Buddhism and in many cases draws directly from it.

In a sociological sense, however, Western Buddhism's more formalized organizational structure and the restraining effects of its long tradition clearly set it off from most of the New Age movement. The movement is, of course, usually considered to include some highly structured organizations of its own such as Scientology and Rev. Moon's Unification Church, but those groups are relatively recent creations with a far weaker affinity to Western Buddhism than the more mystically oriented side of the New Age movement.

In doctrine, practice, and to some degree in organization, Western Buddhism bears the closest resemblance to the groups that have developed around teachers from other Asian traditions—especially the Hindus, Taoists, and Sufis. Although their vocabulary and cultural styles are often quite divergent, the underlying intent is sometimes almost indistinguishable. It is certainly common for Western Buddhist teachers to quote from the likes of Lao Tse, Rumi, and Nisargadatta, and for teachers in those other traditions to quote from various Buddhist masters. Of course, in the case of Hinduism this similarity should hardly be surprising, given the common origins of the two faiths. While there have also been important historical contacts between Buddhism, Sufism (the mystical strain of Islam), and Taoism, the best explanation for their underlying similarities (and those with the Christian mystics and such independent philosophers as Krishnamurti) is the obvious fact that they all embarked on a similar quest in similar circumstances, and therefore they all arrived at a similar destination.

Into the Future

It seems appropriate to end this book with a brief look into the crystal ball, for there are many fascinating questions about what the future may hold for Western Buddhism. Never before in the long history of Buddhism have all of its major traditions entered a new area at the same time, and never before has there been so much contact and exchange among those different traditions. These unique events have led some people to predict that Western Buddhism will eventually turn into an eclectic new amalgam of all Buddhist traditions. We know, for example, that Western Buddhist teachers already borrow freely from one another's traditions and perspectives. As the number of communities with several different Buddhist groups grows, the competition may indeed force them all to adopt whichever characteristics and approaches are most popular with their potential members.

The history of East Asia provides us with some interesting precedents, but unfortunately they point in two different directions. Over the years, the different schools of Buddhism in China, Vietnam, and Korea tended to blend together in an eclectic mix through the same kind of process that many expect to occur here. Yet in Japan numerous Buddhist traditions continue to have distinct sectarian expression.

At the present time, there is still tremendous diversity among the Zen, Vipassana, and Tibetan groups active in the West. In the short run, there is little doubt that there will continue to be four distinctive streams of Western Buddhism—the three just mentioned and a more eclectic, non-sectarian fourth stream in which elements from different Buddhist traditions are synthesized together with a melange of other influences. In the longer run, the likelihood of divergent lexicons, styles, and forms blending together is much greater. Yet there are some fundamental differences in approach that will be difficult to reconcile.

As we have seen, the groups that take a more formal religious approach have sharp differences from those that are closer to the secular end of the spectrum. I am not suggesting that two antagonistic camps are likely to emerge, but neither do these approaches seem to be very compatible companions within the same group. Another pivotal axis is between what Andrew Rawlison has termed the "hot" and the "cool" approaches.[1] The hot approach is emotional, passionate, and visionary. Bright images and complex symbolism abound, and considerable importance is placed on the powers of the cosmic Buddhas and bodhisattvas. The cool approach is more quiet and still. Colors are muted and practitioners tend to see visionary experiences as a distraction from their realization of the vast emptiness within themselves. Once again, it is hard to see how the hot approach favored by most Tibetan groups and such renegades as Kennett Roshi can easily coexist in the same group with the cool traditions of Zen or Vipassana.

Over the last two decades, Buddhist groups throughout the West have been wrestling with the vexing conundrum of power. Up until now, most of the scandals that have rocked Western Buddhism have centered around allegations of some kind of sexual misconduct. But there is good reason to believe that as time goes on that other eternal source of scandal— money—will take on more importance. Most Buddhist groups in the West are still relatively new and have only limited financial assets. But if the history of Asian Buddhism is any guide, we can expect they will eventually become wealthy and influential social institutions. As time goes by, it seems inevitable that some affluent members will bequeath their estates to Buddhist causes and that their assets will grow year by year. Although many Buddhist groups now feel frustrated by their financial constraints, wealth brings its own problems. Today, there is little reason to join a Buddhist group other than a sincere personal quest, but during many periods of Asian history the Buddhist elite lived lives of comfort and ease that were far removed from the deprivation of the average people. As Buddhist groups in the West become wealthier and more influential, they will inevitably attract people looking for something other than spiritual development. Although the years of disciplined training required for top leadership positions will certainly provide some significant protection, even the most sincere teachers will still be faced with a whole host of new temptations for various kinds of financial misconduct.

One approach to the problem of accountability has been to create a code of ethics governing the behavior of the teachers. Although such documents may have considerable symbolic value, they have not proven markedly successful in other kinds of social organizations, and they seem unlikely to be any more fruitful in Buddhist groups. There has, for example, been a growing trend among major corporations to adopt such codes in recent years, but researchers have not found any measurable effect on actual behavior, even when the code contains explicit sanctions. A more promising development lies in the changing structure of power, and the trend to separate the spiritual authority of the teachers from the administrative authority of the board of directors. Even more important is the increasing popularity of various styles of group leadership shared among several different teachers. Since it seems likely that teachers will continue to have enormous prestige and authority within their groups no matter what the official bylaws may say, the active presence of several different teachers of equal authority would seem to provide a natural way to diversify power and discourage abusive behavior.

Some of the most interesting questions concern the Tibetan groups whose Asian leadership, elaborate hierarchy, and tradition of guru devotion have slowed such reforms. Although their future is unclear, three directions seem possible. On the one hand, new generations of Western teachers may eventually take over leadership positions in the Tibetan groups and institute more sweeping structural reforms. But the large community of Tibetan refugees living in difficult conditions in India and Nepal has created a pool of traditionally oriented Asian teachers with a strong motivation to be active in the West. Thus a second possibility is that the Tibetan groups in the West will continue pretty much as they are with close ties to Asian traditions and a more centralized power structure. The most likely scenario, however, is that both will occur. Some of the growing number of qualified Western teachers are likely to start their own groups with a more open style, as Lama Surya Das has done, while other groups continue under Asian leadership with a more traditional approach.

While Buddhism still seems something rather exotic to most Westerners, that too is bound to change over the years. It may ultimately be marginalized as just one more "cult" that has somehow failed to see the importance of worshiping a monotheistic God. There is, however, a good chance that Buddhism will eventually be accepted into the religious mainstream. The demographics of its membership certainly work in its favor. A religion that attracts so many high-status professionals is harder to dismiss than a faith of the poor and minorities, and Buddhism's influence among artists, musicians, and writers may be even more critical. Numerous books, movies, and musical pieces already show a strong Buddhist influence, and there is no doubt about the media's power to influence public opinion. Buddhism's status as a major world religion is another key asset, as is the resonance between the values it advocates and the ideals of Western culture. Western Buddhists may not believe in a personal God, but they are tireless advocates of loving-kindness, compassion, and mutual responsibility.

Real acceptance of Buddhism into Western culture would, however, be no small matter. Most of the generic, nondenominational treatment of religious issues that has become so common in Western public discourse is still predicated on theistic assumptions. In a truly pluralistic society, advocates of religious tolerance would, for example, have to go far beyond the right for everyone to "worship God in their own way." But more important, Buddhism challenges Western society's deepest cultural assumptions about the nature of reality. The mere fact that a respected, religious group would reject the existence of a separate independent self is bound to force some people to think long and hard about the way they look at their lives.

Some of its enthusiasts see Buddhism going well beyond mere acceptance and becoming a mass religion, perhaps someday even challenging the dominant position of Christianity in Western culture. Such a prospect remains, however, very much in doubt. My guess is that Buddhism will grow vigorously for many years to come. As it becomes more familiar to Westerners, its appeal is likely to expand beyond the intellectuals, artists, and bohemians who are willing to experiment with the exotic. But rather than become a mass religion, it seems most likely to continue to draw most of its following from its existing demographic base among well-educated members of the middle and upper classes. It's true that many Buddhist leaders are already expressing concern about the lack of diversity in the Buddhist sangha, and some groups are making serious efforts to reach out to the poor and minorities. But the fact remains that the new Western Buddhism is an intellectually challenging religion that demands an extraordinarily high level of dedication and discipline among its members, and, of course, lots of time to devote to spiritual pursuits. Unlike Asian Buddhism, it lacks the emotional appeal of the devotional faiths that history has shown to hold the greatest attraction for those in the less privileged classes. Those religious elements could still, of course, be imported from the East. But that would require a profound change in the character of many of the Buddhist groups here in the West. Moreover, it is unclear how much mass appeal they would have in competition with the vigorous and well-established traditions of evangelical Christianity.

There is, however, one Buddhist group we haven't considered that has shown itself capable of attracting members from a much wider demographic spectrum. Sokka Gakkai could well prove to be a gateway for Buddhism to reach a wider audience in the West. In earlier times, their aggressive style of proselytization, emphasis on material success, and absence of a meditative tradition, as well as an often brash confidence in the superiority of their approach, left them rather isolated from the wider Buddhist community. Their approach has mellowed with the years, however, and Sokka Gakkai is now playing an increasingly important part in the emerging Western sangha.

Even meditation-oriented Buddhist groups have been effective in reaching out to a broader spectrum of people in one area— prisons. A number of groups now have various kinds of prison dharma projects. Although there are no reliable statistics, interest in Buddhism seems to be growing among prison inmates. It may be that Buddhism is appealing to the same demographic group in prison that it does on the outside, but my own experience with such groups leads me to believe that those prison sanghas have a much broader base. In many ways, the prison is ideally suited for Buddhist practice. Inmates must somehow cope with social stigma and what is often an extremely threatening environment, yet regardless of their class background, they also have lots of time for reading and meditation. Over the years, the growth of "prison dharma" may serve to broaden the demographic horizons of the new Buddhism, although it may ultimately prove to be more of a vehicle for upward mobility for former inmates than anything else.

Whatever place Buddhism ultimately takes in Western society, many prominent members of the Buddhist community would like to see it do more to encourage social change. This movement toward an engaged Buddhism certainly provides an important counterbalance to the tendency of some Buddhists to withdraw their attention from the world in the single-minded pursuit of personal liberation. In another sense, it seems to be a natural corollary of Western Buddhism's focus on everyday life rather than monastic renunciation. Nonetheless, belief in the separation of church and state is strong in the Buddhist community, and there is certainly a great deal of discomfort with the political activism practiced by the religious right. Most members of Buddhist groups I queried said that they did not want their group to become more involved in politics. Their response might have been more favorable if I had asked their opinions about a separate Buddhist organization explicitly devoted to political causes, but it still seems likely that the political activists will remain an influential, high-profile *minority* within the Buddhist community.

There is, on the other hand, much broader support for increased involvement in charity and social welfare. While such efforts are often looked on as more acceptable activities for religious groups than politics, they are still guided by the same ideals that motivate more overtly political activities. So it seems likely that Western Buddhism will continue this trend toward greater social involvement in one way or another.

Buddhism's expanding dialogue with the more liberal elements in Judaism and Christianity may produce important changes in Western Buddhism and in those other faiths as well. Many followers of Western religions already practice Buddhist meditation techniques, and a new synthesis of these religious traditions may well emerge. The history of Buddhism shows that it has often absorbed many elements from the indigenous traditions of the cultures to which it spread or joined with them to create syncretistic new faiths. It wouldn't be at all surprising to see the emergence of some kind of new faith rooted in the Buddhist path of liberation with its highly developed "spiritual technology" which also embraced the theistic language and cosmology of the Judeo-Christian tradition.

The Buddhist perspective is clearly gaining increasing favor among physical scientists and, perhaps more importantly, among therapists and psychologists. Although some traditionalists are afraid that Western science may somehow corrupt Buddhism, if the dharma is really the truth as the name declares, it can hardly be threatened by science. Indeed, many traditional Buddhist leaders from the Dalai Lama on down have not only encouraged a dialogue with Western science, they have been downright enthusiastic about it. The Dalai Lama has gone so far as to say that Buddhist doctrines that are contradicted by the scientific evidence must be changed—a position that few leaders of the world's other major religions are willing to take.

Just as Buddhism was first translated into Chinese using traditional Taoist terminology, it is often presented in the concepts of contemporary social science in the West. But more than just a matter of terminology, the new Buddhism has absorbed a great deal of the Western understanding of personal psychology. For its part, Buddhism certainly has much to offer Western social scientists and especially Western psychotherapists who are struggling to deal with the deepest existential suffering of their patients. While Western psychology has developed considerable knowledge of the workings of the self, it has never taken the leap to question its fundamental reality. The Buddhist belief that the self has no independent existence and that our endless efforts to support, protect, and enhance it are in fact the fundamental source of human suffering provides a challenge to rethink the most basic understandings of Western psychology.

Not surprisingly, therapists themselves appear more likely to participate in Buddhist groups than those in just about any other profession—with the possible exception of college professors. Indeed, Buddhist practice has already had a powerful influence on the way many therapists treat their patients. John Cabat-Zinn, for example, has been extremely successful in promoting a secularized version of Buddhism for use as the basis of a stress reduction program, and other such innovations seem likely to follow. Indeed, some people think that Buddhism actually has more in common with Western psychotherapy than Western religion. Many Buddhist teachers in the West are licensed therapists, and a few have actually begun offering Buddhist teachings and guidance the way therapists offer their services. Rather than the traditional group setting, students schedule individual appointments at their teacher's office and pay by the hour. Whether religion or therapy, in the final analysis the goal remains the same.

How great a social impact will Buddhism ultimately have? Some may dismiss Western Buddhism as a small religious movement of minor social import, but size and importance are not necessarily the same. For one thing, although Buddhism may be unlikely to ever attain the dominant position in the West that Christianity now holds, it is gaining a rapidly increasing number of adherents among those in key positions to influence the direction our culture will take in the years ahead. The Eastern worldview, of which Buddhism is a major part, has already had an influence far beyond those who come to identify themselves as Buddhists. But to really understand the potential impact of the new Buddhism we must take a more global view.

There seems little doubt that we are standing on the verge of a unique new era in human history that will see the world's first truly global culture take shape. So far the influence has been flowing primarily from West to East, but it is naive to think that the rest of the planet will just passively adopt Western culture. Buddhism's greatest impact in the West and in Africa, Latin America, and even much of Asia may well be from its influence on the new synthesis that comes out of this historic cultural encounter. Buddhism's most fundamental attitudes, beliefs, and assumptions are so radically different from those common in the West that they could well contribute to a major change in the trajectory of the evolution of world culture.

Despite its gentle mien, Buddhism is a profoundly subversive force in postmodern consumer society. The structure of our economy, our psychology, our whole social reality is built around the unquestioned assumption that we are each of us separate, autonomous selves. Selves with endless appetites for consumer goods to set us off from the crowd, make us feel good about who we are, and give us a sense of identity. Selves that identify with a particular ethnic group, political party, or ideology. Selves driven by a sense of inadequacy, driven by the desire to be better, richer, or wiser people, driven by the need to prove their worth, driven by dark fears about the future and the fate that awaits us. What would happen if enough people saw through all that? If there was a critical mass for change? Perhaps these are just hypothetical questions about the unlikeliest of events, but then again perhaps not. Of course, no important social transformations ever come from a single cause. But few would deny that there is a kind of restless instability in our personal lives and in the way we structure postmodern society, and it is not hard to imagine that some very fundamental changes await us in the years ahead.

Appendix I: Buddhist Centers in the West

For readers interested in a comprehensive listing of Western Buddhist centers I recommend Don Morreale's *The Complete Guide to Buddhist America* (Boston: Shambhala, 1998) for North America and the Buddhist Society's *Buddhist Directory*, 7th ed. (London: Buddhist Society, 1997) for Ireland and the United Kingdom. Morreale's book is widely available in bookstores. The address of the Buddhist Society is:

59 Eccleston Square
London SW1V 1PH
United Kingdom
Phone: 0171 976 5238

There is space here only to list the largest centers that figure most prominently in the story told in this book. Many of the centers listed here head up a large network of affiliated centers and groups, and readers interested in finding a local group in a particular lineage should contact the main offices listed below.

There are hundreds of Vipassana groups scattered throughout the West, but there are two Vipassana hubs in North America. On the East Coast the most important Vipassana center is:

Insight Meditation Society (IMS)
1230 Pleasant Street
Barre, Mass. 01005
(508) 355-4378

On the West Coast it is:

Spirit Rock Meditation Center
P.O Box 909
5000 Sir Francis Drake Boulevard
Woodacre, Calif. 94973
(415) 488-0164

Zen

Zen groups are more numerous than Vipassana groups in the West, and it is harder to give a short listing of their most influential centers. Those interested in Shunryu Suzuki's lineage should contact the following:

San Francisco Zen Center
300 Page Street
San Francisco, Calif. 94102
(415) 863-3136

Homebase for the lineage of Maezumi Roshi is:

Zen Center of Los Angeles
923 South Normandie Avenue
Los Angeles, Calif. 90006-1301
(213) 387-2351

For the numerous centers in the Korean Zen lineage of Seung Sahn contact:

Providence Zen Center
99 Pound Road
Cumberland, R.I. 02864-1464
(401) 658-1464

To make contact with some of Thich Nhat Hanh's groups in the English-speaking nations, write or phone:

Community of Mindful Living
P.O. Box 7355
Berkeley, Calif. 94707
(510) 527-3741

Other influential centers include Philip Kapleau's:

Rochester Zen Center
7 Arnold Park
Rochester, N.Y. 14607
(716) 473-9180

and Robert Aitken's

Diamond Sangha
2119 Kaloa Way
Honolulu, Haw. 96822
(808) 946-0666

as well as Jiyu Kennett's

Shasta Abbey
P.O. Box 199
3612 Summit Drive
Mount Shasta, Calif. 96067-0199
(916) 926-4208

The largest Western sangha following the Tibetan tradition was founded by Trungpa Rinpoche. Its headquarters is in Nova Scotia:

Shambhala International
1084 Tower Road
Halifax, Nova Scotia B3H 2Y5
(902) 425-2750

Their largest center in the United States is:

Boulder Shambhala Center
1345 Spruce Street
Boulder, Colo. 80302
(303) 444-0190

The U.K. headquarters for Sogyal Rinpoche's Rigpa Fellowship is:

Rigpa
330 Caledonian Road
London N1 1BB
071 700 0185

In the United States it is:

Rigpa North America
P.O. Box 607
Santa Cruz, Calif. 95061-0607

Lama Surya Das's organization is the:

Dzogchen Foundation
P.O. Box 734
Cambridge, Mass. 02140

Nonsectarian

Nonsectarian groups tend to be small and independent and thus are difficult to include in a listing such as this. One exception is the Friends of the Western Buddhist Order:

The London Buddhist Centre
51 Roman Road
Bethnal Green
London E2 oHU
0181 981 1225

Toni Packer's center is:

Springwater Center for Meditative Inquiry
7179 Mill Street
Springwater, N.Y. 14560
(716) 669-2141

An influential college with a Buddhist affiliation is:

Naropa Institute
2130 Arapahoe Avenue
Boulder, Colo. 80302
(303) 444-0202

The Buddhist Peace Fellowship is the leading Western organization expressing the ideals of engaged Buddhism:

Buddhist Peace Fellowship
P.O. Box 4650
Berkeley, Calif. 94704
(510) 525-7973

CYBER RESOURCES

There is a growing wealth of Buddhist resources on the internet. Two good places to start are:

DharmaNet International
http://www.dharmanet.org

and

Buddhist Resources File
http://ccbs.ntu.edu.tn/BRF/

Appendix II: The Questionnaire

This questionnaire was not administered to all the groups surveyed simultaneously. Rather, I focused on one tradition at a time, doing interviews and visits before asking for cooperation in distributing the survey. The first group surveyed was the Berkeley Zen Center (1992) and the last was the White Heron Sangha (1996). Reproduced below is the core of the questionnaire administered to the groups. After analyzing the early returns, I made some minor changes to deal with various problems that arose. The questionnaire below includes those changes. Some groups were also asked additional questions that were specific to their lineage or tradition which are not included here.

Please answer as many questions as you can and return this form in the attached envelope. Feel free to skip any question you do not feel comfortable answering. All answers are strictly confidential. *Thanks for your help*!

1. How long have you participated in the [name of group being surveyed]?

2. How long have you been involved with any Buddhist organization or teacher?

3. In an average month, how often do you attend meditation groups or visit Buddhist centers?

4. If you are involved with other Buddhist organizations/teachers aside from those affiliated with this group, please list them:

5. Would you say that your involvement with Buddhist organizations has been:
   increasing   staying the same   or decreasing
   over the last year? (Please circle your answer.)

6. If you are involved in any non-Buddhist spiritual organizations, please list them:

7. How did you first become interested in Buddhism? (Check one.)
   Friends   Books   Newspapers or television
   Lectures   Other (Please specify):

8. How long have you been practicing meditation?

9. In which tradition has most of your practice been?
   Tibetan   Zen   Vipassana   Other (Specify)

10. About what percentage of your meditation sessions occur at:
    A meditation group or Buddhist center   % Your home   %
    Somewhere else   % (Please specify location.)

11. When you meditate, do you usually (check one):
    Count your breath   Follow your breath without counting
    Label your thoughts and emotions   Sit without focusing your
    attention on any particular object   Work on a koan
    Mantra   Visualization   Other (Please specify.)

12. Approximately how many times have you attended a meditation retreat?

13. What is the longest period of time you have attended a single retreat?

14. In an average week, how many times do you do sitting meditation? For how many minutes (each time)?

15. How often do you do the following?
Walking meditation   Never   Occasionally   Regularly
Prostrations   Never   Occasionally   Regularly
Tantric sexual practices Never   Occasionally   Regularly

16. Please rank each of the following activities commonly carried on by Buddhist groups in order of their importance to you. (1 most important, 3 least important)
Social relations with other members   Meditation
Ceremonies and rituals

17. How great an impact has Buddhism had on your daily life?
Very Significant   Significant   Small   None

18. How often do you read books or articles that deal with Buddhism?
Frequently   Occasionally   Rarely   Never

19. How many of your friends are involved in Buddhism?
All of them   Most of them   Three out of four
Half   One out of four   Only few   None

20. Have you ever taken a psychedelic drug such as LSD, MDMA, or psilocybin (not including marijuana)? No   Yes
If you answered yes, how important were your experiences with such drugs in attracting you to Buddhism?
Very   Fairly   Some   Not at all

21. Have you ever practiced a martial art such as karate or kung-fu?
No   Yes
If yes, how important was it in attracting you to Buddhism?
Very   Fairly   Some   Not at all
Buddhism stimulated my interest in the martial arts

22. Would you say you are a Buddhist?
No   Don't Know   Yes

A Christian?   No   Don't Know   Yes

A believer in Judaism?   No   Don't Know   Yes

23. I feel that discrimination against women is a serious problem in American Buddhism.
Strongly Agree   Agree   Disagree   Strongly Disagree

24. What happens to us in this life is determined by the kind of karma we create.
Strongly Agree   Agree   Disagree   Strongly Disagree

25. After death, we are reborn into another life.
Strongly Agree   Agree   Disagree   Strongly Disagree

26. I think women have equal chance with men in attaining leadership positions in [name of group].
Strongly Agree   Agree   Disagree   Strongly Disagree

27. I became interested in Buddhism in order to help me deal with my personal problems.
Strongly Agree   Agree   Disagree   Strongly Disagree

28. I became interested in Buddhism because of a desire for spiritual fulfillment.
Strongly Agree   Agree   Disagree   Strongly Disagree

29. I became interested in Buddhism because I was attracted by the people I met who were involved with it.
Strongly Agree   Agree   Disagree   Strongly Disagree

30. Buddhist teachers often show little interest in my needs.
Strongly Agree   Agree   Disagree   Strongly Disagree

31. My Buddhist practice has had a very positive influence on my life.
Strongly Agree   Agree   Disagree   Strongly Disagree

32. The meditation periods in the group are too long and difficult.
Strongly Agree   Agree   Disagree   Strongly Disagree

33. Buddhist groups should be more actively involved in charities and other work to benefit the larger community.
Strongly Agree   Agree   Disagree   Strongly Disagree

34. Buddhist groups should be more involved in political causes.
Strongly Agree   Agree   Disagree   Strongly Disagree

35. Buddhist groups should encourage more social activities and contacts among their members.
Strongly Agree   Agree   Disagree   Strongly Disagree

36. If I call on them, the Buddhas and bodhisattvas will help me with my problems.
Strongly Agree   Agree   Disagree   Strongly Disagree

37. Gender: Female   Male

38. Age:

39. Ethnic group:

40. Education: Not a high school graduate   Finished high school
Some college   College graduate   Advanced degrees

41. What was the total income of your family last year?
Under $10,000 $10,000 $30,000 $30,000–$60,000
$60,000-$90,000 $90,000–$120,000   Above $120,000

42. Please place a mark where you feel your political views fall within the range of opinions of the American public as a whole.
Right   1   2   3   4   5   6   7   8   9   10   Left

43. Which political party do you feel closest to?
Republicans   Democrats   None   Other

44. What was the predominate religious orientation of the family in which you were raised?

Notes

The description of traditional Asian Buddhism is based on numerous sources, most of which are discussed in the notes section for the next chapter. My sources for the historical sketch of Western Buddhism are included in the notes for chapter 3. For Max Weber's ideas about the "routinization of charisma," see his *Sociology of Religion*, trans. Ephraim Fischoff (Boston: Beacon, 1963). Thomas Tweed's study of North America's early encounter with Buddhism was published as *The American Encounter with Buddhism, 1844–1912: Victorian Culture and the Limits of Dissent* (Bloomington: Indiana University Press, 1992). Anthony Giddens has written widely about the nature of contemporary society. His most relevant work to the discussion above is *Modernity and Self-Identity: Self and Society in the Late Modern Age* (Stanford: Stanford University Press, 1991). On the question of how many Buddhist there are in the United States, see Barry A. Kosmin and Seymour P. Lachman, *One Nation under God: Religion in Contemporary American Society* (New York: Harmony, 1993). The *Los Angeles Times* article I mentioned is Mary Rourke, "Redefining Religion in America," June 21, 1998, pp. A1, 28–29. The second edition of Don Morreale's *The Complete Guide to Buddhist America* was published by Shambhala in 1998. The *Buddhist Directory* is published by the Buddhist Society in London. A complete list of the questions in my survey appears in appendix A.

1. Barry A. Kosmin and Seymour P. Lachman, *One Nation under God: Religion in Contemporary American Society* (New York: Harmony, 1993), p. 16. The number I used to compute this estimate is 274,634,000, the U.S. Census Bureau population estimate for the year 2000.

2. Martin Baumann, "The Dharma Has Come West: A Survey of Recent Studies and Sources," *Journal of Buddhist Ethics*, 4 (1997), p. 198.

3. Kimberly Winston, "About Books," *Publisher's Weekly*, September 14, 1998, reprinted in *Tricycle: The Buddhist Review*, Winter 1998, pp. 88–93.

TWO: ASIAN ROOTS

Of all the chapters in this book, this one had by far the greatest number of easily available sources upon which to draw. For the sake of brevity, I will list only the most important of the numerous works I consulted. For a general treatment of the history of Buddhism, Peter Harvey's *An Introduction to Buddhism: Teachings, History, and Practices* (Cambridge: Cambridge University Press, 1990); Richard H. Robinson and Willard L. Johnson's *The Buddhist Religion: A Historical Introduction*, 3d ed. (Belmont, Calif.: Wadsworth, 1982); and Edward Conze's *A Short History of Buddhism* (London: Allen & Unwin, 1980). Despite its title, John Snelling's *The Buddhist Handbook* (Rochester, Vt.: Inner Traditions, 1991) also devotes a considerable amount of attention to historical issues. For a collection of articles on various historical issues, there is Charles S. Prebish, ed., *Buddhism: A Modern Perspective* (University Park, Pa.: Pennsylvania State University Press, 1975); and William Theodore de Bary, ed., *The Buddhist Tradition in India, China, and Japan* (New York: Vintage, 1972). Two useful works on the earliest days of Buddhism are Kogen Mizuno, *The Beginnings of Buddhism* (Tokyo: Kosei, 1980); and Walpola Rahula, *What the Buddha Taught*, 2d ed. (New York: Evergreen, 1974). Two sources that covered both the earliest teachings of the Buddha and the intricacies of Mahayana philosophy are A. K. Warder, *Indian Buddhism* (Delhi: Motilal Banarsidass, 1980); and David J. Kalupahana, *A History of Buddhist Philosophy* (Honolulu: University of Hawaii Press, 1992). Another good source was Paul Williams, *Mahayana Buddhism: The Doctrinal Foundations* (London: Routledge, 1989). A rather specialized work that nonetheless sheds light on a number of important issues in Buddhist philosophy is Paul J. Griffiths's *On Being Mindless: Buddhist Meditation and the Mind-Body Problem* (La Salle, Ill.: Open Court, 1986). For Indian sociocultural context, A. L. Basham's *The Wonder That Was India,* 3d rev. ed. (New York: Taplinger, 1967) is still my favorite work, although Romila Thapar's *A History of Buddhism,* vol. 1 (Harmondsworth, U.K.: Penguin, 1966) is also extremely useful. Charles Drekmeier's *Kingship and Community in Early India* (Stanford: Stanford University Press, 1962) is also quite helpful. For Tibet, I used Thubten Jigme Norbu and Colin M. Turnbull's highly readable *Tibet* (New York: Clarion, 1968), as well as Tulku Thondup Rinpoche, *Buddhist Civilization in Tibet* (New York: Routledge & Kegan Paul, 1987). For Chinese history, I like Charles O. Hucker, *China's Imperial Past* (Stanford: Stanford University Press, 1975). On Chinese Buddhism there is Arthur F. Wright's *Buddhism in Chinese History* (Stanford: Stanford University Press, 1959) and covering both Ch'an and Zen are Heinrich Dumoulin, *Zen Buddhism: A History*, vols. 1–2 (New York: Macmillan, 1988, 1990); Thomas Hoover, *The Zen Experience* (New York: New American Library, 1980); and John R. McRae, "The Story of Early Ch'an" in *Zen: Tradition and Transmission*, ed. Kenneth Kraft (New York: Grove, 1988). J. C. Cleary's *Introduction to A Buddha from Korea: The Zen Teachings of T'aego* (Boston: Shambhala, 1988) contains an excellent treatment of the fundamentals of East Asian Buddhism. Another good source on Korean Buddhism is Mu Soeng Sunim, *Thousand Peaks: Korean Zen-Traditions and Teachers* (Berkeley, Calif.: Parallax, 1987); and for Korean history, Carter J. Eckert et al., *Korea Old and New: A History* (Seoul: Ilchokak, 1990). For Japanese history, W. Scott Morton, *Japan: Its History and Culture* (New York: McGraw-Hill, 1984); and H. Paul Varley, *Japanese Culture: A Short History* (New York: Praeger, 1973).

1. Kogen Mizuno, *The Beginnings of Buddhism*, trans. Richard L. Gage (Tokyo: Kosei, 1980), pp. 16–17.
2. Edward Conze, *Buddhism: Its Essence and Development* (Oxford: Cassirer, 1957), p. 94.
3. Edward Conze, *A Short History of Buddhism* (Belmont Calif.: Dickenson, 1970), p. 45.
4. Richard H. Robinson and Willard L. Johnson, *The Buddhist Religion: A Historical Introduction*, 3d ed. (Belmont, Calif.: Wadsworth, 1982), p. 175.
5. Heinrich Dumoulin, *Zen Buddhism: A History* (New York: Macmillan, 1988), 1:172.

THREE: WESTERN FLOWER

There are three excellent treatments of the history of Western Buddhism. For the earliest period there is Thomas Tweed's *The American Encounter with Buddhism, 1844–1912: Victorian Culture and the Limits of Dissent* (Bloomington: Indiana University Press, 1992). Rick Fields, *How the Swans Came to the Lake: A Narrative History of Buddhism in America*, rev. ed. (Boston: Shambhala, 1986); and Stephen Batchelor, *The Awakening of the West: The Encounter of Buddhism and Western Culture* (Berkeley, Calif.: Parallax, 1994) cover roughly the same ground, although Fields focuses more on North America and Batchelor more on Europe. Fields updated his work in Rick Fields, "The Changing of the Guard: Western Buddhism in the Eighties," *Tricycle*, Winter 1991. The *Wind Bell* published by the San Francisco Zen Center published several good articles on its history, and Abbot Mel Weitsman published a history of the Berkeley Zen Center in *Old Plum Mountain Shogakku-ji*, which the center published in 1989. Catherine Ingram has written a good history of Vipassana in the West, "Awakening the Mind," *Yoga Journal*, March-April 1987, pp. 28–33. Another good source on Vipassana is Gil Fronsdal, "Insight Meditation in the United States: Life, Liberty, and the Pursuit of Happiness," pp. 163–180, in *The Face of Buddhism in America* ed. Charles Prebish and Kenneth Tanaka (Berkeley. University of California Press, 1998). On Thich Nhat Hanh and engaged Buddhism, see Kenneth Kraft, "Meditation in Action: The Emergence of Engaged Buddhism," *Tricycle*, Spring 1993, and Donald Rothberg, "Responding to the Cries of the World," pp. 253–265, in *The Face of Buddhism in America*. The autobiographies by Alan Watts, *In My Own Way* (New York: Vintage, 1972) and Chogyam Trungpa, *Born in Tibet* (Baltimore, Md.: Penguin, 1971) are highly valuable. D. T. Suzuki's *The Training of the Zen Buddhist Monk* (New York: University Books, 1965) and Jack Kornfield's *A Path with Heart* (New York: Bantam, 1993) also contain some autobiographical material.

Among the interviews I conducted, the most useful for this chapter were those with Abbot Norman Fischer of the San Francisco Zen Center, Abbot Mel Weitsman of the Berkeley Zen Center, Bodhin Kjolhede Sensei of the Rochester Zen Center, Abbot Bernard Glassman of the Zen Community of New York, Taizan Maezumi Roshi of the Los Angeles Zen Center, Anna Douglas, Julie Wester, and Nancy Taylor of the Spirit

Rock Meditation Center, Richard Streitfeld and Ellen Sidor of the Providence Zen Center, Soen Sa Nim of the Kwan Um School of Zen, Reggie Ray, Robert Spellman, and Richard Authure of Vajradhatu, Helen Tworkov of *Tricycle* magazine, and numerous informal talks with Toni Packer.

1. Thomas Tweed, *The American Encounter with Buddhism, 1844–1912:Victorian Culture and the Limits of Dissent* (Bloomington: Indiana University Press, 1992), p. 18.
2. *Wind Bell* 8 (Fall 1969): 8.
3. John Snelling, *The Buddhist Handbook* (Rochester, N.Y.: Inner Traditions, 1991), p. 203.
4. Jack Kerouac, *The Dharma Bums* (New York: Viking, 1959), p. 78.
5. Alan Watts, *In My Own Way: An Autobiography* (New York: Vintage, 1972), p. 358.
6. Alan W. Watts, *Beat Zen, Square Zen, and Zen* (San Francisco: City Lights, 1959).
7. Watts, *In My Own Way,* pp. 359–360.
8. Ibid., p. 421.
9. Ibid., p. 54.
10. Ibid., p. 224.
11. Peter Stafford, *Psychedelics Encyclopedia,* 3d ed. (Berkeley, Calif.: Ronin, 1992), p. 38.
12. Jacob Needleman, *The New Religions,* rev. ed. (New York: Pocket Books, 1970), p. 49.
13. Quoted in Richard Baker, introductioni to Shunryu Suzuki, *Zen Mind, Beginner's Mind* (New York: Weatherhill, 1970), p. 18.
14. Suzuki, *Zen Mind,* p. 28.
15. Shunryu Suzuki, "Sesshin Lecture," *Wind Bell,* June 1971.
16. Rick Fields, *How the Swans Came to the Lake: A Narrative History of Buddhism in America,* rev. ed. (Boston: Shambhala, 1986), p. 230.
17. Ken McLeod, "The Three-Year Retreat," in *Buddhist America: Centers, Retreats, Practices,* ed. Don Morreale (Santa Fe: John Muir Publications, 1988), p. 218.
18. Fields, *How the Swans Came,* p. 282.
19. Chogyam Trungpa, *Born in Tibet* (Baltimore, Md.: Penguin, 1971), pp. 252–253.
20. Quoted in Fields, *How the Swans Came,* p. 303.
21. Chogyam Trungpa, *Cutting through Spiritual Materialism* (Boulder: Shambhala, 1973), p. 3.
22. Quoted in Jeremy Hayward, *Sacred World: A Guide to Shambhala Warriorship in Daily Life* (New York: Bantam, 1995) p. 129.
23. Stephen T. Butterfield, *The Double Mirror: A Skeptical Journey into Buddhist Tantra* (Berkeley, Calif.: North Atlantic, 1994), pp. 151–152.
24. Jack Kornfield, *A Path with Heart* (New York: Bantam, 1993), pp. 6–7.
25. Quoted in Tony Schwartz, *What Really Matters* (New York: Bantam, 1996), p. 331.
26. Kornfield, *Path with Heart,* pp. 8–9.
27. Quoted in Stephen Batchelor, *The Awakening of the West: The Encounter of Buddhism and Western Culture* (Berkeley, Calif.: Parallax, 1994), p. 366.
28. Batchelor, *Awakening of the West,* p. 337.
29. Quoted in William Elliott, *Tying Rocks to Clouds: Meetings and Conversations with Wise and Spiritual People* (Wheaton, Ill.: Quest, 1995), p. 174.

30. Quoted in Elliott, *Tying Rocks,* p. 173.

31. Ibid., p. 169

32. Ibid., p. 174.

33. Ibid., pp. 174–175.

34. Batchelor, *Awakening of the West*, p. 358.

35. Thich Nhat Hanh, *For a Future to Be Possible: Commentaries on the Five Wonderful Precepts* (Berkeley, Calif.: Parallax, 1993), pp. 3–4.

36. Quoted in Kenneth Kraft, "Meditation in Action: The Emergence of Engaged Buddhism," *Tricycle,* Spring 1993, p. 47.

FOUR: AT THE MARROW

Most of the hundreds of books published in the West by various Buddhist teachers contain some kind of description of their practices and beliefs, and they are far too numerous to list here. A few that I found most useful are as follows: For Zen, Philip Kapleau's classic book *Three Pillars of Zen,* rev. and exp. ed. (Garden City, N.Y.: Anchor, 1980) answers many basic questions that others often neglect. Kapleau's is a more Rinzai-oriented style, and I think nothing captures the spirit of Soto Zen better than Shunryu Suzuki's *Zen Mind, Beginner's Mind* (New York: Weatherhill, 1970). Jack Kornfield and Joseph Goldstein represent the two poles of Western Vipassana practice and I would recommend Joseph Goldstein, *The Experience of Insight* (Boston: Shambhala, 1987); and Jack Kornfield, *A Path with Heart* (New York: Bantam, 1993). Stephen T. Butterfield's autobiographical work, *The Double Mirror: A Skeptical Journey into Buddhist Tantra* (Berkeley: North Atlantic, 1994) is full of insights into the practices and problems in Trungpa Rinpoche's Vajradhatu centers. The fall 1991 issue of *Inquiring Mind* is devoted to a comparison of the different Buddhist traditions active in the West and is very useful. Don Morreale's encyclopedic listing of North American Buddhist centers, *The Complete Guide to Buddhist America* (Boston: Shambhala, 1998) is a vital statistical resource and includes some extremely useful short articles on various groups, traditions, and practices. *The Buddhist Directory,* published by the Buddhist Society in London performs much the same function for the British Isles that Morreale's book does for North America except that it started earlier (1979) and is updated more often. A critical academic literature on Western Buddhism is just now beginning to emerge. One of the best sources is Charles Prebish and Kenneth Tanaka's collection of articles, *The Faces of Buddhism in America* (Berkeley: University of California Press, 1998). I found Gil Fronsdal's "Insight Meditation in the United States: Life, Liberty, and the Pursuit of Happiness," G. Victor Sogen Hori's "Japanese Zen in America: Americanizing the Face in the Mirror," Amy Lavine's "Tibetan Buddhism in America: The Development of American Vajrayana," and Donald Rothberg's "Responding to the Cries of the World: Socially Engaged Buddhism in North America" to be especially useful.

Most of the interviews I conducted touched on issues of practice and belief. Among the most useful were those with Abbot Norman Fischer of the San Francisco Zen Center; Abbot Mel Weitsman of the Berkeley Zen Center; Bodhin Kjolhede Sensei of the Rochester Zen Center; Abbot Bernard Glassman of the Zen Community of New York; Taizan Maezumi Roshi of the Los Angeles Zen Center; Anna Douglas, Julie

Wester, and Nancy Taylor of the Spirit Rock Meditation Center; Ellen Sidor and Do An Sunim of the Providence Zen Center; Soen Sa Nim, Richard Streitfeld, and Mu Deung Sunim of the Kwan Um School of Zen; Reggie Ray, Robert Spellman, and Richard Authure of Vajradhatu in Boulder, Colorado; Judith Simmer-Brown of the Naropa Institute; Lama Surya Das of the Dzogchen Foundation;Rob Crow-Mains of the FWBO's London Centre; and Helen Tworkov of *Tricycle* magazine. Finally, the single essential source of data for this chapter was participant observation at the meetings and retreats of groups from the four of the main streams of Western Buddhism.

1. Don Morreale, ed., *The Complete Guide to Buddhist America* (Boston: Shambhala, 1998); and Morreale, ed., *Buddhist America: Centers, Retreats, Practices* (Santa Fe: John Muir Publications, 1988).

2. Shunryu Suzuki, *Zen Mind, Beginner's Mind* (New York: Weatherhill, 1970), pp. 43–44.

3. Thich Nhat Hanh, *Peace Is Every Step* (New York: Bantam, 1991), pp. 27–28.

4. This rendering is based on four popular English translations: Paul Reps, *Zen Flesh, Zen Bones: A Collection of Zen and Pre-Zen Writings* (New York: Anchor, 1961); Katsuki Sekida, *Two Zen Classics: Mumonkan and Hekiganroku* (New York: Weatherhill, 1977); Robert Aitken, *The Gateless Barrier: The Wu-Men Kuan* (San Francisco: North Point, 1990); and Thomas Cleary, *No Barrier: Unlocking the Zen Koan* (New York: Bantam, 1993).

5. Robert A.F. Thurman, "Talking Tantra: An Interview with Robert A.F. Thurman," *Inquiring Mind* 8 (Fall 1991): 6.

6. West Abrashkin, "All-Night Vigil to Yumka," in *Complete Guide*, pp. 227–228.

7. Ken McLeod, "The Three-Year Retreat," in *Buddhist America*, p. 218.

8. These quotations are from personal interviews conducted by the author.

9. Gil Fronsdal, "Life, Liberty, and the Pursuit of Happiness: Insight Meditation in the United States" (Stanford: Department of Religious Studies, Stanford University, 1995), p. 1.

10. Armstrong, "Path of the Buddha."

11. Sharon Salzberg, "A Lovingkindness Retreat," in *Complete Guide*, p. 19.

12. Joseph Goldstein, *The Experience of Insight: A Simple and Direct Guide to Buddhist Meditation* (Boston: Shambhala, 1976), pp. 5–6.

13. Manjuvajra, "Aryaloka," in *Complete Guide*, p. 327. Text in parentheses is original.

14. Henry Shukman, "Friends of the Western Buddhist Order: Friends, Foes, and Files," *Tricycle*, Summer 1999, p. 117.

15. Donald Rothberg, "Responding to the Cries of the World: Socially Engaged Buddhism in North America," in *The Faces of Buddhism in America*, ed. Charles S. Prebish and Kenneth K. Tanaka (Berkeley: University of California Press, 1998), p. 268.

16. Thich Nhat Hanh, *Peace Is Every Step*, p. 91.

17. Quoted in Joseph Goldstein, "Liberation through Nonclinging Is the Point Where All Buddhist Traditions Agree," in *Complete Guide*, p. xxxi.

18. Kazuaki Tanahashi, ed., *Moon in a Dewdrop: Writings of Zen Master Dogen* (San Francisco: North Point, 1985) p. 70.

19. Stephen T. Butterfield, *The Double Mirror* (Berkeley: North Atlantic, 1994), p. 103.

20. Suzuki, *Zen Mind*, pp. 59–60.

21. Thurman, "Talking Tantra," p. 7.
22. Barbara Gates, ed., "Western Teachers' Forum on the Schools of Buddhism," *Inquiring Mind* 8 (Fall 1991): 10.
23. Stephen Batchelor, "Deep Agnosticism: A Secular Vision of Dharma Practice," in *Buddhism in America: Proceedings of the First Buddhism in America Conference*, ed. Al Rapaport (Rutland, Vt.: Tuttle, 1998), p. 177.
24. Toni Packer, *The Work of This Moment* (Boston: Shambhala, 1990), pp. 38–39.
25. What followers are ideal types in the Weberian sense. See Max Weber, *Theory of Economic and Social Organization* (New York: The Free Press, 1947).
26. Jack Kornfield, *A Path with Heart* (New York: Bantam, 1993), p. 236.
27. Chogyam Trungpa, *The Myth of Freedom and the Way of Meditation* (Boston: Shambhala, 1976), pp. 137–138.
28. C. Victor Sogen Hori, "Japanese Zen in America: Americanizing the Face in the Mirror," in *Faces of Buddhism*, p. 66.

FIVE: SEX, POWER, AND CONFLICT

There are numerous books devoted to the issues of women and Buddhism. One of the best is Sandy Boucher, *Turning the Wheel: American Women Creating the New Buddhism* (San Francisco: Harper & Row, 1988). A more theoretical analysis can be found in Rita M. Gross, *Buddhism after Patriarchy: A Feminist History, Analysis, and Reconstruction of Buddhism* (Albany: State University of New York Press, 1993). Other useful books include Marianne Dresser, ed., *Buddhist Women on the Edge: Contemporary Perspectives from the Western Frontier* (Berkeley, Calif.: North Atlantic, 1996); Karma Lekshe Tsomo, ed., *Sakyadhita: Daughters of the Buddha* (Ithaca, N.Y.: Snow Lion, 1988); and Ellen S. Sidor, *A Gathering of Spirit: Women Teaching in American Buddhism* (Cumberland, R.I.: Primary Point, 1987).

The best single source on the role of sex in Buddhism is probably John Stevens, *Lust for Enlightenment: Buddhism and Sex* (Boston: Shambhala, 1990). However, Stevens's primary focus is on East Asian Buddhism; for the tantric approach I would recommend Miranda Shaw, *Passionate Enlightenment: Women in Tantric Buddhism* (Princeton: Princeton University Press, 1994). The most complete source on homosexuality and Buddhism is Winston Leyland, ed., *Queer Dharma: Voices of Gay Buddhists* (San Francisco: Gay Sunshine, 1998); also see Roger Coreless, "Coming Out in the Sangha: Queer Community in American Buddhism," in *The Faces of American Buddhism*, ed. Charles Prebish and Kenneth Tanaka (Berkeley: University of California Press, 1998), pp. 253–265. On Issan Dorsey see his biography: David Schneider, *Street Zen: The Life and Work of Issan Dorsey* (Boston: Shambhala, 1993).

Numerous publications have covered the scandals in Western Buddhism. One of the first, and still among the most useful, is Katy Butler, "Encountering the Shadow in Buddhist America," *Common Boundary*, May-June 1990. Stephen T. Butterfield's *The Double Mirror: A Skeptical Journey into Buddhist Tantra* (Berkeley, Calif.: North Atlantic, 1994) offers insight into many aspects of Vajradhatu, and Rick Fields covered these issues in "The Changing of the Guard: Western Buddhism in the Eighties," *Tricycle*, Winter 1991, pp. 42–49. A thorough discussion of the charges against Sogyal Rinpoche can be found in Mick Brown, "Scandal and the Living Buddha," *Telegraph Magazine*, February 25, 1995, pp. 20–29. For the charges against the Friends of the Western Buddhist Order, see Henry Shukman, "Friends of the Western Buddhist Order: Friends, Foes, and Files," *Tricycle*, Summer 1999, pp. 66–68, 112–118. On Jetsunma Ahkon Lhamo see Martha Sherrill's fascinating book *The Buddha from Brooklyn* (New York: Random House, 2000). There is also a fascinating video documentary by Anne Cushman about the Zen Center of Los Angeles, *Zen Center: Portrait of an American Zen Community*, which happened to be filming just as the crisis exploded in that community.

I conducted many useful informal interviews concerning the material in this chapter, and I will not list the names of the subjects here. Among the Buddhist leaders I found most helpful were Judith Simmer-Brown of the Naropa Institute, Abbot Norman Fischer of the San Francisco Zen Center, Lama Surya Das of the Dzogchen Foundation, Bodhin Kjolhede Sensei of the Rochester Zen Center, Anna Douglas of the Spirit Rock Meditation Center, Ellen Sidor of the Providence Zen Center, Richard Authure of Vajradhatu, and Helen Tworkov of *Tricycle* magazine.

1. Alan Sponberg, "Attitudes toward Women and the Feminine in Early Buddhism," in *Buddhism, Sexuality, and Gender,* ed. Jose Ignacio Cabezon (Albany: State University of New York Press, 1992), p. 8.

2. Quoted in Miriam L Levering, "Lin-chi Ch'an and Gender: The Rhetoric of Equality and the Rhetoric of Heroism," in *Buddhism, Sexuality, and Gender,* p. 139.

3. Rita M. Gross, *Buddhism after Patriarchy: A Feminist History, Analysis, and Reconstruction of Buddhism* (Albany: State University of New York Press, 1993), p. 80.

4. Miranda Shaw, *Passionate Enlightenment: Women in Tantric Buddhism* (Princeton: Princeton University Press, 1994), p. 3.

5. The statistical test Chi^2 was significant at the .02137 level.

6. Gil Fronsdal, "Life, Liberty, and the Pursuit of Happiness: Insight Meditation in the United States" in *The Faces of Buddhism in America,* ed. Charles S. Prebish and Kenneth Tanaka (Berkeley: University of California Press, 1998).

7. Quoted in Sandy Boucher, *Turning the Wheel: American Women Creating the New Buddhism* (San Francisco: Harper & Row, 1988), p. 356.

8. Quoted in Boucher, *Turning the Wheel,* pp. 328–329.

9. Carol Ochs, *Women and Spirituality* (Totowa, N.J.: Rowman & Allanheld, 1983), p. 19.

10. Jane Baraz, "Parenting as Spiritual Practice," *Inquiring Mind*, February-August 1996, p. 14.

11. $Chi^2 = .034$

12. $Chi^2 = .042$

13. $Chi^2 = .014$

14. Quoted in John Stevens, *Lust for Enlightenment: Buddhism and Sex* (Boston: Shambhala, 1990), p. 22.

15. Ibid., p. 23

16. Ibid., p. 45.

17. Ibid., p. 24.

18. Ibid., p. 97.

19. Ibid., p. 124.

20. Ibid., p. 142.

21. Stephen T. Butterfield, *The Double Mirror: A Skeptical Journey into Buddhist Tantra* (Berkeley, Calif.: North Atlantic, 1994), p. 113.

22. Michael C. Hyman, "Practicing Together as a Gay Couple," in *Queer Dharma: Voices of Gay Buddhists,* ed. Winston Leyland (San Francisco: Gay Sunshine Press, 1998), p. 136.

23. Jose Ignacio Cabezon, "Homosexuality and Buddhism," in *Queer Dharma,* p. 43.

24. "Dalai Lama Meets with Lesbian and Gay Leaders," *Turning Wheel: Journal of the Buddhist Peace Fellowship,* Fall 1997, p. 25.

25. David Schneider, *Street Zen: The Life and Work of Issan Dorsey* (Boston: Shambhala, 1993), pp. 128–129.

26. Kobai Scott Whitney, "Vast Sky and White Clouds: Is There a Gay Buddhism?" in *Queer Dharma,* pp. 16–17.

27. Stephen T. Butterfield, *The Double Mirror: A Skeptical Journey into Buddhist Tantra* (Berkeley, Calif.: North Atlantic, 1994), p. 110.

28. Rick Fields, "The Changing of the Guard: Western Buddhism in the Eighties," *Tricycle,* Winter 1991, p. 47.

29. Henry Shukman, "Friends of the Western Buddhist Order: Friends, Foes, and Files," *Tricycle,* Summer 1999, p. 114.

30. Judith Simmer-Brown, no title, *Shambhala Sun,* January 1994, p. 41.

31. Jack Kornfield, "Sex Lives of the Gurus," *Yoga Journal,* July-August 1985, pp. 26–28, 66.

32. Katy Butler, "Encountering the Shadow in Buddhist America," *Common Boundary,* May-June 1990, p. 20.

33. Quoted in Boucher, *Turning the Wheel,* p. 218.

34. Ibid., p. 229.

35. Ibid., p. 217.

36. Quoted in Mick Brown, "Scandal and the Living Buddha," *Telegraph Magazine,* February 25, 1995, pp. 20–29.

37. Mariana Caplan, *Halfway Up the Mountain* (Prescott, Ariz.: Hohm, 1999), pp. 17–18.

SIX: WHY BUDDHISM?

Most of the data for this chapter came from surveys and depth interviews that I conducted. The most useful interviews were those with the average participants I contacted in Buddhist groups, and I will not try to list their names here. I would, however, like to thank Gil Fronsdal for the extremely helpful comments he made on this chapter in his review of an earlier draft of the manuscript for this book.

For a useful summary of the theories of religious conversion, see Brock Kilbourne and James T. Richardson's "Paradigm Conflict, Types of Conversion, and Conversion Theories," *Sociological Analysis* 50 (1988): 1–21; also see John Lofland, "Becoming a World Saver Revisited," in *Conversion Careers: In and Out of the New Religions,* ed. J. T. Richardson (Beverly Hills, Calif.: Sage, 1978). For readers interested in the sociology of religion, I would recommend Joachim Wach's classic work, *Sociology of Religion* (Chicago: University of Chicago Press, 1944). They might also look at Rodney Stark and William Sims Bainbridge, *The Future of Religion: Secularization, Revival, and Cult*

Formation (Berkeley: University of California Press, 1985). Two good current works are Steve Bruce's *Religion in the Modern World: From Cathedrals to Cults* (Oxford: Oxford University Press, 1996), which provides an insightful historical review of the process of secularization in Western society, and Malcolm B. Hamilton's *The Sociology of Religion: Theoretical and Comparative Perspectives* (London: Routledge, 1995), which is mainly concerned with the many theoretical disputes in the sociology of religion. For an examination of the question of who is or is not a Buddhist, see Jan Nattier, "Who Is a Buddhist: Charting the Landscape of Buddhist America," in *The Faces of Buddhism in America,* ed. Charles S. Prebish and Kenneth K. Tanaka (Berkeley: University of California Press, 1998), pp. 183–195. The idea of explaining human behavior in terms of motivation and opportunity has a long tradition in criminology. I explored this approach more fully in my work on white-collar crime. See, for example, James William Coleman, "Toward an Integrated Theory of White Collar Crime," *American Journal of Sociology,* September 1987, pp. 406–439; Coleman, "Crime and Money: Motivation and Opportunity in a Monetarized Economy," *American Behavioral Scientist* 35 (July 1991): pp. 827–836. On the evolution of consciousness I recommend Erich Neumann, *The Origins and History of Consciousness* (1954; reprint, Princeton: Princeton University Press, 1993); and Ken Wilber, *Up from Eden: A Transpersonal View of Human Evolution* (Boulder: Shambhala, 1983). For an insightful sociological analysis of the current state of the human psyche, see Anthony Giddens, *Modernity and Self-Identity: Self and Society in the Late Modern Age* (Stanford: Stanford University Press, 1991). A considerable amount of material has been published on Buddhism and the use of psychedelics. The entire fall 1996 edition of *Tricycle: The Buddhist Review* was devoted to articles on this subject, and Charles Tart has conducted some useful survey research on this topic. See Tart, "Influences of Previous Psychedelic Drug Experiences on Students of Tibetan Buddhism: A Preliminary Exploration," *Journal of Transpersonal Psychology* 23 (1991): 139–173. Most of the publication figures I used for recent Buddhist books came from Kimberly Winston's article in the September 14, 1998, issue of *Publisher's Weekly*.

1. Quoted in Gil Fronsdal, "Insight Meditation in the United States: Life, Liberty, and the Pursuit of Happiness," in *The Face of Buddhism in America,* ed. Charles S. Prebish and Kenneth K. Tanaka (Berkeley: University of California Press, 1998), pp. 163–180.
2. Quoted in Kimberly Winston, "About Books," *Tricycle,* Winter 1998, p. 89.
3. Thich Nhat Hanh, "The Work of a Sangha," *White Heron Sangha Newsletter,* November 1997, p. 1.
4. Rodney Stark and William Sims Bainbridge, *The Future of Religion: Secularization, Revival, and Cult Formation* (Berkeley: University of California Press, 1985), pp. 4–5.
5. Thomas F. O'Dea, *The Sociology of Religion* (Englewood Cliffs, N.Y.: Prentice-Hall, 1966), p. 60.
6. "Domains of Consciousness: An Interview with Jack Kornfield," *Tricycle* 7 (Fall 1996): 36.
7. $\text{Chi}^2 = .00003$.
8. Charles T. Tart, "Influences of Previous Psychedelic Drug Experiences on Students of Tibetan Buddhism: A Preliminary Exploration," *Journal of Transpersonal Psychology* 23 (1991): 139–173.

9. Stark and Bainbridge, *Future of Religion*, p. 411.

10. Steve Bruce, *Religion in the Modern World: From Cathedrals to Cults* (Oxford: Oxford University Press, 1996), p. 4.

11. Determining how often people actually attend religious services turns out to be unexpectedly difficult, but such attendance is undoubtedly less common that it used to be. See Bruce, *Religion,* pp. 29–37, for a review of some of the data.

12. Stark and Bainbridge, *Future of Religion*, p. 402.

13. Erich Neumann, *The Origins and History of Consciousness* (1954; reprint, Princeton: Princeton University Press, 1993), p. 131.

14. Michelle Z. Rosaldo, "Toward an Anthropology of Self and Feeling," in *Culture Theory: Essays on Mind, Self, and Emotion*, ed. Richard A. Shweder and Rober A. LeVine (Cambridge: Cambridge University Press, 1984), p. 147.

15. Anthony Giddens, *Modernity and Self-Identity* (Stanford: Stanford University Press, 1991), p. 5.

16. Jack Kornfield, *A Path with Heart: A Guide through the Perils and Promises of Spiritual Life* (New York: Bantam, 1993), pp. 40–42.

17. Mark Epstein, *Thoughts without a Thinker: Psychotherapy from a Buddhist Perspective* (New York: Basic, 1995), p. 3.

18. Joseph Goldstein, "Liberation through Nonclinging Is the point Where All Buddhist Traditions Agree," in *The Complete Guide to Buddhist America,* ed. Don Morreale (Boston: Shambhala, 1998), p. xxxii.

19. Chogyam Trungpa, *The Myth of Freedom and the Way of Meditation* (Boston: Shambhala, 1976), pp. 19–20.

20. Robert Thurman, *Inner Revolution: Life, Liberty, and the Pursuit of Real Happiness* (New York: Riverhead, 1998), p. 68.

21. Quoted in Charlotte Joko Beck, *Nothing Special: Living Zen* (San Francisco: HarperSanFrancisco, 1993), p. 275.

SEVEN: THE NEW BUDDHISM TAKES SHAPE

1. Andrew Rawlison, *The Book of Enlightened Masters: Western Teachers in Eastern Traditions* (Chicago: Open Court, 1997), pp. 96–142. I have modified Rawlison's typology to better fit an analysis that is confined solely to the Buddhist experience.

Index

Abhisheka, 107

Activism, 117–19, 227–28

Age. *See* Demographics

AIDS, 87, 166, 170–71

Aitken, Robert, 68, 90, 118

Amida Buddha, 52

Amitabha Buddha, 37, 46–47

Ananda, 31

Anderson, Reb, 168

Arhat, 32, 33. *See also* Monks

Arnold, Sir Edwin, 56, 188

Ashvaghosha, 165

Asia. *See specific countries*

Asoka Maurya, King of Magadha, 35

Authority. *See* Power

Avalokitesvara, 36. *See also* Dalai Lama

Avatamsaka Sutra, 46

Awakening the Buddha Within (Surya Das), 189

Bainbridge, William Sims
  on Buddhism's appeal, 206, 207
  on cults, 198
  on drug use, 202

  on theism, 195

Baker, Richard, 86, 167–68

Baraz, Jane, 148

BASE (Buddhist Alliance for Social Engagement), 118

Batchelor, Stephen, 82, 127, 180

Baumann, Martin, 19

Bays, Jan Chozen, 148, 176, 178

Beat Generation
  contrasted to Bohemians, 64–65
  Watts and, 63–64
  Zen and, 8, 60–63

"Beat Zen, Square Zen, and Zen" (Watts), 63

Beck, Joko, 126, 150

Being Peace (Nhat Hanh), 188–89

Blavatsky, Helena Petrova, 56, 58, 81

Bodhidharma, 47

Bodhisattvas, 6, 14, 122
  in Mahayana Buddhism, 36
  way of, 37

Bohemians
  contrasted to Beats, 64–65
  drugs and, 65–66

O'Dea, Thomas F., 197
Olcott, Colonel Henry Steel, 56–57, 58
Opportunity, to practice Buddhism,
    202–7

Packer, Kyle, 84
Packer, Toni, 83–85, 115, 126
    practice style of, 150
    on religious tradition, 128
    retreats of, 92
    teacher's ego and, 133
Padmasambhava, 43
Pandaka, 164
Pandita, U, 80
Paramitas, 37, 107
Parenthood. See Family life
Peace Corps, 78, 79
Personal awakening. See Enlightenment
Platform Sutra, 48
Plum Village, 89
Political affiliations, of Western
    Buddhists, 193, 228
Postmodern society
    Buddhism in, 207–15
    characteristics of, 21–22
Posture, 100–101
Power
    practice centers and, 176–81
    sex and, 172–76
    sharing of, 224–25
    women's exclusion from, 145
Practice centers
    crimon at, 85, 88, 178, 81
    power and, 176–81
    see also specific centers
Prajnaparamita sutras, 37–38
Priests. See Monks
Prison dharma projects, 227
Psychedelic drugs, 65–66
    as entry into Buddhism, 200–201
    gender differences and, 152–53
    Kornfield and, 79
    meditation and, 201–2
Psychedelic Experience, The, 66
Psychotherapy, 228–29

Pure Land Buddhism
    in China, 46, 50
    in Japan, 51, 52
    in Korea, 51
    in Vietnam, 51
Pygmies, 75

Race, in Western Buddhism, 192
Ranji Ambedkar, Bhimrao, 82
Rational secularism, 204–5
Rawlison, Andrew, 224
Rebirth, 122
Reincarnation
    of lama, 45, 132
    in Tibetan Buddhism, 44, 45
    Trungpa line and, 74
Religion
    Buddhism as, 4–5, 6, 23, 34, 126–28,
        194–95
    sociology of, 194–99
    Western Buddhists background in,
        192
Retreats
    families and, 147–49
    of groups, 113
    for meditation, 14–15, 67, 102–3,
        107–8, 120
    in new Buddhism, 16
    of Toni Packer, 92
    at Spirit Rock Center, 166
    street, 119
    of Surya Das, 92
Rhodes, Barbara, 147–48
"Right livelihood" business, 115–17
Rinzai, 49
Rinzai sect, 50, 60, 94
    samurai and, 53
    walking meditation and, 99
Rituals, 97, 127
Robinson, Richard, 47
Rochester Zen Center, 68, 94
    gender differences at, 151, 152, 192
    Toni Packer and, 83, 84, 86
Rosaldo, Michelle, 209–10
Rutter, Peter, 174, 180

Sahn, Sueng, 69, 94, 136, 215
Sa Nim, Soen, 69, 169–70, 172, 177
Sakayamuni. *See* Siddartha Gautama
  (the Buddha)
Sakyas, 44
Salzberg, Sharon, 78, 80, 112, 150
Samadhi, 123
Samantabhadra, 36
Samayas, 105
Samurai, 53
San Francisco Zen Center, 96
  activism of, 118
  crisis at, 86–87, 167–68
  ethics codes of, 179–80
  families and, 149
  meditation at, 91–92
  sexuality and, 165
Sandoz Corporation, 65
Sangha, 28
  the Buddha and, 32
  demographics of, 191–94
  in new Buddhism, 190, 200
  as reason to practice Buddhism,
    197–99
Sangha Trust, 82
Sangharakshita, Urgyen, 81–82, 115–17,
  144
Satori, 58. *See also* Kensho
Scripture of Golden Eternity, The
  (Ginsberg), 63
Secrecy, in Vajrayana Buddhism,
  104–5
Self-clinging, freedom from, 213–14
Self-identity/self-consciousness
  birth of, 208–11
  Buddhism and, 203–15, 230
  ego and, 123
  in post-modern society, 21–22,
    211–13
Senauke, Alan, 180
Senzaki, Nyogen, 59–60
Sesshin, 67, 102–3
Sex in the Forbidden Zone (Rutter), 180
Sex, Power, and Buddha Nature
  symposium, 180

Sexuality
  the Buddha and, 154–56
  new Buddhism and, 159–62
  power and, 17
  practice center crises and, 86–88,
    166–71
  teacher-student relationships and, 130
  traditional Buddhism and, 156–59
Shaku, Soyen, 7, 58
Shakubuku (proselytizing), 9
Shamatha meditation, 75–76
Shambhala Meditation Center, 149
Shambhala Publications, 189
Shambhala training, 74, 76
Shasta Abbey monastery, 68
Shaw, Miranda, 143, 158, 175
Shikantaza, 53, 101, 125
Shobogenzo (Dogen Zenji), 157
Shrines, 35
Siddha, 39
Sitting groups, 114–15
Sitting meditation, 100
Snelling, John, 60
Snyder, Gary, 59, 62, 167
Social activism, 117–19, 227–28
Sodnam Gyatsho, 45
Sogen Hori, C. Victor, 136–37
Sogyal Rinpoche, 181
Sojiji Temple, 68
Soka Gakkai, 9, 196, 227
Sokoji temple, 70
Soto Zen sect, 94
  founding of, 50, 53
  spread of, to U.S., 67
  walking meditation and, 99
  women in, 143
Sound, as primary sense, 40
Spirit Rock Meditation Center
  1993 conference at, 88, 180
  ethics codes of, 179–80
  families and, 149
  founding of, 78, 80
  meditation at, 92
  retreats of, 166
  teachers at, 110–11, 127, 133

World Congress of Religions (1893), 7,
57–58, 60
Wu, Emperor of Liang, 47

Yi dynasty, 51

Zazen, 53, 71, 100
Zen Buddhism, 7–8, 47, 52–53, 58
"Beat" generation and, 60–64
beliefs/practices of, 93–103, 104, 125
in Japan, 59
meditation in, 120

psychedelic drugs and, 201
retreats and, 120
sexuality and, 156–58
teacher-student relationships in,
129–30
women and, 53, 142
see also Rinzai Zen sect; Soto Zen sect
Zen Center of Los Angeles, 87, 168–69
Zen Mind, Beginner's Mind (Suzuki), 189
Zendo, 59
Zeoli, Alyce, 171